The Old Northwest Territory

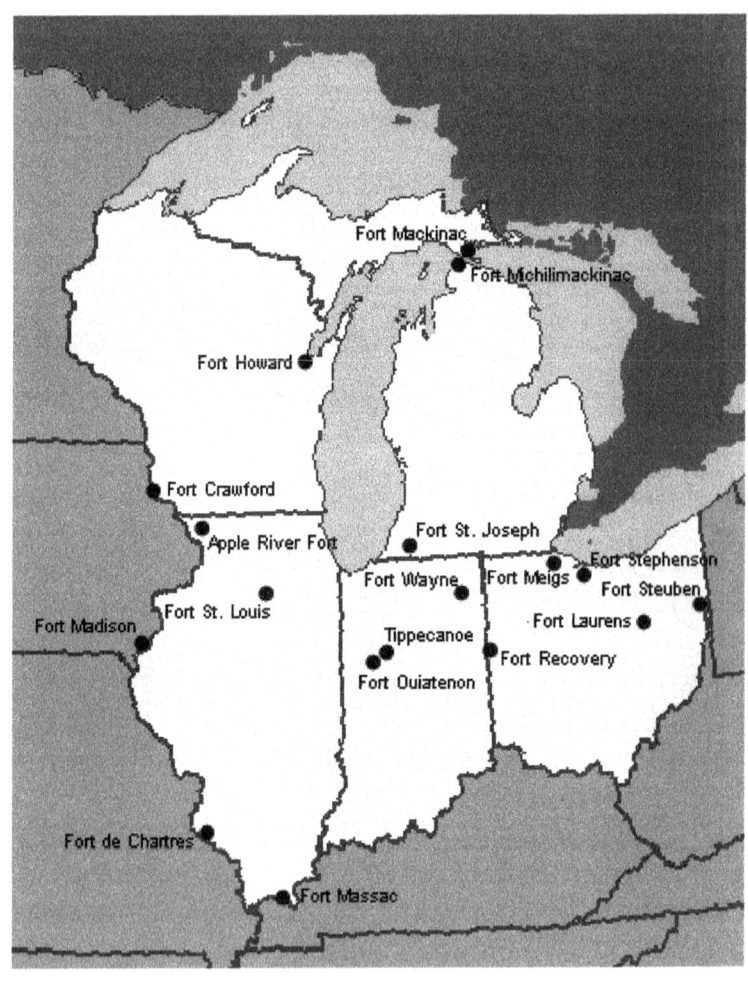

Reconstructed Forts
of the
Old Northwest Territory

Jonathan N. Hall

Edited by
Daniel Steilen

HERITAGE BOOKS
2008

HERITAGE BOOKS
AN IMPRINT OF HERITAGE BOOKS, INC.

Books, CDs, and more—Worldwide

For our listing of thousands of titles see our website
at
www.HeritageBooks.com

Published 2008 by
HERITAGE BOOKS, INC.
Publishing Division
100 Railroad Ave. #104
Westminster, Maryland 21157

Copyright © 2008 Jonathan N. Hall

Cover photo: Fort de Chartres
courtesy of Illinois Historic Preservation Agency
Fort de Chartres State Historic Site

All rights reserved. No part of this book may be reproduced or transmitted in any form or by any means, electronic or mechanical, including photocopying, recording or by any information storage and retrieval system without written permission from the author, except for the inclusion of brief quotations in a review.

International Standard Book Numbers
Paperbound: 978-0-7884-4776-1
Clothbound: 978-0-7884-7528-3

Table of Contents

Acknowledgements vii
Introduction ix

Ohio

Fort Laurens 1
Fort Steuben 13
Fort Recovery 23
Fort Meigs 35

Indiana

Fort Ouiatenon 49
Fort Wayne 57
Battle of Tippecanoe 71

Michigan

Fort Michilimackinac 87
Fort Mackinac 101

Illinois

Fort Massac 115
Fort de Chartres 127
Apple River Fort 139

Wisconsin

Fort Howard 151
Fort Crawford 159

Iowa

Fort Madison 173

Appendix I – Glossary 187
Appendix II – Additional Fort Sites 189
Appendix III – Personnel Lists 199

Bibliography 203
Index 211

Acknowledgements

I would like to thank the following people for their assistance in acquiring many of the photos and images for this book: Kathy Atwell, Linda Baxter, Judith Bratten, Rick Finch, Susan Gordy, Brian Jaeschke, Nancy Knapke, Ted Kolbet, Charles Pelky, Kim Shuette, Ken Sorg, Vicky Space, Susanna Steilen, Linda Norbut Suits, Dennis Thomas, and Eugene Watkins.

Introduction

The French, the British, and the Americans all built forts in what is now the Midwest to advance their territory and to protect their traders, missionaries, and settlers. Beginning with the French in the seventeenth century and ending with the Americans in the nineteenth century, the various governments or their citizens established literally hundreds of forts. Most of the large and important forts were constructed on government orders with government money. Usually, the government acted as the vanguard for the settlement of a region, drawing settlers into the safety of a fort's shadow. The governmental authorities charged with construction carefully located the forts in good defensive positions at the strategic water transportation points of the day—on rivers, lakes, and portages. Each government also attempted to regulate trade at different forts where the local military had the power to enforce the law. Thus many forts contained trading posts or houses with licensed traders either within or in the near vicinity of the fort.

The French built the first forts in the Old Northwest Territory, an area that encompasses the present Midwestern states of Ohio, Michigan, Indiana, Illinois, and Wisconsin. They constructed Fort Michilimackinac in Michigan, and Fort Ouiatenon in Indiana to promote trade with the surrounding tribes, to protect their traders, and to store trading goods. They built Fort de Chartres to protect their Illinois settlements and as an administrative center for their possessions in the Mississippi Valley. Finally they built Fort Massac to prevent British penetration of the region from the Ohio or Tennessee rivers and to aid in supplying their forts further up the Ohio valley.

The British principally obtained forts in the Northwest Territory by taking them over from the French and the Americans. They received Michilimackinac, de Chartres, Ouiatenon, and others from the French after the signing of the Treaty of Paris. They did build Mackinac during the American Revolution, replacing the more vulnerable

Michilimackinac. They also constructed Fort Miamis prior to General Anthony Wayne's victory at Fallen Timbers in 1794. During the War of 1812, they recaptured Mackinac from the Americans.

The Americans constructed all of the Ohio forts. Fort Laurens became the only fort to be built in Ohio during the American Revolution. Fort Steuben was built in 1786 to protect the first surveyors of the Old Northwest Territory from Indian attacks. General Arthur St. Clair ordered the construction of Fort Recovery as a supply depot in his 1791 campaign against the Miami Confederacy. William Henry Harrison decided to build Fort Meigs to protect Ohio from a British-Indian invasion. In Indiana, Anthony Wayne ordered the construction of Fort Wayne on the site of the Miami town of Kekionga in present Fort Wayne, Indiana, to establish control over the Indians of the Northwest. Finally, in Iowa, the army constructed Fort Madison along the Mississippi to protect a trading post planned to bring the Indians into the American sphere of influence.

Usually, one of the first acts that settlers of a new territory performed was to build a fort to provide safety from attack. In many other cases, settlers only built small forts later when hostilities were impending. For example, during the War of 1812 and the Black Hawk War, settlers constructed dozens of fortified blockhouses and small forts in anticipation of attack. The Apple River Fort built during the Black Hawk War is a good example of this. The successful defense of a fort sometimes meant not only survival for the occupants, but the continuing possession of the territory, while conversely defeat could mean death or the loss of territory. In all of the colonial wars, the wars for independence, and the Indian wars, forts played a prominent role in housing supplies and troops, providing a stronghold against attack, and serving as a meeting place for the signing of treaties. For each government and its citizens, forts played an important role in maintaining their presence and control. Consequently, they became magnets for enemy attacks.

Many exciting stories of battles and sieges contribute to the legends of these forts. Fort Meigs, Fort Wayne, and Fort Madison were all under siege for substantial periods of time. The heavy fighting at Fort Meigs and Fort Recovery was so important as to affect the course of the war. Forts served in brokering peace as well. At Fort Crawford in 1825, over five thousand Indians from thirteen tribes submitted to a treaty promising peace among them and outlining specific boundary lines.

Important historical figures, including U.S. presidents, manned these forts. Zachary Taylor supervised the construction of Fort Crawford, where Jefferson Davis also served. William Henry Harrison commanded the defense against the siege of Fort Meigs and relieved the siege of Fort Wayne. Dr. William Beaumont conducted important medical experiments on the digestive system at Fort Mackinac and Fort

Crawford. Individuals performed heroic deeds, such as George Miller, whose attack on the British batteries at Fort Meigs earned him instant fame. These and many other stories form the history of forts in the Old Northwest Territory.

While most forts were built of wood and did not last much more than a decade without extensive repairs, some were built of stone—Fort de Chartres for example, of which parts still stand today. The architecture differs, as some represent French forts, some British forts, and others American forts. At a few locations the French, British, and Americans all built forts at different times.

Though there were numerous forts built in the lands of the Old Northwest Territory from the time of the first French explorers to the end of the Black Hawk War, this book will focus primarily on those which have been fully or at least partially reconstructed today. Fort Madison in Iowa, while not in the Northwest Territory, is included due to its proximity, the role it played with the Indians in Illinois and Wisconsin, and its significance in the War of 1812. Though no part of Fort Laurens in Ohio has been reconstructed, it is included since there is a museum and an outline of the fort on the original site, and an organization is trying to raise funds to reconstruct the fort. In addition, the Tippecanoe battlefield is highlighted because visitors can walk on the actual battlefield site and learn about the battle and its participants at a museum that houses artifacts. It is also close to Fort Ouiatenon.

In addition to displaying the fort itself and its location, reconstructions today show visitors how the inhabitants lived two hundred to three hundred years ago. Visitors can view artifacts, uniforms, weapons, utensils, tools, and various other items used in past eras. They also have the opportunity to see mock battles, various foods and methods of cooking, musical instruments, toys, and furniture. Re-enactors at the sites answer questions and provide a real sense of what living meant at that time. Additionally, visitors learn of the interaction between the inhabitants and the surrounding Indians, the role of the fort in the settling of the area, and its role in fighting wars.

This book is arranged geographically by state and chronologically within each state. First the historical background prior to each fort's existence and the reasons for its construction will be explained in the context of the times, including a physical description of each fort. Then the role it played will be explained, highlighting the major events that occurred during war, the settling of the territory, the important people who occupied it, life at the fort, and various other functions of the fort. Finally, information will by provided on what can be experienced and seen at the fort today, including the fort itself with dates and hours of operation, as well as any museums, re-enactments, or other educational activities taking place today. Always call ahead as hours of operation could change.

There are also three additional fort sites described in the appendix where forts have not been reconstructed but are still worth visiting. At Fort Stephenson, young George Croghan fought a heroic battle against great odds during the War of 1812. The battle was fought shortly after the second siege of Fort Meigs in present day Fremont, Ohio, which is only about thirty miles from Fort Meigs. The fort site is occupied by a library that contains the Fort Stephenson Museum, where five cases of artifacts are on display. Information and artifacts concerning Fort St. Joseph can be found in Niles, Michigan, at the Fort St. Joseph Museum. The fort was a significant fur trading center and is noteworthy for having been captured by the Spanish during the American Revolution. There is also an organization hoping to reconstruct the fort. Finally, Starved Rock, the site of Fort St. Louis, built by Robert La Salle's lieutenant Tonti, is included because of its interesting history and the scenic beauty of the site.

Fort Laurens

The events that led up to the construction of Fort Laurens began when western frontiersmen begged Congress to help stop British instigated Indian attacks during the Revolution. Congress appointed three commissioners in the fall of 1777 to travel to Fort Pitt and make recommendations based on their assessment of the situation. They sent two reports to Congress in the following spring recommending the construction of a fort in the Indian country and the stationing of two Continental Army regiments in the West.

By the summer of 1778, Congress realized the need for offensive action against the British at Detroit. From there the commander, Lieutenant Governor Henry Hamilton, plotted against American strongholds such as Fort Pitt. One such raiding party he had outfitted and sent out succeeded in capturing Daniel Boone and twenty-six other frontiersmen at Blue Licks, Kentucky, in February. Because the British could distribute trading goods from Detroit, they could maintain their influence over the western tribes. The Americans needed to neutralize Detroit if they were going to halt Indian depredations on the frontier and win over any other tribes to their side. A portion of the Delaware tribe had agreed to help the Americans, due solely to the efforts of the Moravian missionaries David Zeisberger and John Heckewelder. Congress decided to take the war to Detroit rather than remain on the defensive. Thus on May 2, 1778, it resolved to raise two regiments of Continental Army troops, three thousand men, to defend the frontier.

On the authority of Congress, and upon the recommendation of its president, Henry Laurens, George Washington appointed Lachlan McIntosh to the command at Fort Pitt and the Western Country. Born in 1725, McIntosh had been appointed the commander of Georgia's troops at the beginning of the war. George Washington learned of his success in several engagements and appointed him a brigadier general in 1776. In writing to Colonel William Russell, Washington stated, "I have great expectations from his prudence, good sense and knowledge of negotiation in Indian Affairs, in which I imagine he has been convergent during his long residence in Carolina and Georgia." The two regiments he was to command consisted of twelve companies from the Thirteenth Virginia and four from the Eighth Pennsylvania. About one hundred men the Eighth Pennsylvania regiment had been in Daniel Morgan's Rifle Corps. While the men moved from Valley Forge towards Fort Pitt, which they reached August 10, McIntosh gathered supplies. Meanwhile, Congress appointed commissioners to negotiate with the Delaware and Shawnee to obtain permission for an army to cross their land in a march on Detroit. The treaty was supposed to be signed July 23, and it was necessary that it be completed before the expedition began. Simultaneously with this expedition, an attack would be made on the Iroquois homeland around Fort Niagara. This would serve to divert British attention away from Detroit.

The expedition received a blow before it began. The Virginia executive council voted against the expedition for the ostensible reason that it would weaken the frontier. The Tory and Indian attack headed by Colonel John Butler on the Wyoming Valley in Pennsylvania pointedly verified this danger. In early July, Butler's force of over 100 Rangers and 400-500 Indians had killed as many as 400 men, women, and children. Though Virginia's Council was persuaded to change their position, the outlook was not good. McIntosh was finding it difficult to raise sufficient transportation and food for the expedition. Many farmers did not want to sell supplies to the army as they did not think they would get a fair price. McIntosh complained that though the expedition was for their own protection, the frontier people were taking advantage of the situation by "demanding more than double the price for their Grain, then they got last summer before I arrived here." Eventually, he did get more cooperation when he appealed to county authorities.

The Virginia Council feared that time was running out and stated that the expedition should not proceed unless it could leave Fort Pitt by September 1. Foreseeing difficulty in meeting its goal of attacking Detroit, Congress postponed it. Instead Congress ordered an attack with 1,500 men against the Indian towns on the Sandusky. Joining the expedition were about 40 North Carolina Dragoons, 900-1,000 Virginia militia, some Delaware, and several French officers including the engineer Louis Antoine Jean-Baptiste, chevalier de Cambray-Digny, who would supervise the building of forts. However, the treaty with the Delaware scheduled for July 23 was not signed until later in September. The treaty established an alliance between the Americans and the Delaware, allowed passage of the American army through Delaware land, and provided for the construction of a fort to protect the Delaware from hostile British allied Indians.

Due to the delays, McIntosh did not leave Fort Pitt until October 23. He arrived two days later at Fort McIntosh, built earlier in October by Virginia militia in preparation as a storehouse for the main army. As was often the case, McIntosh did not have the projected number of men assigned to the expedition. He left 150 men at the fort under the command of Colonel John Richard Campbell and set out on November 4, much later than originally thought feasible, with 1,200 men, consisting of 900 militia and 300 regulars, on the trail Colonel Henry Bouquet had followed in 1764 toward the Muskingum during Pontiac's Rebellion. The frontiersman Samuel Brady, later famous for his exploits against the Indians and the leader of a band of Rangers, was also a part of the expedition. The army only averaged about five miles per day. The horses were very tired, could not get good forage, and thus could not carry a normal load.

On November 18, after fourteen days, the army crossed the Tuscarawas River and halted to make camp on an open plain on the west bank of the river with some Delaware who had met them there. The march had been uneventful except for the killing and scalping of two men, Lieutenant James Parks and David Ross, who had ventured away from camp without permission to hunt. McIntosh did have disciplinary problems, especially with men shooting off their guns. At one point he stated that anyone who reported "another shooting a gun hereafter without leave, shall, upon conviction of the offender, be entitled to a month's pay extra, and any who will not detail or inform against such offenders shall be confined as guilty of the crime himself, & forfeit one month's pay." McIntosh proved very unpopular with the troops. Later Daniel Brodhead wrote George Washington, "General McIntosh is unfortunate enough to be almost universally hated by every man in this department both Civil and Military. Therefore whatever his capacity may be for conducting another Campaign I fear he will not have it in his Power to do any thing Salutary."

The day after their arrival, McIntosh ordered the men to begin gathering material for fort construction. Already supplies were low, and McIntosh reduced rations to the point that the men received only four ounces of spoiled flour and eight ounces of spoiled beef per day. Yet, at the same time he bragged of the resources at his command and of his power to subjugate any Indians that would not make peace with the Americans. In a speech he ordered all the Delaware, Shawnee, Wyandot, Chippewa, and Ottawa to come to the fort within 14 days to make peace. He told them that "if any nations or tribes refuses this offer now, I will never make it again nor rest or leave this Country, but pursue them While any of them remain upon the face of the earth for I can fill the woods with men as the trees, or as the Stones are on the Ground." Following the speech he pleaded with the Delaware to furnish more food, for which he would reimburse them. Additionally, he told the Delaware that any who did not "join us heartily by taking up the Hatchet with us....should be looked upon as enemys to the United States of America." They did supply him, but his arrogance and hypocrisy nearly drove them into the enemy camp as did their fear that the Americans were weak and would not be able to protect them from their enemies. Even so, several supposedly allied Delaware killed one of his men, wounded several others, and shot three horses later in the winter when a detail from the garrison traveled to their villages to obtain more food. Only the efforts of Zeisberger, Heckewelder, and the Indian agent George Morgan kept them safe from their supposed to be allies.

Construction of the Fort

Though McIntosh stated that he would be going to Detroit, he put the men to work building a fort, which he named Laurens for Henry Laurens, the president of Congress at that time and also a personal friend. The fort would meet a treaty obligation to the Delaware, though it was too far away (forty miles) to offer them any real protection. By the twenty-ninth he could store weapons and provisions in one of the bastions. On December 1 in a meeting with the officers, McIntosh made a decision to return back to Fort McIntosh with most of the army, because they lacked adequate supplies, even with four men from each regiment out hunting each day. Plus the term of service for the militia ended January 1. McIntosh knew that it was too late to make a move even toward the closer Indian towns, but the fort would serve as a jumping off place for an expedition the following year. By December 9 McIntosh considered the fort sufficiently completed for defensive purposes, and he departed. While it had taken fourteen days to reach the Tuscarawas River from Fort McIntosh, it only took four days on the return trip. He left only 150 men of the Thirteenth Virginia Regiment under Colonel John Gibson. Gibson was an experienced Indian fighter highly respected by the Delaware. He was married to Chief Logan's sister-in-law.

Back at the fort, the men continued to work with little to eat. They did receive some additional provisions brought in by twenty men form the Eighth Pennsylvania, who had been sent back to Fort McIntosh at the start of the construction of the fort. The men were pushed hard to complete the fort and had to work in a colder and harsher than normal winter without sufficient clothing. They began to criticize the effort and called the fort "Fort Nonsense." By December 21 the low morale resulted in a brief mutiny that was put down by Gibson. By the third week in December, all the pickets were set. Conditions were so poor by January 1 that Gibson wrote McIntosh, "Unless a Supply of Cloathing soon Arrives, I shall not have fifty men fit for duty in a short time." Later in

January he sent the Fort commissary, Samuel Sample, to go to Coshocton, the chief village of the Delaware to obtain more food.

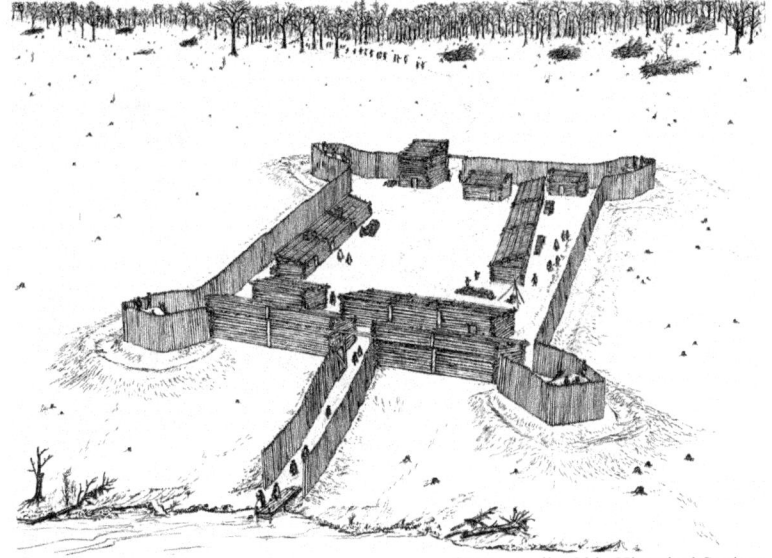

Image credit: Ohio Historical Society

The fort itself covered about an acre—each side about 240 feet in length—and started about 20 feet from the river. The French engineer Digny supervised the construction. It had pickets twelve to fourteen feet high with a gate on the river side and one on the opposite side. Pickets were placed on each side of the riverside gate from the gate to the river. A ditch about four feet wide and three feet deep surrounded the fort on three sides. There were also four bastions, a blockhouse, and huts along the inside walls of the fort capable of accommodating up to two hundred men. Altogether eleven buildings were eventually completed both inside and outside of the fort. One defect in the fort's defense was the lack of any artillery. McIntosh had left all six cannon behind at Fort McIntosh. As recorded by historian Lyman Draper, John Cuppy of the Hampshire County militia left the following description of the fort:

> There was one block-house, about 20 feet square, which was directly to the right of the gate, [land gate] and next to it, and formed a part of the outside in place of picketing: the block-house, about six feet above the ground, the block-house was made a foot wider on the wall side, and made to over-jut, so if the Indians came up, the garrison could shoot down through this open jut directly upon an enemy below; and the floor of puncheons on a level with the over-jut and the timbers

built up some eight feet, so as completely to protect those within from the enemy without, and port-holes all around about five feet from the floor, and some two or three feet apart, through to which for the garrison to fire in case of an attack, with a rude roof slanting one way, and that within the fort.

Aware of the necessity to discover what the Americans were doing at Fort Laurens, Lieutenant Governor Hamilton sent Simon Girty on a reconnaissance mission in early January. Girty left the Upper Sandusky villages for Fort Laurens with seven or seventeen Mingoes (depending on the source) on January 6. Girty learned that friendly Delawares entered the fort by wearing a deer tail on their head as a sign. He planned to do the same and take Gibson's scalp in the process. Zeisberger sent Gibson a warning about Girty, and said that the enemy planned on besieging the fort at the beginning of March. Gibson sent Captain John Clark with fifteen men, who had brought much needed clothing into the fort on January 21, back to Fort McIntosh to obtain help. About three miles from the fort, Girty's party ambushed them, killing two, wounding four and capturing one. Gibson and the rest of the men returned to the fort, bringing the wounded with them. Girty captured the man who carried Gibson's dispatches to McIntosh, but Girty could not read. However, when he brought the dispatches to Captain R. B. Lernoult, the British learned that McIntosh had written that the fort was too short on supplies to sustain a siege by Indians.

Supplies at the fort were again getting low. Additionally, Gibson wanted to help the Delaware who were allied with the Americans. These Delaware wanted to remain with the Americans, yet pressure from the other tribes would sway them to the other side. They requested powder, lead, and flints. In response McIntosh ordered Major Richard Taylor (Father of future president Zachary Taylor) to bring relief to the fort. At Taylor's suggestion, instead of marching on land, McIntosh gave permission for him to bring the supplies by water, down the Ohio and up the Muskingum to Fort Laurens. With one hundred men as an escort, Taylor journeyed as far as twenty miles up the Muskingum before Indians ambushed his force and killed two men. Warned by Heckewelder that he would not be able to reach the fort because of a large force of three hundred Indians in the area—and the fact that he was still 130 miles from the fort, battling to move upstream against high water—he was persuaded to turn back.

The Siege

Captain Richard Lernoult commanded in place of Hamilton, who had marched to recapture Vincennes from George Rogers Clark's Americans.

He sent Colonel Henry Bird along with 10 British regulars, Simon Girty, and about 180 predominantly Wyandot under Chief Pomoacan (but also including Shawnee, Mingo, and Delaware) to besiege the fort. While recruiting the war party at the Sandusky villages, the British watched the Indians torture the prisoner recently captured by Girty and stick his head on a post. A Wyandot chief, Half King, sent messengers to the Delaware to convince them to join the alliance. He threatened any pro-American Delaware with death if they tried to warn the Americans of their arrival. After Bird distributed powder and ball, he led the British-Indian force towards Fort Laurens arriving in the vicinity undetected on February 22.

Unaware of the war party's presence, Gibson sent a wagoner and eighteen men to gather horses and wood. The horses were allowed to roam free for forage. They wore bells so the garrison members could easily find them. The men could not see the horses from the fort, but could hear the bells not too far away. They did not realize that the Indians had stolen the bells from the horses the previous night and were ringing them to attract the soldiers. Within sight of the fort, but out of musket range, they had hidden themselves in tall prairie grass. Consequently, the party of soldiers walked unaware into their ambush. The Indians destroyed the entire force, killing seventeen and capturing two. That evening the Indians paraded in sight of the fort, circling around a knoll to exaggerate their numbers. One of the garrison's men counted 847 of them, a number that intimidated the fort's 172 inhabitants of which only about 100 were fit for duty. Knowing he needed help, Gibson sought reinforcements. On the night of February 28, a man (possibly a Delaware) slipped out of the fort to race for help. He reached General McIntosh on March 3.

In one of those strange historical coincidences, George Rogers Clark deceived Henry Hamilton at Vincennes on the same day, marching his men repeatedly to mislead Hamilton as to the real strength of his force. In Clark's case he convinced Hamilton to surrender without a fight, while Gibson doggedly determined to defend his post to the end. Prior to the siege he had written McIntosh on February 13 stating, "You may depend on my defending it (Fort Laurens) to the last extremity and of my care to prevent surprise." When McIntosh had learned of the threat to the fort, he sent out 123 Virginia militiamen with supplies for Fort Laurens. However, the militia turned back when they neared the vicinity of the fort and learned that the British and Indians had surrounded it.

The Indians had taken a position across the river to keep the fort under surveillance. Occasionally, they would approach the fort to hold conversations in which they protested against white occupation of their lands, but they did not actively try to attack the fort—other than firing at it without injuring anyone. Instead, they attempted to starve out the garrison. Fortunately, under these threatening conditions, Gibson did not have to hang on to the last extremity. His Delaware allies came to his rescue. Chief Killbuck sent Delaware "wise men" to the enemy camp to persuade them to desist from any further attacks on the Americans. Eventually their argument that the Americans would soon have the upper hand due to their new alliance with France succeeded in weakening the resolve of the hostile Indians. After a while, only about sixty were left watching the fort. The Indians had been suffering in their vigil around the fort as the winter was exceptionally harsh with two to three feet of snow on the ground and temperatures around zero most of the time. Of course their suffering was less than those inside the fort. Additionally, there is the unproven legend that Gibson offered the besiegers a barrel of flour if they would leave. He supposedly did this to persuade them into believing the garrison contained abundant supplies and could sustain a prolonged siege. The besiegers were also already suffering from a lack of food.

The garrison suffered immensely on a starvation diet. By the third week of the siege, there was hardly any food left. Their rations were cut to about five ounces of spoiled meat and flour per day. A week later they were down to half a biscuit a day, and finally they resorted to cooking dried beef hides, roasting and eating their moccasins, and eating roots and herbs that could be gathered immediately outside the fort's walls. Two died from the poisonous roots, and many were weak and sick from malnourishment. At one point they received a brief respite when two men who had snuck out of the fort brought back a deer they had killed. The famished soldiers devoured the uncooked meat in minutes.

After learning of the garrison's plight, McIntosh strove to gather all the provisions available from several Virginia counties. With two hundred militia and three hundred continentals from Fort Pitt and Fort McIntosh, he began marching on March 19 to relieve Fort Laurens. They traveled much quicker than they had in the fall, reaching the fort in four days. Upon their approach, the remaining besiegers abandoned the siege. Tragically, in the exhilaration of sighting the relief column, some of the garrison fired off their muskets into the air. This frightened many of the packhorses, which quickly bolted and scattered their loads throughout the woods. It was late evening when the column had arrived, and a search could not be conducted until the next day. A large portion of the flour was destroyed, and much of the provisions were either unfit for use or never recovered, despite a day spent scouring the woods. Again, the garrison's own actions brought tragedy on itself when the starving men gorged themselves on the now abundant provisions. With stomachs unaccustomed to so much food many of the men fell ill and three died.

McIntosh not only had come to relieve the fort but to renew his campaign to capture Detroit. However, his officers unanimously rejected the plan as impractical. They argued that forage could not yet be obtained, the roads were under water and, there were not enough provisions due to the loss from the stampede. In the end McIntosh reluctantly bowed to their opposition. He replaced Colonel Gibson and his garrison with Major Frederick Vernon and 106 men and officers of the Eighth Pennsylvania. Afterwards, he returned with the rest of the army to Fort Pitt. There McIntosh, a Georgian, requested and received a transfer to the Southern colonies where he would be closer to home.

Colonel Daniel Brodhead replaced McIntosh as commander of the Western Department. He immediately wanted to abandon Fort Laurens. He wrote Washington stating that the fort was difficult to supply and that it could be besieged and captured before a relief force could arrive. Washington wanted to maintain the fort to deceive the British and Indians to further the objective of his plans. He planned an expedition to destroy the Iroquois in New York. General John Sullivan's men were to march up the Susquehanna. Brodhead would participate by marching up the Allegheny to convince the other Indians from aiding the Iroquois. Fort Laurens worked in the role of a decoy. Brodhead did remove some men from the fort and by the end of May the garrison only numbered twenty-six men. Near the end of May, a Delaware named Big Cat informed Brodhead that a British force with Wyandots, Shawnees, and Mingoes would attack the fort with cannon.

Henry Bird and Alexander McKee had gathered about two hundred warriors, mostly Shawnee. Fortunately for Vernon and his men at Fort Laurens, they did not have to defend the fort against cannon (for which it was not designed) or anyone else. Just prior to leaving the Sandusky villages, the Indians—already discouraged by George Rogers Clark's capture of Vincennes—learned that Colonel John Bowman and three hundred Kentucky militiamen had burned the Shawnee town of Chillicothe on the Little Miami River. In the attack Bowman's men wounded the Shawnee chief Blackfish, plundered the village, and stole 170 horses. The Indians then abandoned the expedition as they hurried towards their villages to defend them from expected attacks. Without assistance from the Shawnees, the British gave up on the attack.

Brodhead sent orders for Lieutenant Colonel Richard Campbell and his men who had relieved Major Vernon in July to abandon the fort. Sullivan's expedition was underway and the fort's usefulness was at an end. The beginning of the fort's history had not gone well and neither did the end. Campbell did not have sufficient pack horses to carry all the provisions and had to burn what he could not transport. The garrison finally left the fort on August 2, but not before an Indian raiding party had killed two more men outside the fort walls. Upon returning to Fort Pitt, these soldiers joined Brodhead's expedition up the Allegheny which began August 11. The people of the northwestern frontier were now left without Continental government protection.

Aftermath

After the abandonment of the fort in 1779, which was the only American built fort in the Ohio country during the Revolutionary War, no military force ever reoccupied it, and it slowly deteriorated. A man named Carpenter reported that the fort was still in good condition in 1782. He had escaped captivity from the Indians and had spent one night in the fort. By the terms of the Treaty of Greenville in 1795, the fort was used as a reference point in defining the boundary line. In 1832 the construction of the Ohio and Erie Canal resulted in the destruction of the two eastern bastions. In 1850 the president of the Northern Ohio Historical society, Charles Whittlesey, reported that part of the fort was obliterated but traceable, and other parts were still visible.

In 1915 the state of Ohio purchased eighty-one acres for a park on the ground where the fort had stood. The Ohio Archaeological and Historical Society then acquired the site in 1917, but did little in the next fifty years to improve the site. The construction of Interstate 77, which passed nearby, revived interest in the fort. In 1970 construction began on a museum and interpretive center which was completed in 1973. Meanwhile, Professor Gramly directed archaeological diggings in 1972 which uncovered artifacts and showed that part of the fort was under the new museum. They also found the mass grave of the seventeen men that the Indians had killed. The remains of these men were buried in a crypt in the museum wall and at the Tomb of the Unknown Patriot of the American Revolution.

The Present

Today a visitor can see the outline of the fort and learn much more about the fort in the round museum built and operated by the Ohio Historical Society. Inside the museum's forty seat auditorium, visitors can watch a video explaining the fort's history. Artifacts are also on display, and there is a small gift shop. The museum is open Wednesdays through Sunday from Memorial Day weekend until Labor Day, 9:30 a.m. to 5 p.m. Currently the Friends of Fort Laurens Foundation are raising funds to build a replica of the fort on the original site. Call 1-800-283-8914 toll free for further information.

Image credit: Ohio Historical Society

Fort Steuben

The story of Fort Steuben is rooted in the events surrounding the end of the American Revolution. At the Treaty of Paris, signed September 3, 1783, America acquired the lands from the Allegheny Mountains to the Mississippi River. Congress intended to use sales of land to fill the treasury and to pay the soldiers who had served in the Revolutionary War. Back in 1776, in the early days of the Revolution, Congress had offered bounties of land to serve as an inducement to enlist soldiers. As part of the deal, Congress had promised five hundred acres to a colonel, one hundred acres to a private, and proportionately to the other ranks. In 1783, Timothy Pickering made an appeal to Congress known as the Newburgh Petition, which was signed by 288 officers. Pickering proposed that Congress purchase the land from the Indians and then give portions to the soldiers to fulfill its obligations from 1776. In 1784, as part of a committee, Thomas Jefferson proposed that the states that included Massachusetts, Connecticut, New York, and Virginia relinquish the lands which they claimed in the region. He envisioned seventeen future states emerging from the territory, and even suggested names for the new states, including Metropotamia, Polypotamia, Washington, Michigania, and Illinoia. The proposal was not adopted at that time.

In order to sell the land, Congress had to first remove squatters and secure proper title. It issued a prohibition against "all persons from making settlements on lands inhabited or claimed by Indians, without the jurisdiction of any particular state." The state of Virginia agreed to surrender its claims to the Ohio region on the premise that her war veterans would receive Ohio land. Finally, Congress conducted two treaties with the Indian tribes that claimed possession of the region. At Fort Stanwix, where a treaty signed in 1768 had guaranteed the Iroquois the land north of the Ohio, a new treaty was signed in 1784 whereby the Iroquois relinquished any claim to the land. In 1785, in a treaty at Fort McIntosh, the elders of the Wyandot, Delaware, Ottawa, and Ojibwa

(Chippewa) tribes relinquished their claims to the American commissioners Richard Butler, George Rogers Clark, and Arthur Lee. The Americans told them the land was theirs by right of conquest and forced them to sign away the lands south of a line extending from Fort Laurens to the head of the Maumee River. The Miamis and Shawnees did not participate in the treaty, and before long all the tribes of the region repudiated the terms of the treaty.

Before Congress could begin to conduct any land sales, it first had to survey the land. Thus Congress passed the Land Ordinance of 1785 partly in response to the demands of soldiers for land. Under its terms Thomas Hutchins, who later became Chief Geographer (Surveyor-General) of the United States, headed a crew of geographers that would include former General Benjamin Tupper, Absalom Martin, Rufus Putnam, Winthrop Sargeant, and Isaac Sherman. They would survey the region between the Ohio River and Lake Erie. The land was to be divided into townships six miles square further subdivided into thirty-six sections a mile square each (640 acres). The townships were to be arranged in north and south columns called ranges. They were to start at the point where the 233 mile Mason-Dixon Line, drawn by Charles Mason and Jeremiah Dixon from 1763 to 1768, crossed the Ohio River north of modern East Liverpool Ohio (a granite marker identifies this location today).

In the fall of 1785, Hutchins began surveying the line that was to extend forty-two miles west to make up the first seven ranges. There were thirteen surveyors, one from each state. It was hoped that they would be able to survey thirteen ranges in 1785. However, surveying work proceeded slowly through the wilderness. Since a clear line of sight was required, the axmen with the surveying team had to first remove any trees in the way. They could only survey in 33-foot increments—the distance two chainmen stretched the surveyor's chain. Finally, in the face of rumored Indian troubles, specifically an attack by Shawnee warriors on two traders, the work was halted with only four ranges completed by the end of December.

The Army

The Army performed the task of providing protection for the surveyors. After the Revolutionary War ended, Congress disbanded the Army except for eighty men to guard the stores at West Point and Fort Pitt. Congress realized military force would be needed to protect the Northwest. It passed a resolution on June 3, 1784, to establish a regiment of over seven hundred men, incorporating the existing eighty men. Pennsylvania, New Jersey, New York, and Connecticut supplied the recruits for the Army. Since Pennsylvania supplied the most men it chose the commanding officer. At the rank of lieutenant colonel, Josiah Harmar assumed command. He instigated discipline into the new force using Baron von Steuben's *Regulations for the Order & Discipline of the Troops of the U.S.* written at Valley Forge during the Revolutionary War. (Steuben's *Revolutionary War Drill manual* was used through the first quarter of the nineteenth century and can still be purchased today).

Many of the men recruited for the new army were of the lowest class in the economic order, unable to make a living elsewhere. The recruits had to be over 5' 6" tall, between the ages of eighteen and forty-five, and had to sign up for a three year term. They were promised the following clothing for a yearly allowance:

1 regimental coat	1 pair of woolen breech
4 pairs of shoes	1 pair of mitts
2 pairs of woolen socks	1 blanket
2 pairs of stockings	1 hat
1 woolen vest	1 hunting frock
1 pair linen overalls	1 stock clasp*
4 shirts	1 hunting frock

*every two years

In reality they were often short on clothing, and to begin with they were given clothing of assorted kinds and colors left from the Revolutionary War. Due to the economic conditions, they were not outfitted in a uniform way and the clothing was of very poor quality. In 1786 Harmar complained to Secretary of War Henry Knox:

> The shirts are in general of a sleezy linen, very scanty made...not more I believe than 2 & 3/4ths yds 7/8ths linen in them...they will not last a soldier a week...The shoes which Hodgdon shewed me are too small, fit only for boys of twelve or fourteen years of age, and of a bad quality...The coats are also of the worst quality being made of a kind of stroud or duffel which would wear out before the troops arrive at Fort Pitt, were it not for the benefit of having fatigue coats.

To prepare the land for settlement, Congress ordered the army under Colonel Josiah Harmar to remove squatters. Commanding a total of only seven hundred men, Harmar could only spare twenty men under Ensign John Armstrong to complete the task. Beginning in April his small force succeeded in evicting some squatters. However, many of them avoided the army or returned to their homes after the army left the area. Harmar realized the need to establish forts in the territory to enforce the law. Thus he sent men down the Ohio River to establish two forts: Fort

Marietta near the mouth of the Muskingum and Fort Finney by the mouth of the Miami.

After learning that many squatters had returned to their homes, Major John Wyllys, now in command of Fort McIntosh, sent another force to remove them in April 1786. Captain John Hamtramck would repeat Armstrong's mission of the previous year. A month later Wyllys departed for Fort Harmar and left Hamtramck in command. Meanwhile Harmar received a letter from the surveyor Hutchins requesting a military escort to protect his surveyors, who were beginning their work again. In response, Harmar ordered Hamtramck to join Hutchins with three companies of troops.

Fort Construction

After building several blockhouses in September, Hamtramck decided to build a regular fort to relieve the surveyors from their fear of an Indian attack. Their fear was real. In the past year, Captain Johnny, a Shawnee war chief, had told the Americans: "We can almost hear the noise of your axes felling over trees and settling our country." He also threatened that if the Americans crossed the Ohio, "We shall take up a rod and whip them back to your side of the Ohio." On October 11 Hamtramck crossed the Ohio from near present-day Weirton, West Virginia to find a suitable location for a fort. He found some high ground, a plateau about fifty or sixty yards from the river (in present-day Steubenville) that was not in danger of flooding, and began construction that very day on redoubts and a blockhouse. However, his men were hampered by lack of clothes and shoes. To motivate them to build the additional three blockhouses (he would need to make a square fort) he inaugurated a contest. He assigned each company to build a blockhouse and announced that the first to finish would receive a prize of six gallons of whiskey, the second company to finish would receive four gallons, and the last would have the task of digging the ditch for the pickets.

The men started the race on Friday morning, October 27. By noon on Sunday the blockhouses were completed, except for the roofs. At that point Hamtramck ordered the companies to erect two buildings for officer's quarters. The weather turned foul and began to snow. The men had to obtain stones from across the river to build the chimneys before they could complete the roofs and floors. They finally were able to move into their new quarters on November 4. It was of great benefit to them that they were able to move in then because by December 5 there was two and a half feet of snow on the ground. Though the men had completed the buildings, it would be another two months before the outer defensive works, pickets, and gates were finished. The men completed the fort on January 8. Hamtramck noted that if the days that no work could be done were subtracted from the total, the fort had been built in thirty-three days (not including were additional auxiliary buildings such as a quartermaster's store or artificer's shop yet to be built). On January 2 Hamtramck wrote Harmer suggesting Fort Steuben as the name of the fort (rather than naming it for himself as had Harmer) after the Prussian General Frederick William Baron von Steuben.

Both Hamtramck and Lieutenant Ebenezer Frothingham made sketches of the fort. It can be seen from the sketches that the blockhouses were set at forty-five degree angles from the pickets. From this position the soldiers in the blockhouses could fire from the second story gun ports and thus forming a cross-fire, could rake the entire area in front of the pickets. Hamtramck stated that the blockhouses were twenty-five feet square from the inside and eleven feet high, while Frothingham reported that they were twenty-eight feet square from the outside. Therefore the walls must have been eighteen inches thick. The second floor walls would have only been about four feet high on the outside, but with the steeply pitched roof, a man could stand up and fire through the porthole. The first floor of the blockhouse was divided into two rooms of twenty by twelve and a half feet for accommodating fourteen men in each room. There was not enough room for the entire garrison to occupy the blockhouses at the same time. However, there was always a portion of men on sentry duty or patrol.

Separate from the blockhouses, an officer's quarters housed the fort's twelve commissioned officers. There were the three captains, John Hamtramck, John Mercer, and William McCurdy; the three lieutenants, Russell Bissell, Ebenezer Frothingham, and William Kersey; the three ensigns, John Armstrong (the one who first ejected the squatters from the territory in 1785), Francis Luse, and Cornelius Ryker Seydam. In addition, Lieutenant John Mills (later a captain) served as the commissary, Lieutenant William Peters served as quartermaster, and Lieutenant Mahlon Ford served as a messenger.

The other fort buildings consisted of the commissary's store where the beef, flour, whiskey, salt, and molasses were stored. There was a quartermaster's store, which held non-food items, such as uniforms, armaments, and camp equipment. The uniform supplies included hats, coats, vests, breeches, shirts, gloves, and stockings. For armaments Lieutenant Peters listed 4 muskets, 4 bayonets, 3 gun boxes, 4 bayonet bolts, 4 bayonet scabbards, 1 gun worm, and 1,665 cartridges, which amounted to roughly 16 per man. The remaining equipment stored included tents, camp kettles, axes, a shovel, a spade, and a pickaxe. A small shed inside the pickets served as the magazine for storing the fort's gunpowder and munitions. The artificer's or blacksmith's shop would have probably had a bellows, an anvil and a sledge, a pair of tongs, a hammer, a vise, and iron. A hospital/infirmary was not shown on

Frothingham's sketch, yet a separate building was standard on any post and was probably built for Dr. John Elliott, the post surgeon. The last structure, the guardhouse, was the tallest. It was built over the sally port on the river side of the fort. Two piers, each twelve feet in width and projecting eighteen feet to the inside and eighteen feet to the outside, supported a tower. Soldiers stored items in the lower floor of one pier. The other pier was secured to hold prisoners and was called a "black hole" by the garrison.

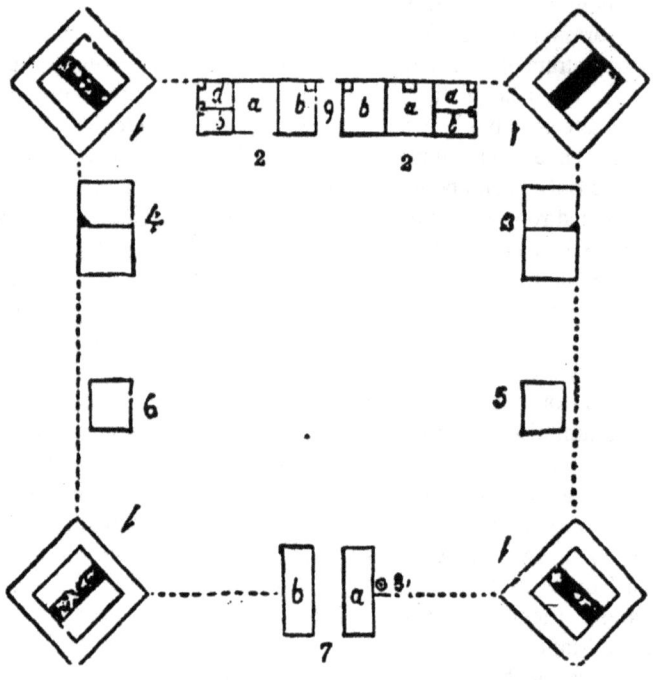

The Frothingham Sketch of Fort Steuben, drafted some time between January 8, 1787, when the fort was completed, and February 6, 1787, when the drawing was entered into Ekuries Beatty's diary. The present whereabouts of the original is unknown. The original publication in the December 6, 1881 *Herald* included the following legend, corresponding to the numbers on the sketch: 1, block houses; 2, officers' barracks; a, parlors; b, bedrooms; d, kitchens; 3, commissary's store; 4, quartermaster's store; 5, magazine; 6, artificer's shop; 7, guard house built on two piers, a, b, with a piazza looking inwards and a sally port between the piers; pier a, common store; pier b, black hole (place of confinement); 8, flagstaff; 9, main gate looking toward the river. The small squares in the sides and corners of the rooms represent chimneys. (Image and caption from Old Fort Steuben Project, Inc.)

Like many other soldiers serving in the early days of the U. S. Army, the soldiers at Fort Steuben received their pay irregularly. Some still had not received their pay from their Revolutionary War services. The paymaster of the army, Major Ekuries Beatty, did visit the fort several times to pay the soldiers. Their pay would have been as follows:

Major	$45.00
Captain	$35.00
Lieutenant	$26.00
Ensign	$20.00
Surgeon	$45.00
Surgeon's mate	$30.00
Sergeant	$6.00
Fife & Drum	$5.00
Corporal	$4.00
Private	$4.00

The officers had hopes for better pay, especially with a promotion. In the wake of "Shay's Rebellion" in 1786, the Government decided to expand the army from 700 to 2,040 or more. In fact the fort's commissary, John Mills, was promoted to captain.

Unfortunately for a soldier, if he lost or damaged any of his equipment, the cost for replacing it was deducted from his pay. His firelock could equal a third of his earnings for an entire year as a soldier. The following list of pay deductions was established by General von Steuben's manual:

Firelock	$16.00
Cartridge Box	$4.00
Bayonet	$2.00
Bayonet Belt	$1.00
Ramrod	$1.00
Scabbard	$2/3
Cartridge	$1/6
Flint	$1/20

The men endured harsh punishment for their crimes. They suffered twenty-five to one hundred lashes on the back for such crimes as swearing at officers, drunkenness, falling asleep while on guard duty, and minor thefts. For more serious crimes—including murder, desertion, assaults on Indians or civilians, or aiding a prisoner to escape—a soldier could be punished by death or running the gauntlet and being drummed out of the army. In running the gauntlet, the convicted man ran between two ranks of soldiers facing each other. As he ran stripped to the waist through the column, each soldier struck him with a switch or pounded him with his fists, all to the beat of a drum. Sometimes he had to run the gauntlet multiple times.

In mid February, five weeks earlier than anticipated (before spring had arrived) the surveyors were ordered back to work to try to get three more ranges done. Congress wanted the land to be ready for auction by the end of the summer. Thus Hamtramck had to supply soldiers in separate detachments to protect them. Fortunately, his men had just received new clothes and pairs of shoes brought by Beatty. Prior to the arrival of additional clothing the soldiers had to share clothes. While one dressed soldier performed his duties, one in his underwear shivered in the blockhouse wrapped in a threadbare blanket. The hardships caused by lack of clothing and a poor food supply encouraged some soldiers to desert before morning roll call on February 15. Though Hamtramck sent out eight search parties to apprehend the men, none were found.

The period from early March to the middle of May found Hamtramck absent from his command. First Beatty requested him for an escort back to Fort Pitt, where he remained for a month. Then a few days after his return, Colonel Harmar ordered him to take command at Fort Harmar. Meanwhile part of the fort's garrison under Ensign Cornelius Ryker Seydam again engaged in the onerous duty of removing squatters from Ohio land. He reported on April 4 that he had destroyed twelve houses at the Short Creek settlement. Simultaneously, the surveyors continued to work their way south until they were now closer to Fort Harmar than to Fort Steuben. Upon his arrival back at Fort Steuben on May 19, Hamtramck met four surveying teams led by Martin, Ludlow, Smith, and

Simpson all demanding troops for protection. Hamtramck released fifteen soldiers for each party, though the surveyors argued for twenty. With his troops stretched thin, Hamtramck contemplated garrisoning Fort Steuben with only fifteen men. He even suggested that an artillery company replace his men. This became a moot point when he received orders from Harmar to evacuate the fort and proceed to Fort Harmar. Hamtramck began marching all of his soldiers south with the exception of thirty shoeless men of Mercer's company who would have to travel by boat. By May 30, the fort that had at one time held as many as 150 men stood empty except for quartermaster Matthews who departed with the remaining fort provisions the next day bound for Wheeling, Virginia. Soldiers would never occupy the fort again. How long it took no one has recorded, but the fort disappeared as hordes of settlers floating down the Ohio River absconded with finished lumber from the fort.

Note: This Fort Steuben should not be confused with a second Fort Steuben. At the mouth of the Great Miami River, Captain Walter Finney constructed the first Fort Finney. After abandoning this fort, another Fort Finney was built in the early summer of 1787 about a half mile above the Rapids of the Ohio. Soon after Finney resigned from the army in November 1787, the garrison changed its name to Fort Steuben.

Ordinance of 1787

The auction for the surveyed land was completed by October 9. Only 108,431 acres out of more than 1.5 million were sold for $176,090. Not counting the expenses for the military, it cost the government $14,876 for the surveyors. However, in 1787 Congress, still under the Articles of Confederation, passed the Ordinance of 1787, which provided terms for the establishment of government in the new territory. Beginning in 1788 with Marietta—the first settlement northwest of the Ohio under the Ordinance of 1787 founded by forty-eight men of the Ohio Company—settlers began to pour into the new territory. Under the conditions of the Northwest Ordinance, the settlers in a district would be allowed to elect a legislature and send a nonvoting member to Congress when the population reached five thousand free males. When the population reached sixty thousand free males, the district would be eligible for statehood. In 1799 the first condition was met and in 1800 Congress divided the Northwest Territory into two parts. The eastern half, still called the Northwest Territory consisted for the most part of present Ohio and eastern Michigan. The remainder was the new Indian Territory. In 1803 Congress admitted Ohio to statehood.

Consequently, the men of Fort Steuben played a role in aiding the earliest settlement in the Northwest Territory and subsequently the establishment of the Ordinance of 1787, which served as a model for all state constitutions which followed. The Ordinance was extremely important for America's future development since it provided a way for new territory to become a state equal with those that preceded it. It also provided for freedom of religion, trial by jury, the setting aside of land for public education, and in addition prohibited slavery in the new territory.

Present

Archaeological digging has been progressing since 1986, when it was begun under the direction of the Franciscan University of Steubenville. The digging and research inspired the reconstruction of the fort, which is owned and operated by the Old Fort Steuben Project Inc., a non-profit organization from the local community. Today Fort Steuben is located at 120 S. Third Street, Steubenville, Ohio. It is open May through October from 11:00 a.m. to 4:00 p.m., Monday through Saturday, and noon to 4:00 p.m. on Sunday. A special event, The Fort Steuben Festival, which is held annually the third weekend in June, features an archaeology dig. There are lectures given at various time and the Visitors Center houses a Museum, gift shop, and Exhibition Hall with displays of some artifacts and local history. As one tours the fort, items in use at the time are displayed in the various buildings of the fort, including Hamtramck's sword, various personal items of the officers and enlisted men, cooking utensils, hand forged blacksmith's tools, the enlisted men's bunks etc. In addition, the First Federal Land Office of the Northwest Territory, built in 1801, is located adjacent to the fort. It is the original structure and houses antiques and historical documents. Call 740-283-1787 for more information.

Image credit: Old Fort Steuben Project, Inc.

Fort Recovery

One of the many problems George Washington faced as the new president of the United States concerned the Indians of the Northwest Territory. After Congress passed the Ordinance of 1787, land companies, including the Ohio Company which purchased 1.5 million acres of land, began selling land to settlers. In April 1788, General Rufus Putnam led forty-eight men to the mouth of the Muskingum River and began the first settlement in Ohio, named Marietta for Queen Marie Antoinette of France. The movement of settlers onto their land infuriated the Indians of Ohio and they determined to resist encroachment. They stated, "No white man shall plant corn in the Ohio Country." The people of Kentucky already were fighting the Indians, and raiders from both peoples were stirring up hatred between the races. The Kentuckians demanded that the federal government take action against the Indians. One of Washington's friends, Harry Innes, claimed that from 1783 to 1790 the Indians had killed or captured 1,500 people. To protect the people, the government finally authorized General Josiah Harmar to take the offensive against the Indians.

Harmar began his campaign in September 1790 with an army of about 350 regulars and 1,100 militiamen. He departed from Fort Washington, which had been constructed the previous year on the future site of Cincinnati, and headed toward Kekionga. Kekionga was the Miami Indian stronghold located at the junction of the St. Mary's and St. Joseph rivers, where the Maumee River forms. The Shawnee and Delaware also had villages near this future site of Fort Wayne and the British had established an important trading post there. The government believed that by destroying this center of power they could force the tribes to make peace. Chief Little Turtle of the Miami learned about General Harmar's advance from the British and quickly sent out runners to seek help from the other tribes. Believing Harmar's army to consist of over three thousand men, the Indians abandoned their village rather than attempt to fight directly against Harmar's superior force with only about six hundred warriors. Harmar's army burned Kekionga—where at least 185 log cabins and many other traditional dwellings had stood—and all the fields of corn and Indian gardens. Harmar then mistakenly allowed detachments to seek out other villages and Indians in the area. Little Turtle twice ambushed detachments, killing 183 of Harmar's men.

When Harmar returned to Fort Washington a month after he had departed, he declared his expedition a success. However, the other Indian tribes, particularly the Shawnee and Delaware, became more determined than ever to resist white offensives. A confederacy of all the tribes of the Northwest—Miami, Wyandot, Kickapoo, Chippewa, Ottawa, Potawatomi, Delaware, and Shawnee—formed as a result of Little Turtle's repulse of Harmar's expedition. They increased their attacks on whites and discarded any idea of making peace. Secretary of War Henry Knox wrote of the expedition after hearing various reports: "The general impression upon the result of the late expedition is that it has been unsuccessful; that it will not induce the Indians to peace, but on the contrary encourage them to a continuance of hostilities, and that, therefore, another and more efficient expedition must be undertaken."

St. Clair's Campaign

In the fall of 1791, Northwest Territory Governor Arthur St. Clair, a former British officer and an American veteran of the Revolutionary War, marched out of Fort Washington in command of an army of approximately 2,300 men. Due to its size, it was one of the largest armies ever to battle against the Indians on the North American continent. President Washington and Henry Knox had approved his plan to construct forts at thirty to forty mile intervals on his way to his destination at the Miami main village at Kekionga, where he would build another fort to establish control over the Indians. Yet, the army had many problems: a late start, inadequate provisions, many untrained and undisciplined troops, and weaknesses in leadership. Many experienced Indian fighting frontiersmen viewed St. Clair's expedition as a regular army operation and refrained from volunteering their services.

After building Fort Hamilton and Fort Deposit, St. Clair's army of about 1,400 arrived at a site by a little creek, a tributary of the Wabash about fifty miles from Kekionga on the evening of November 3. The army had recently been reduced when St. Clair sent three hundred of his battle hardened regulars under Major John Hamtramck after deserters. The next morning St. Clair's army disintegrated after three hours of carnage, commencing in a surprise attack as they prepared for breakfast. Many of the militia refused to fight. Hidden marksmen from Little Turtle's surrounding army of 1,500 warriors fired until they tore the heart out of the army. Many of the regulars fought desperately, repeatedly charging their foes only to see them return again to continue firing from cover. Finally, after losing most of his officers and artillerymen, and seeing the futility of battling from an indefensible position, St. Clair led the remnants of his army in a desperate charge through the Indian lines. The retreat did not end until one hundred miles later when the army literally straggled back into Fort Washington a week afterward.

Little Turtle's confederation of Miami, Shawnee, Delaware, Wyandot, and other tribes of the Northwest Territories had inflicted the worst defeat ever suffered by the U.S. army against the Indians. The casualties suffered by St. Clair's army in killed, wounded, or captured have been estimated at around 900, easily exceeding George Armstrong Custer's losses of around 250 men at the Battle of the Little Bighorn. Panic soon subsided on the frontier, and as in Custer's defeat, the U.S. Government responded with a new military force to subdue the recently victorious Indians. Unlike Custer, St. Clair survived the battle and received vindication from Congress.

Construction of the Fort

After the defeats of Harmar and St. Clair, President Washington desperately searched for a new army commander who would complete the task. He settled on General "Mad Anthony" Wayne then forty-seven years old and a veteran of the Revolutionary War. Wayne had fought at Brandywine, Germantown, and earned hero status for his victory at Stony Point. Wayne traveled to Pittsburgh in June 1792 to begin to shape what Secretary of War Henry Knox had newly named "The Legion of the United States" into a competent well trained army. Author Wiley Sword said of him, "Anthony Wayne was above all a determined and ardent competitor. Given the means to accomplish a task, he would win by finesse or by brute force, by deception or direct assault, but inevitably he would find a way to preserve until the object was at hand." His later victory against the Indians demonstrated that he succeeded. The Indians called him the "Chief Who Never Sleeps."

When Wayne took command he immediately installed a strict discipline. Within a five week period he ordered the execution of seven deserters. He constantly drilled the men and enacted sham battles. He also changed their ammunition from a single ball and a small load of powder to a cartridge loaded with one ball and heavy buckshot for their French Charleville smoothbore muskets remaining from the Revolutionary War.

In preparation to initiate offensive operations against the confederation of Indians the next spring, Wayne sent Major Henry Burbeck, his chief of artillery, forward from Fort Greeneville on

December 23, 1794, with eight companies of infantry and a detachment of artillery. Burbeck had fought in the Battle of Bunker Hill and had been a commandant at West Point. The expedition of three hundred men arrived on the site of Arthur St. Clair's defeat the next day, twenty-three miles north of Greeneville. Following Burbeck's design they immediately began construction of four blockhouses that were twenty feet square. Wayne joined them on Christmas day with additional men and supplies on packhorses. Hundreds of bones, many with sinew attached still covered the site. At Wayne's command the men gathered the bones (over five hundred skull bones) and buried them in a large pit, while others worked on constructing the fort.

Wayne also instigated a search for the eight pieces of artillery St. Clair had abandoned in his defeat. He had left behind three brass 6-pounders, three brass 3-pounders, and two iron carronades. In the nearby creek his men found one 6-pounder and one 3-pounder which they mounted in the fort. Wayne named the new fort Recovery since the land had been recovered from the Indians. The men quickly enclosed the four blockhouses with a fifteen foot high stockade and cleared the grounds around the fort of large trees for a distance of about one thousand feet. One difference from the typical stockade was the shutters Burbeck added on the musket portholes that could be closed for protection while reloading. Unfortunately, in testing the recovered cannon, an explosion of loose powder burned Burbeck. Nevertheless, the fort was sufficient for defense, and Wayne began the trip back to Fort Greeneville with most of his men on December 28, leaving behind Captain Alexander Gibson in charge of his own infantry company and a company of artillery. Burbeck stayed for a few weeks more to supervise completion of the fort. Not one Indian had been spotted during the fort's construction.

Upon his return Wayne quickly acted to strengthen Fort Recovery. He ordered Captain Richard Greaton at Fort St. Clair to send him the remainder of the men belonging to Gibson's and Bissell's companies under the command of Sergeant Samuel Dold. Gibson reported on January 12 that the reinforcements had increased his garrison to a total of 138 enlisted officers and enlisted men. The newly constructed fort was closer to the Indian villages than any previous fort. Wayne warned Gibson of the Indians, writing, "You will on no pretence admit them within the walls of your Garrison; and all risqué and danger must be removed in your intercourse with them." Gibson put his men to work digging a 36-foot deep well and removing remaining underbrush and fallen trees so that the area was cleared around the fort for 250 yards. He also had them build a twelve foot by fourteen foot ice house to store meat and a detached blockhouse by the stream. Additionally, the men added a second story to each blockhouse with a cupola on top to function as a lookout post. Because the well water was sulfurous to the taste, Gibson built a tunnel to the Wabash River. The garrison finally completed the fort on March 31.

Meanwhile the men continued their search for St. Clair's remaining cannon. While they did find pick axes, musket balls, and a blacksmith's anvil, the cannon continued to elude them until two more were uncovered in May between the fort and the rear redoubt. Finally, in June captured Potawatomi Indians revealed the location of more cannon. Gibson now had six of the eight cannon from St. Clair's army. Significantly, in mid-March Gibson also received additional powder for the cannon. In late February only one keg of cannon powder had been available. Despite shortages of gunpowder, Gibson's garrison of two hundred men practiced musketry. They were ready for battle and would not have to wait long.

In preparation for his planned offensive, Wayne continually sent out scouts and spies. One of his best was Captain William Wells (known as "Blacksnake' among the Indians). The Indians had captured Wells when he was a boy. He had become one of them, and had even married Little Turtle's daughter. In addition he had fought ferociously against his own race in St. Clair's defeat. A turning point came in 1792 when Wells met Samuel, one of his white brothers, while serving as an interpreter for a party of Wea Indians. The meeting prompted Wells to leave the Miami and Little Turtle, whom he had lived with as an adopted son for nine years. Wells left on good terms and was a friend of Little Turtles for the remainder of his life, frequently aiding him in his relations with the Americans.

Naturally, Wells possessed valuable skills that the Americans desired to use. Wells appreciated how his talents could benefit himself, and accepted the position as captain of scouts. An elite group under his command tried to capture enemy Indians to acquire information. On one such attempt, his men sighted three Indians in a camp. They shot the Indians on the right and left. Surprisingly the man in the center turned out to be Christopher Miller, who had been captured in 1782 by the Shawnee. His brother Nicholas helped to convince him to join the American side. Miller soon informed Wayne that the British were dissuading the Indians from making peace. Instead they were giving them aid and encouraging them to fight the Americans.

Difficulties in obtaining and transporting sufficient supplies due to a shortage of packhorses delayed Wayne from striking against the Indians. On May 1 the Legion possessed only enough meat for eight days and flour for twenty. The garrison of Fort Recovery endured an even worse threat when on May 12 their supply of all provisions had been reduced to one day's worth. Indian attacks on the supply lines to the forts made the situation hard to remedy. Their attacks had begun in early March and had increased in April and May, creating a dangerous situation where encounters occurred almost daily. Wayne resorted to heavily escorted columns to get supplies through. However, by the middle of June, the supply problem had been resolved.

Fortunately, Wayne had received additional help in the form of Choctaw and Chickasaw allies. Different groups arrived in April, May, and June until almost one hundred of them were aiding the Americans. They were enemies of the northern Indians and were intent on obtaining scalps. Their leaders only requested that they receive a hat with feathers in it to indicate respect and that no whiskey be given to their men. To distinguish them from the enemy, they wore a yellow ribbon tied to the tuft of their hair. Unfortunately for Wayne, his scouts would bring him some bad news. From captured prisoners they learned that the British had begun building a fort (Fort Miamis) in early April under orders from Sir Guy Carleton (Lord Dorchester, the Canadian governor-general) on the site of an earlier post on the west bank of the Maumee near the rapids. One hundred and twenty regulars of the Twenty-Fourth Regiment and a Royal Artillery detachment would man the fort along with four 9-pounders and four 6-pounders. This fort was eleven miles from the mouth of the river at Lake Erie in U.S. territory—definitely a hostile act. In addition he learned the strength of the Indians. They could muster 300 Shawnee, 480 Delaware, 100 Miami, 150 Wyandot, and an unknown but numerous force of Chippewa and Ottawa warriors. Wayne thought that he may be facing more than just an Indian army and one stronger than his own. It was estimated that there were as many as 2,000 Indians and 1,500 British facing the 1,400 to 1,700 soldiers in the Legion.

The Attack

The Indians held a council at the Grand Glaize in mid June, where they gathered an army and forced the British servants, enlisted men, and all but the senior of the fourteen British officers to join them. They began to move toward Wayne's outposts with the intention of attacking his tenuous supply lines. Based on their previous victories over Harmar and St. Clair, they again expected success. They advanced slowly in a line with about one hundred to two hundred paces between each of them. They stopped about one o'clock each day to hunt. To feed their army they killed as many as two hundred dear and about as many turkeys each day. Due to the prominent number of Chippewa and Ottawa, the Bear Chief, an Ottawa, was the titular head of the army. A scouting party of his encountered four Choctaws that Wayne had sent out. They killed one of the Choctaws. Stimulated for more battle, the Indians decided to attack nearby Fort Recovery despite pleas from British officers to stay with the original plan. On the night of June 29, the Indian army camped undiscovered close to the fort.

Wayne's Choctaw scouts reported on the twenty-eighth that numerous Indians were advancing and that "there was a great number of white men with the Indians." Wayne then sent Major McMahon commanding fifty dragoons and ninety riflemen to the fort with 1,200 kegs of flour. McMahon's force arrived without seeing any hostiles and camped outside the fort on the night of the twenty-ninth. Firing had been heard in the woods but this was not considered that unusual as small parties of Indians had been in the vicinity over the course of the past few months. The next morning as McMahon's force prepared to depart, a Chickasaw scout arrived at the fort and reported that he had seen many tracks. Gibson sent out four scouts who returned without seeing any Indians. He then allowed the packhorse drivers to move their horses down the road back to Greenville to graze. After moving their herd about a half mile down the road, they were suddenly attacked. McMahon quickly shouted for his men to follow him (about one hundred did) as he charged down the road toward the firing. At point blank range the Indians fired from ambush, killing McMahon and about a third of his command. The remainder of McMahon's men began to retreat toward the fort. Aided by reinforcements under the command of Lieutenant Drake and Ensign Dold, whom Gibson had sent out, most of them made it back into the fort. Many of them also retreated to the detached blockhouse. It is believed that the men in the detached blockhouse, who were severely attacked, actually killed more Indians in the following fight then the men in the fort.

In their initial attack the Indians had only lost three men killed. However they began to suffer casualties as they closed to within fifty yards of the fort from all sides. Though some carried hatchets and axes to cut the pickets, they could not scale them. The intense fire from the fort forced them to retreat to whatever available cover they could find. They then kept up a heavy though rather ineffective continual fire on the fort throughout the day. One soldier, Isaac Paxton, later stated, "The balls were heard continually striking against the pickets and logs of the blockhouses, and whizzing over the heads of those in the garrison." Gibson ordered his men to fire deliberately to conserve on ammunition. They fired solid shot, canister, and shells from the cannon at the enemy in the woods. The Indian army could not return the cannon fire though not for lack of trying. The British had sent along six artillerymen and ammunition with the Indian army to utilize the cannon hidden around the battlefield to aid in capturing the fort. During the battle Gibson's men saw the Indians overturning logs as they searched for the cannon. Though it was later learned that the Indians did find one of the remaining cannon, a British officer stated that they could not use it due to a lack of gunpowder. Without artillery the Indians could not effectively attack the fort. Though they did try another attack that night, it was as ineffectual as the first attack in the daytime.

The next morning only a few Indians fired at the fort. The western Indians decided that they had fulfilled their commitment and decided to leave. They complained that the other Indians, particularly the Shawnee, had shot some of their people during the battle. In reality some of the American allied Chickasaws and Choctaws had infiltrated into the rear of the hostiles and had shot them in the back. In addition the western Indians had heard of an outbreak of smallpox and wanted to get home. With the departure of eight hundred western Indians, only about five hundred remained. By the early afternoon, the remaining army had departed. Throughout all of the battles they killed twenty-two and wounded thirty, but only managed to kill one member of the garrison inside the fort. After talking to participants over the years, William Wells estimated that the Indians lost about forty to fifty men and one British officer (a Captain Beaubion), who had been shot by a Chickasaw Indian using a double charge of powder. Wells stated that in his opinion, "This was the severest blow I ever know the Indians to receive from the white." Of the campaign a Briton commented, "I must observe with grief that the Indians had never it in their power to do more and have done so little." Afterwards Little Turtle of the Miami did not want to continue fighting the Americans unless the British would send twenty regulars and two cannon to assist in a future attack on Fort Recovery. Weighing the lack of

British commitment, Little Turtle sensed that it was in the Indian's best interest to seek peace. The Shawnee did not agree, and leadership of the Indian resistance then began to shift to the Shawnee under Blue Jacket and Captain Johnny.

Wayne's Campaign

At Fort Greeneville twenty-four miles away, firing had been heard. That it was an attack was confirmed to Wayne when Corporal Thompson and Private Hunter, who had volunteered to carry a message from Gibson through the lines, arrived on July 1 in the afternoon. Wayne praised the men of Fort Recovery for their defense against one of the largest Indian armies ever gathered in one place. He did not reach the fort until nearly a month later when he finally started the Legion on their campaign to subdue the Indians—Indians who were now less numerous and divided in their councils.

Finally, Wayne started his legion of 3,500 men toward the confluence of the Auglaize and Maumee Rivers where the Indians had gathered. He was determined to subdue the Indian Confederation, consisting of Miami, Shawnee, Wyandot, Potawatomi, Ottawa, and other tribes. The tribes were no longer led by Little Turtle. Now Blue Jacket of the Shawnee and Buckongehelas of the Delaware led the Indians when Little Turtle relinquished leadership shortly after the Indians were defeated in an attack on Fort Recovery. When Wayne's army reached the Auglaize villages, the Indians fled to the vicinity of Fort Miamis.

Little Turtle stated that the Indians should make peace since "we have beaten the enemy twice under different commanders. We cannot expect the same good fortune to attend us always. The Americans are now led by a chief who never sleeps. The nights and days are alike to him, and during all the time that he has been marching on our villages, notwithstanding the watchfulness of our young men, we have never been able to surprise him. Think well of it. There is something whispers me, it would be prudent to listen to his offers of peace." Nevertheless, the Indians prepared for battle under the overall leadership of Blue Jacket and Buchongehelas.

On August 18 the Indians attacked some of Wayne's scouts and captured one, William May. From information gathered by interrogators, they set an ambush on a three quarter of a mile line on August 19 in a tornado devastated area called "Fallen Timbers" that was in the line of Wayne's advance. Unfortunately for them, instead of advancing, Wayne stopped first to build Fort Defiance on the nineteenth. The Indians had fasted on the eighteenth, the day before the expected battle. Thus, when Wayne advanced on the twentieth, many were on their third day without food. Some left prior to the battle to obtain food, which further weakened the Indian combatants waiting for Wayne's advancing army.

The Indians, along with about seventy Canadians, began the battle by attacking and pushing back Wayne's advancing mounted militia. Wayne then ordered his regular infantry directly toward them, the first rank with fixed bayonets. On the Indian flanks he sent the Legion cavalry under James Wilkinson and John Hamtramck. The Indians scattered and ran for Fort Miamis where British commander Major William Campbell refused to let them enter through the gates. In the decisive battle lasting little more than an hour, at the cost of around thirty to forty killed and eighty-seven wounded, Wayne had inflicted a terrible defeat to the Indian Confederation. The refusal of the regular British soldiers to aid them convinced the Indians that further resistance to the Americans would only result in defeat. Their demoralized leadership would now seek peace, culminating in a peace treaty at Greenville the following summer.

Aftermath

Fort Recovery suffered another small attack on August 4 when Indians ambushed a four-man detail near the detached blockhouse. The men escaped with no losses, and the soldiers began firing on the Indians who in return opened up fire on the southeast blockhouse of the fort. They withdrew without inflicting any losses. In another incident later after Indian resistance had mostly collapsed, Indians killed two soldiers from the garrison within a mile of the fort. With the signing of the Treaty of Greenville on August 3 in 1795 and the ceding of 25,000 square miles to the United States, the fort was no longer needed. However, a small force remained to garrison the fort for several years before it was entirely abandoned. Settlement arrived in the area in the early 1800s and what remained of the fort served as a playground for children. Part of the stockade stood as late as the 1830s.

In 1851, boys playing along the Wabash River found some bones. This sparked a renewed interest in the battles surrounding the fort as excavations exposed the bones of those buried there sixty years ago. The citizens conducted ceremonies for their re-interment and a Fort Recovery Memorial Association was formed. Petitions were sent over the years to prod the Federal government to build a monument on the site. In 1913 a monument 101' 4" tall was erected on the battlefield site of St. Clair's defeat. In 1936, the Ohio State Archaeological and Historical Society and the Works Progress Administration oversaw construction of a fort approximately one-third size of the original. Though the exact dimensions of the original fort were unknown, the discovery of the base of the flag staff of the fort indicated the approximate location. The flagstaff itself had been unearthed in 1836 during the digging of a well.

The Wabash River was no longer close to the fort since it had cut a new channel. In 1938 the Works Progress Administration built a museum on the site. A new fort was again reconstructed in 1956, this time consisting of only two large blockhouses with a stockade in front.

Present

Today the fort reconstruction of 1956 still stands and the museum houses the largest collection of Indian artifacts on display in the State of Ohio. Exhibits of mannequins illustrate the dress of the participants of the time and tell the history of the fort. Other exhibits portray the history of the Indian wars of the 1790s. There is also a two-story log house and a log cabin displaying blacksmith tools and products made for the pioneers.

Image credit: Fort Recovery Historical Society

Museum hours are from 12-5 p.m. daily in June, July, and August and weekends 12-5 p.m. in May and September. Call ahead at 419-375-2065 as these may change.

Fort Meigs

After relieving Fort Wayne on September 12, 1812, General William Henry Harrison dispatched various detachments to attack nearby Indian villages and destroy their crops in the hope of dissuading them from future hostile actions due to lack of food. In the third week of September, three different parties destroyed towns belonging to the Ottawas on the Auglaize River, the Potawatomis at Elkhart, and the Miami towns at the forks of the Wabash River. Other expeditions mounted in Indiana and Illinois territories attacked Indian villages at Peoria, Illinois, and on the Mississinewa River in Indiana.

Taking over from Harrison at Fort Wayne, General James Winchester began to march toward the Maumee Rapids (near present day Toledo Ohio). An advance party from Winchester's force clashed with another from Major Adam Muir's British and Indian force while Muir was still advancing toward Fort Wayne. In the face of Winchester's superior army, Muir retreated back down the Maumee to a position to battle Winchester. However, when a majority of his Indian allies left him, he abandoned any thought of fighting and retreated all the way back to Amherstburg, Ontario. Meanwhile, Harrison worked to collect additional men and supplies (he wanted a million rations for ten thousand men) in preparation for a campaign against the British at Detroit. However, a lack of sufficient supplies for his army forced him to delay.

Though he still hoped for a winter campaign by crossing the ice over Lake Erie to attack Fort Malden, an unforeseen disaster to one of his subordinates thwarted his plans. Unfortunately, General Winchester responded to appeals from Frenchtown inhabitants on the River Raisin to protect them from British-Indian pillagers. Winchester marched the forty miles away from his quarters at the Maumee Rapids to their aid. He then battled about six hundred Canadian militiamen and Indians and drove them from the town on January 18 at the cost of thirteen killed and fifty-four wounded. However, his army was now in an exposed position close to additional British forces at Fort Malden. Colonel Henry Proctor, with a mixed force of 1,100 to 1,500 Canadian militia, British regulars, Indians, and six 3-pound cannon, surprised Winchester's 800 Kentucky militiamen and 175 army regulars—killing, wounding, and capturing all but a few of them.

Harrison had been advancing to join General James Winchester's army at the River Raisin. He halted and turned around just north of the Maumee River Rapids after learning of Winchester's defeat by the British. After conferring with his officers, Harrison decided that his force of nine hundred men was insufficient to battle Proctor's, but once joined by Virginia militia under Brigadier General Joel Leftwich, he again started moving toward the British forces. Upon reaching the Maumee Rapids, he ordered the building of a stockade on the south bank on a plateau sixty feet above the river. In honor of Ohio Governor Return Jonathan Meigs, he named the new fortification Fort Meigs. At this location the water became shallow, and shipping moving up the river from Lake Erie could proceed no further. Any goods bound for the interior had to be unloaded and transferred to smaller vessels. Thus Harrison could control the transfer of supplies here and protect the territory from invasion crossing Lake Erie.

Image credit: Ohio Historical Society

Due to the illness of chief engineer Captain Charles Gratiot, Captain Eleazor Wood, another West Point graduate (the seventeenth), oversaw construction of the fort. Fifteen foot logs set vertically 3 feet in the ground enclosed approximately 10 acres in the shape of an ellipse, 2,500 yards in circumference—400 yards in length and 200 yards in length. When completed towards the end of April, the fort included various storehouses, two earthen powder magazines, and a quartermaster's building. Seven two-story blockhouses, each housing an artillery piece and its crew on the first floor with riflemen and musket men on the second floor, greatly strengthened the stockade. Four batteries were positioned to enfilade an enemy. The men also cleared trees and brush from the area surrounding the fort and strategically positioned abates formed from branches and brush.

Harrison did attempt to mount several attacks against the British, however, the weather insured that the two antagonists would not meet. When the ice broke up and opened Lake Erie for navigation in the spring, Harrison believed a British expedition would be heading his way. On March 6 Harrison left for Cincinnati and did not return until mid April. Captain Wood also left at the same time as Harrison to build Fort Stephenson. During their absence Brigadier General Joel Leftwich, a militia officer, commanded the garrison. Leftwich allowed discipline to disintegrate and permitted the men to stay in their tents all day. Since he "couldn't make the militia do anything, they might as well be in their tents as to be kept out of the mud and water," he said in his own defense. Under Leftwich the undisciplined men actually began to dismantle the fort for use as firewood. Wood returned on March 20 and restored discipline and put the men back to work repairing the fort.

Some of the men resented the reestablishment of discipline. One private, John T. Mosby, made it known that he intended to blow up the post's powder magazine and desert to the British. Before he could act on his words he was apprehended, tried by a court martial, and found guilty. His sentence: "To be confined, tied to a post or log in a tent by himself one month, to have a handcuff on his right hand, to ride a wooden horse 30 minutes once a week for a month with a six pound ball fastened to each foot, to wear a ball and chain the whole time, to have one eyebrow and one side of his head shaved, and to be fed on bread and water only. After the time of confinement expires, he is to be drummed out of camp." Captain Daniel Cushing recorded similar punishment given to others who attempted to desert.

First Siege

A party of Indians attacked a seven man work detail on April 8. On April 18 Frenchmen from the River Raisin informed Harrison, who had returned to the fort on April 12, that the British expedition had already begun and would arrive at the fort in ten to twelve days. On the twenty-sixth a few mounted British scouts and Indians appeared on the north side of the river to observe the fort.

The fort held 1,100 effectives, half of which were regulars and volunteers, and half of which were militia from Kentucky and Ohio. The fort contained artillery under the command of Captain Daniel Cushing, consisting of four 18-pounders, four iron 12s, one brass 12, four 6s, and five howitzers. For the 18-pounders Harrison only had 360 rounds of ammunition. The artillery was placed around the stockade in five batteries with abates in front of the positions.

Harrison made final preparations to protect his men. He ordered them to throw up a mound of dirt—called a traverse—twenty feet thick and twelve feet high from one end of the fort to the other, about three hundred feet parallel with the river. To do the work he divided the garrison into three groups and ordered them to work in eight hour shifts around the clock on the traverse. On April 28 an observation party returned to the fort and reported that they had witnessed a large body of the enemy only about three miles from the fort. Harrison then sent Captain William Oliver accompanied by one Indian and one white man on a mission to find General Green Clay and hand him a message urgently appealing him to lead his 1,200 Kentucky militia to relieve the fort. To prepare his troops for the battle ahead he addressed them on the twenty-ninth, saying in part, "Can the citizens of a free country who have taken up arms to defend its rights think of submitting to a band composed of reluctant Canadians goaded to the field by the bayonet and wretched naked savages?" With that the men awaited the expected attack.

General Proctor knew he had to take the offensive. He wrote on April 17, "If I tamely permit the enemy to await his reinforcements and mature his plans, he will become too formidable." Proctor had departed from Fort Malden on April 24. Traveling down the Detroit River across Lake Erie to the Maumee in six ships and two gunboats, Proctor transported 522 regulars—mostly from the Forty-First Regiment—462 Canadian Militia, some volunteers, siege artillery, and howitzers. At Swan Creek, thirteen miles northwest of Fort Meigs, the Shawnee Tecumseh and the Wyandot Chief Roundhead joined him with over 1,000 Indians, giving him a total force of about 2,400. Proctor then made the ruins of old Fort Miamis his base. From April 28-30 both armies prepared their defensive positions. The Americans dug in and the British set up their batteries on the higher ground across the river. Prior to the battle Tecumseh challenged Harrison to battle, stating, "I have with me 800 braves. You have an equal number in your hiding place. Come out with them and give me battle. You talked like a brave man when we met at Vincennes and I respected you, but now you hide behind logs and earth like a ground hog. Give me your answer." Harrison did not reply, perhaps remembering his orders to stay on the defensive until the U.S. naval squadron could take command of Lake Erie.

Proctor sent two gunboats, *Eliza* and *Myers*, to the foot of the rapids the night of the thirtieth to fire into the fort; however, they did little or no damage. The British began to sight the guns in their four batteries across the river in the morning. To their surprise, Harrison ordered the tents struck and moved to the other side of the fort's traverse for protection. There they started to dig out little caves at the base of the mound for shelter from the coming bombardment. The British then began to batter the Americans, firing 240 rounds the first day, May 1, from their 24, 12, and 6-pound cannon, and an 8-inch mortar.

Proctor reported, "The Enemy had during our Approach so completely entrenched, and covered himself as to render unavailing every Effort of our Artillery." Due to a limited supply of cannon balls, 360 shot for the 18-pounders and about the same for the 12s, the Americans responded with a restrained fire. To augment his supply, Harrison issued orders that the quartermaster provide a gill (four ounces) of whiskey to each American who retrieved a cannon ball fired by the British into the fort and turned it in for a redemption. During the course of the siege, the troops earned over one thousand gills of whiskey.

In order to further protect one of the powder magazines, Captain Wood ordered a fatigue party of Ohio militia to throw up an entrenchment. The work was very dangerous, and the men did not want to do it. Colonel Alexander Bourne commanding the men noted,

> The ground was much exposed, being nearly in range of the magazine, at which the enemy were throwing red hot balls to blow it up, and these balls passed between the men, and hissed and boiled in the bank. The men would leave their work, and declare they could not stand it. I informed Captain Wood that the men could not be kept at work. He then gave me an unlimited order on the Commissary for whiskey, and directed me to give it to them every half hour, and make them drink it until they were insensible to fear, but not too drunk to stand and work. He said "There is no other way, it must be done in extreme cases!" And so I did it; the men then kept at their work, reeling and cursing the British and their hot balls, until the work was finished. There were none killed or badly wounded.

On the second day of the siege, the British began to aim at the fort's powder magazines and to throw red hot cannon balls at them. The constant bombardment began to steadily erode the protection of layers of wood, and leather hides covered with earth over the magazines. A party of volunteers was sent to repair the damage, and in the course of their work, undoubtedly saved the fort from great destruction. According to one account:

While we were desperately at work, a bomb shell fell upon the roof, and lodging in one of the braces, commenced spinning. Instantly we fell prostrate on our faces, and, in breathless horror, awaited the tremendous explosion which was expected to end our earthly career. Only one of the party exercised his calm reason, and silently argued that, as the shell had not exploded as quickly as usual, something might be wrong in its arrangement. In any event, death was inevitable if it was not extinguished, and the brave fellow, springing to his feet, seized a boat hook, pulled the hissing bomb to the ground, and jerked the burning fuse from its socket.

Image credit: Ohio Historical Society

Throughout the siege the British batteries proved to be largely ineffective, never killing or wounding more than a few men on any day. Partially, this result can be attributed to the initiative of one brave and unlucky militiaman. From his dangerous observation post, where he had stationed himself, he diligently forewarned his fellow soldiers where the shots were headed. When he saw the smoke from a gun muzzle he would shout "shot" or "bomb," or "Look out, main battery," or "Blockhouse number one," or whatever location he deemed in danger of being hit. Yet, he froze in place when he saw that he was in the direct line of fire from one cannon ball and failed to remove himself in time. Another cannon ball almost made Harrison a casualty when it struck the bench upon which he was seated

The British were able to destroy the roofs of all the blockhouses and expose the garrison's provisions to ruin from the rain. However, the rain had saturated the wood and prevented the burning of the fort. Frustrated by Harrison's traverse, Proctor tried to enfilade the fort by constructing two additional batteries only three hundred yards away from the picket walls on the fort side of the river. Two companies of militia, two companies of regulars, and Indian allies under the overall command of Captain Richard Bullock protected the works. Harrison countered this by building lateral transverses perpendicular to the main traverse.

In addition to the artillery fire, Indians kept sniping into the fort from any cover they could find, including treetops. They greatly annoyed the garrison and managed to kill and wound several men when they climbed into the trees to fire down into the fort. One "buck" particularly bothered the garrison by firing from a tall elm tree on the north bank of the Maumee. He also pantomimed insults toward the fort when the soldiers fired at him. Finally an officer remembered that there was a rifle somewhere around General Harrison's headquarters that was too heavy for any soldier to carry while marching. Determined to try anything to put an end to the annoying Indian, the soldiers molded bullets for the rifle and put it into the hands of a marksman. After two or three shots the Indian fell out of the tree and was not heard from again. One witness reported, "At the siege of Fort Meigs, there was a large tree into which an Indian climbed and thus obtained a view of the interior of the fort. A man named Bronson brought him down with a rifle."

Amazingly, it was not until the fourth that a well was finally completed, thus freeing the garrison from its dependence on rainwater. During the day Proctor sent a demand for surrender. Harrison mocked the British commander by replying that taking the fort by fighting would give them more glory. At the close of the day Captain Oliver managed to reenter the fort, bringing news that Clay's relief force was only a few hours away from the fort. Harrison then sent a message instructing Clay to divide his force to attack and destroy British batteries on both sides of the river.

Lieutenant Colonel William Dudley took one force and landed eight hundred men, including seven Shawnee scouts from Black Hoof's band, undetected on the north side of the river and successfully drove off the British manning the batteries in a bayonet charge. However, his men, probably confused over their orders, failed to spike the guns and retreat to the south side of the river. Instead, despite having been forewarned to keep their discipline, they rushed off to continue an unauthorized pursuit of the Indians, who were firing at them from the woods. Desiring vengeance for the massacre of their fellow Kentuckians at the River Raisin, they shouted "Remember the Raisin" as they pursued the Indians. After the Indians drew the Americans away from the fort, the British rallied, and in conjunction with Tecumseh's Indians who had crossed the river and placed themselves behind and to the flank of the Americans, counterattacked the scattered Americans and surrounded them. Many of the Americans could not defend themselves as they had entered the battle with wet weapons that could not fire. In a three hour battle, the British and Indians virtually destroyed the entire detachment—killing 80, including Dudley, wounding 250-300, and capturing the remainder. Only about 150 of Dudley's men managed to escape to the relative safety of Fort Meigs. Harrison had offered a $1,000 reward to any volunteer who would cross the river to call Dudley's men to the fort when they began their pursuit of the Indians. A Lieutenant Campbell had accepted the offer, but could not cross the swift current.

After Dudley's Kentucky militia surrendered, the British marched them back to their base in the ruins of old Fort Miamis. Before entering into the British camp, the Indians formed a gauntlet where they clubbed and tomahawked some of the prisoners and fired into their midst after entering the fort. An urgent message brought Tecumseh to the fort. Instantly enraged at the ongoing murder of prisoners, he physically thrust himself between the Indians and the prisoners, and halted the killing after about forty had been murdered, including one British soldier who had attempted to intervene to save an American. Legend passed down reports that Tecumseh asked where Proctor was, and upon seeing him nearby, asked why he did not stop the massacre. "Sir" replied Proctor, "Your Indians cannot be commanded." Tecumseh retorted, "Begone, you are unfit to command, go and put on petticoats." John Norton later wrote of the incident, "A worthless Chippewa of Detroit, [later identified as Split Nose, a 'petty chief of the Chippewas'] having with him a number of wretches like himself, who had not the courage to kill their enemies while in arms, but yet desirous of obtaining the repute of having killed them, they assailed the unfortunate prisoners and killed a sentry of the 41rst Regiment that stood forth in their defence."

Meanwhile Clay's detachment of four hundred men successfully landed on the south side of the river under fire, and with the help of a sortie from the garrison, fought their way into the fort. Harrison ordered them to reform and sent them out to re-engage the enemy. In two successive efforts, they drove the Indians away from the stockade. In addition, Colonel John C. Miller led 350 in an attack on the British battery to the east of the fort. Emerging from a ravine close to the British position, his men poured a lethal volley from less than fifty yards away, driving the British off. There he captured forty-two prisoners and spiked the guns. On his retreat, 130 Canadian militia and 300 Indians attacked his men, killing 30 and wounding 90.

In the evening Proctor observed a white flag over the fort. Once again he demanded that Harrison surrender the fort. Again, Harrison refused the demand. He just wanted to negotiate a prisoner exchange. The next day both commanders met for the first time. They agreed to an exchange of twenty-one American prisoners for two British officers and thirty-nine enlisted men. Proctor would later release the captured Kentucky militiamen on parole on the north shore of Lake Erie.

Proctor planned to resume the siege. However, his army rapidly began to melt away. Realizing that the promised short siege would be prolonged, many Indians departed with the plunder they had appropriated from Dudley's men. The day following the battle, only Tecumseh and less than twenty other Indians remained in camp. Many of the Canadian militia made their living as farmers. They faced ruin if they did not swiftly return to plant their crops, so many of them just left. Dysentery had begun to reduce the number of effectives. Also, Proctor learned on the seventh that the Americans had captured Fort York. Proctor feared that the Americans would then move to block his return to Fort Malden. Consequently, he felt compelled to abandon the siege.

By the ninth after thirteen days of besieging the Americans, the British forces departed, leaving the Americans triumphant though they had suffered greater losses. Two American-born men deserted from the British gunboats on that day also. They told Harrison's men that the Indians had left because they thought all the white flags they had seen during negotiations had signified American surrender and that Proctor was denying them their share of the spoils of victory. The Americans lost a total of 340 killed and wounded, and 600 captured. Of this total the British artillery bombardment of nearly 1,700 shot and shell accounted for 70-80 killed and 189 wounded. By comparison, Proctor reported losses of fourteen killed, forty-seven wounded, and forty-one captured, excluding Indians. Harrison's victory saved the northwestern army and frontier since nearly all of the artillery and military stores of the army were stored at Fort Meigs.

> Note: Harrison had brevetted Eleazor Wood a major for his exceptional service in the Battle of Fort Meigs. Later for his performance commanding the artillery at the Battle of Lundy's Lane, General Jacob Brown had Wood brevetted lieutenant colonel. Amazingly he was being considered for a third brevet promotion for his repulse of a British attack at Fort Erie when he was mortally wounded during another British attack. Later the army named a new fortification after him, "Fort Wood" on Bedloe Island in New York Harbor, the land now under the Statue of Liberty. Finally, Ohio named Wood County, the location of Fort Meigs, in his honor.

Second Siege

Succumbing to Indian pressure to attack Fort Meigs a second time, Proctor embarked on an expedition and reached his old camp at Fort Miamis on July 20 with about 350 regulars, around 3,000 Indians (the largest force Tecumseh ever led), and a few light field pieces. This time General Green Clay commanded the fort with about two thousand men and plentiful supplies. He confidently believed that the fort could withstand a siege. The Indians surrounded the fort and ambushed a patrol on the twenty-first, killing and capturing half a dozen men. Captain Joseph McCune slinked into the fort early on the twenty-fourth and informed Clay that Harrison was busily gathering reinforcements, Governor Meigs had called out the militia, and that he could expect to receive reinforcements in two to three days.

For five days the British and Indians ineffectively fired artillery and sniped at the fort. Cushing wrote on July 26, "This is the sixth day of siege and not a man killed except what were killed at the picket guard the first day." Suddenly about four in the afternoon on the sixth day, the garrison heard heavy firing from the direction of the Sandusky road about a mile distant. To them it seemed that the expected reinforcements were already near. Unknown to them Proctor had agreed to Tecumseh's plan to draw out the garrison into an ambush by pretending an attack on a relief column. Clay sought advice in a council which was all for sending out a detachment to aid the expected reinforcements. Standing alone in his position, Clay wisely resisted the arguments to send the men out, fearing an ambush. He believed that McCune had reported accurately and that the firing was a ruse. An hour later a severe thunderstorm quelled the mock battle. On the seventh day, only a few of the enemy were seen. Cushing calculated that they could hold out for at least two months due to the amount of pork, flour, and salt that they had stored in the fort. By the twenty-eighth the British had departed to try to subdue the weaker

Fort Stephenson. After the British left the area, Harrison ordered the construction of a smaller stockade about 150 feet square with corner blockhouses. With the coming of peace in 1815, the use of the fort ended, and it was abandoned in May.

Life at the Fort

Fortunately, Captain Daniel Cushing of the Second United States Artillery kept an orderly book and a diary while posted at Fort Meigs. He served from the beginning of its construction on February 7 through both sieges. In his writings he recorded the rules the men lived by, the living conditions, and various activities and events, providing an interesting glimpse into what life was really like at the fort. Unfortunately, he died shortly after the war ended in 1815 while trying to ford the Auglaize River.

A primary duty of the officers was to work to maintain the cleanliness and health of the men under their command. The fact that Cushing mentions more than several occasions where the men had to be ordered to remove filth, demonstrates the battle they fought to achieve this. They commanded their men to dig sinks (latrines) at least ten feet deep in appropriate locations and cover the waste with fresh dirt daily. They prohibited the soldiers from urinating within two hundred yards of the picketing of the garrison except in a sink. In addition, when necessary the men had to drain water from stagnant ditches. The militia officers exercised their men a minimum of four hours a day in practicing marching maneuvers and allowed them to bathe and swim in the river before seven o'clock in the morning. Finally, the officers made sure that the men kept themselves clean, properly dressed, and that they properly cooked their food and ate regular meals.

In spite of the best efforts by the officers, heavy rains and scarcity of firewood combined to make miserable and sickly conditions. Cushing states that eight inches of mud covered the camp on March 3, and on March 18 water covered the ground everywhere. The men could only use wood for cooking fires as most of the wood near the fort had already been cut down. Apparently there was a sufficient supply of food. In early March Cushing reported, "We have 600,000 weight of pork salted, and will have as much more by the time they are done salting, and as much beef." On April 29, General Harrison ordered a ration and a half a day for the men until further notice. However, the wet ground and lack of fire created the unhealthy conditions that caused two to three men to die each day.

The men could supplement their diet by hunting, fishing, and gardening. Whether or not Cushing was a fisherman is unknown, however, he considered fishing important enough to report on it more than several times. The men were ordered to take their weapons with them when fishing. They could not fish until after seven o'clock in the morning, and they were limited to staying fairly close to the fort. Cushing mentions that they caught fish for the first time on March 25, and amazingly on May 20, Cushing states that two lieutenants caught 375 fish while using hooks. Sergeant Keen noted,

> Great quantities of fish are caught. Of (the) different sorts, perch from 3 to 10 pounds, muskellunge from 3 to 40 pound weight, sturgeon from 1 to 100 weight, cat 100. These fish are taken with a spear, the handle to be 12 feet in length.... About the break of day myself and one more went to the river to spear some fish. In the space of thirty minutes we had 67 fish which weighed from 1 to 7 pounds. We caught them all by walking up the shore and plunging our spears in by random. Caught sometimes 3 and frequently 2 at a stroke.

Past to Present

In June 1840, in the largest political rally of the nineteenth century, General Harrison, as the Whig nominee for president spoke to a crowd, estimated between 35,000 and 40,000 people, gathered on the grounds of Fort Meigs. In 1908 a granite monument eighty-two feet high was dedicated on the fort grounds and a law was enacted to provide for the maintenance of the grounds and the monument.

The Ohio Historical Society reconstructed the original fort in the 1960s and opened the museum in 1974 as one of its major projects to celebrate the bicentennial. Beginning in the year 2000, the Society tore down the deteriorating stockade and rebuilt it with hand-hewn timbers, completing the work in May 2003. It is now one of the largest log forts in America. Today it also contains a fourteen thousand square foot Museum and Education Center, newly built in 2003. The museum contains three thousand square feet of exhibits and artifacts from the era, illustrating Ohio's role in the War of 1812. Included for display are weapons, uniforms, maps, and soldier's letters and diaries. There is also a gift shop, classroom and conference room. The fort is open from May 28 to October 31, but closed on Mondays and Tuesdays. The museum is open year-round. Hours are 9:30 a.m. – 5 p.m., Wednesday through Saturday, and 12 p.m. – 5 p.m. on Sunday. For information call 419-874-4121 or 800-283-8916.

Fort Meigs

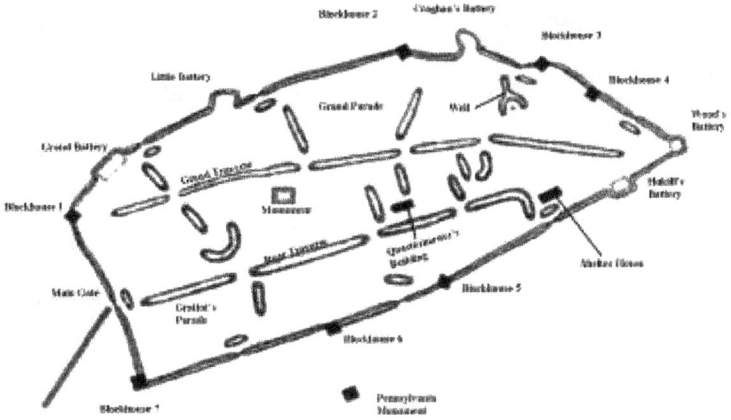

Image credit: Ohio Historical Society

Blockhouse 1: During special events volunteers transform this building into a field hospital. During the first siege many of the blockhouses performed this role.

Grand Battery: Up to four guns were mounted here, the largest artillery emplacement in the fort, to prevent the enemy from crossing the river.

Little Battery: The Little Battery defended the entire length of the wall between the Grand Battery and Blockhouse 2.

Blockhouse 2: The appearance of this blockhouse is the same as it was in 1813.

Blockhouse 3: During the first siege, this blockhouse was destroyed. Henderson's battery, named for an Ohio militiaman who volunteered to serve the cannons, took its place after the siege.

Croghan's Battery: Captain George Croghan, who served with distinction at Fort Meigs, oversaw the construction of this battery. He later earned fame for his defense as commander of Fort Stephenson against an overwhelming British and Indian force under Colonel Henry Proctor.

Hukhill's Battery: This battery was named for Pennsylvanian Major Levi Hukhill, who oversaw its construction.

Blockhouse 5: This blockhouse contains modern restrooms for visitors. The soldiers of 1813 dug sinks (holes) one hundred yards outside the fort walls to "ease" themselves. Only the sick were allowed the comfort of the sinks inside the stockade.

Blockhouse 6: This blockhouse exhibits showcases of the two sieges of the fort including excerpts from participant's diaries.

Main Gate: The walls of the fort included eight gates that were built high off the ground for ease of opening in mud and snow. Their open construction allowed troops to fire through at an enemy attempting to gain entry. Today, the Main Gate posts stand only three feet from the original location.

Quartermaster's Building: The building was used to store supplies for the army. This building is not in the original location, which is unknown. Today it serves as offices for staff and volunteers.

Well: Soldiers dug the well in the first days of the siege. A log cabin built just for Harrison's 1840 campaign was torn down after the rally held at Fort Meigs. Afterwards, the cabin was demolished and the logs were tossed into the well. One of these logs is now on display in the museum.

Grand Traverse: The original was twelve feet high, twenty feet wide, and three hundred feet long. Today it is much smaller due to erosion, but is the only original part of the fort still standing.

Rear Traverse: This traverse has been completely reconstructed to the original specifications.

Fort Ouiatenon

The French constructed their first fortified settlement in what is now Indiana about five miles southwest of Lafayette in 1717. They built Fort Ouiatenon "where the water shines white" on the north side of the Wabash River right across from a village of the Ouia (usually spelled as Wea, which will be used henceforth), a branch of the Miami tribe. The Wea had invited them the area and had requested that they send a missionary and a blacksmith. Not until May 1725 did Governor of Canada Philippe de Rigaud Vaudreuil send a Jesuit missionary, R. P. Guimoneau, to the Wea.

The French had attempted to persuade the Wea and Miami tribe to move further west to keep them away from British traders who had already started crossing the Appalachian Mountains in the early 1700s. However, most refused.

Therefore, the French sent Captain Charles Renaud Dubuisson to the Miami to maintain French influence. Under Dubuisson, Francois-Marie Vincennes commanded a post at Ouiatenon that generally consisted of twenty to thirty traders and soldiers. The outpost consisted of a ten foot high stockade surrounding a double row of fourteen houses, a chapel, and a blacksmith's shop in an area 120 by 150 feet. Vincennes was promoted in 1726 and moved down to found the town that was named after him, Vincennes, Indiana, in 1729. Still he retained overall command of the post until 1736 when he was killed by the Chickasaw Indians while leading an expedition against them. During this time about 1,600 Wea lived around the post. There were never many permanent French residents who established farms around the post—a different situation from most French posts. Instead, most residents practiced the fur trade. The post produced more bales of fur (over four hundred) to be traded than Fort Miami or Vincennes, but fewer beaver and more of the less valuable deer.

Other Indians, including Piankashaw, Kickapoo, Mascouten, and Shawnee moved near the post. In 1733 they all suffered many deaths from a smallpox outbreak. Meanwhile, the French intermarried with the Wea and relations remained friendly most of the time, yet trouble did occur in 1734. Bent on revenge after losing a fight to a Frenchman, one young Wea and some friends pillaged the post while the commander was absent. The commandant requested assistance from Detroit. By the time a force of 120 Frenchmen, 115 Huron, and a larger number of Ottawa were ready to descend on the Wea from Fort Miami, word was received that the stolen goods had been returned and peace had been restored—thus ended the so called Ouiatenon war. In the next few years, Wea joined the French in campaigns against the Fox and Chickasaw Indians. In 1724 Simon Reaume led twenty-eight Frenchmen and four hundred Wea against the Fox. Nevertheless, the French struggled to maintain the friendship of the Wea due to the lure of cheaper British trade goods. The commandant there gave a large number of presents to the Wea in 1739 to keep them from abandoning their village. The French also had to mediate disputes between the Wea and other tribes. For example, they helped mediate peace after a Wea killed a Miami.

During King George's War (1744-1748), the Wea, who could field as many as six hundred warriors in 1746, aided the French by raiding English settlements.

Pontiac's Rebellion

As the French lost their grip on North America, Detroit fell into English possession in November 1760. The commander sent Ensign Wait to take possession of Fort Miami and Fort Ouiatenon to the south. On November 6, 1761, Lieutenant Edward Jenkins was sent to Fort Ouiatenon with twenty men to relieve Ensign Wait of the Rangers. Many of the Indians did not like the English and believed the French would return. Jenkins wrote Gladwin in March 1763,

> The Canadians here are eternally telling lies to the Indians...One La Pointe told the Indians a few days ago that we should all be prisoners in a short time (showing when the corn was about a foot high), that there was a great army to come from the Mississippi, and that they were to have a great number of Indians with them; therefore advised them not to help us. That they would soon take Detroit and these small posts, and then they would take Quebec, Montreal, &c., and go into our country. This, I am informed, they tell them from one end of the year to the other.

He also added that the Indians favored trading with the Frenchmen and would give six beaver-skins for one blanket even though an Englishman would accept three for one.

After the capitulation of the French in Canada, the British had gained sole control of the Indian trade. Sir Jeffery Amherst, commander-in-chief of the British forces in North America, regarded the Indians with contempt. Despite warnings from men who understood Indians, such as Sir William Johnson and George Croghan, he treated the Indians harshly. In fact he had once written that "the only true method of treating the savages is to keep them in proper subjection and punish without exception, the transgressors." The practical result was that Amherst prohibited his military commanders from providing any free goods, such as clothing, food or ammunition to the Indians. He also prohibited the sale of rum and restricted trade to the forts. The Indians reacted in anger. As early as 1761, the Seneca attempted to form an alliance to attack the English. However, the English learned of the plot, and the western Indians still resented the Seneca attack on them at Fort Niagara in 1759, so the plans were abandoned.

By 1762 conditions worsened for the Indians, who resented the high prices of the traders, the shoddy goods, and the British indifference to their needs. They also still maintained hope that the French, who were still at war with Britain and now allied with Spain, would send a new army to retake Canada and reestablish relations with them. In the hope of French aid, one powerful Ottawa Chief, Pontiac, well known for his oratory skills and undoubtedly experienced in fighting the British throughout the French and Indian War, persuaded as many as a dozen tribes to follow him in an uprising against the British. On May 9, 1763, Pontiac, who lived at a village on the north side of the Detroit River, began an uprising by attacking the fort at Detroit. Forts Sandusky, St. Joseph, and Miami all fell to his allies in the month of May. Pontiac's emissaries reached the Indians around Fort Ouiatenon on May 31, 1763. They informed the Wea, Kickapoo, and Mascouten of Pontiac's successes and persuaded them to seize the fort. When the Indians presented themselves on the next day, they requested Jenkins to come to a council with several chiefs at a cabin outside the fort. He readily accepted. Upon entering the cabin, the Indians revealed their treacherous design by binding him and immediately demanding that he order the rest of his soldiers to surrender or they would kill all of them. Noting that the Indians had already captured some of his men, he submitted to their demands.

The Weas and Kickapoos who seized him when he entered the cabin did not wholeheartedly approve of Pontiac's plans. They permitted Jenkins to write a letter to Gladwin in which he defended them stating that they had apologized and told him that the other tribes had forced them to enter the war. He also mentioned that two French fur traders, Mr. Maisongville and Lorain had given the Indians wampum so they would not kill the garrison. Instead of killing the lieutenant and his men after they surrendered, the tribesmen brought them down to Fort de Chartres on the Mississippi River after holding them captive for several months. Jenkins eventually traveled down the Mississippi River to New Orleans and there obtained passage on a ship to New York.

Image credit: Susanna Steilen

Meanwhile, Pontiac's Uprising continued, forts Michilimackinac, Venango, Le Boeuf, and Presqu' ile all had fallen by the end of June, and the post at Green Bay, Fort Edward Augustus, had been abandoned. Only three of twelve British forts west of the Alleghenies held out—Detroit, Niagara, and Pitt. The tide began to turn in August when the following events occurred: an army under Colonel Henry Bouquet defeated and Indian army at Bushy Run, Pennsylvania; a schooner arrived at Detroit bringing relief and much needed supplies; and Pontiac's allies began to wither away due to the failure of the siege at Detroit and their desire for a resumption of trade. The final blow came in October 1763, when Cadet Dequindre, who had arrived at Detroit from Fort de Chartres, informed Pontiac that no French armies would be coming to continue the fight against the British.

In 1764 British armies of 1,200 men under Colonel John Bradstreet and 1,500 men under Colonel Bouquet began marching into Indian country. The pressure of British armies entering Indian country caused the uprising to collapse and the tribes to sue for peace. Pontiac fled to Illinois to seek help from the French at Fort de Chartres and to gain additional allies. He finally accepted defeat in the spring of 1765 and in April made peace in a meeting with British agent Lieutenant Alexander Fraser at Fort de Chartres. He then headed back to his tribe at Detroit. During this time a band of Kickapoos and Mascoutens captured George Croghan and killed many of his party when he entered the Illinois country on a peace mission. They brought him to Ouiatenon where he met Pontiac in July 1765. While there he obtained terms from the Wabash tribes that they would allow the British to take possession of Forts Miami and Ouiatenon.

Ouiatenon was never re-garrisoned by the British. However, the British did maintain representation at Ouiatenon through a civilian "commandant" and a blacksmith stationed at the post. French fur traders remained there as did a large number of Indians. By 1778 only twelve households lived there, while a Wea village nearby was inhabited by one thousand warriors. During the American Revolution, British Lieutenant Governor Henry Hamilton sent weapons and prodded the warriors to attack the Americans. Appalled by George Rogers Clark's conquest of Vincennes and Kaskaskia in the summer of 1778, Hamilton planned an expedition to retake them. On his way he stopped at the Wea village in early December and held artillery practice. He then recaptured Fort Sackville in Vincennes, and the one man Clark had stationed there, Captain Leonard Helm. Hearing of Vincennes' fall to Hamilton in January, Clark responded by gathering about 130 men to make his famous 180-mile march in the middle of winter, which included wading through chest-deep, icy water. Through a ruse Clark induced Hamilton to surrender without a battle. Afterwards he sent troops to Ouiatenon to establish American control.

War in the Northwest Territory

After the American Revolution, the Americans began to penetrate the Northwest Territory. The Wea joined the Miami Confederacy under Chief Little Turtle and participated in resisting the American invaders. As governor of the Northwest Territory, Arthur St. Clair advocated an expedition against the Wea in large part to punish them and satisfy Kentucky's thirst for revenge on account of all the devastating Indian raids in the state, and also to keep the Indians off balance in regard to the American objectives in striking them. St. Clair planned to attack Kekionga (the principal Miami town) in his campaign to crush the Miami

Confederacy in 1791. A raid was planned under the leadership of Brigadier General Charles Scott of the Kentucky Militia to keep the Wea from joining their allies in the defense of Kekionga. In late May, Scott, with James Wilkinson as second in command, began crossing the Ohio River and marched north with his mounted column of almost eight hundred volunteers.

In the meantime, the Indians had learned from a captured prisoner that another army would again be attempting to penetrate into their territory. British agent Alexander McKee estimated that in response to urgent requests from the Miami and Shawnee, around two thousand warriors gathered in Kekionga and its vicinity. Indian scouts observed Scott's column heading seemingly toward the Miami villages and noted that it consisted of militia without any artillery. However, Scott fooled them by changing his line of march toward the Wabash region to the northwest. He was following Secretary of War Henry Knox's instructions to proceed to the Wea, or Ouiatenon, towns and assault them. Fortune shined on Scott when two days before he approached the Wea villages, five hundred warriors departed for the Miami towns surrounding Kekionga to assist in defending them against the Americans. Thus Scott attacked villages that were virtually defenseless.

When Scott's men were only two miles from Ouiatenon, a lone Indian, Captain Bull, discovered them. The now alerted Indians started to evacuate immediately, loading what they could into their canoes to cross the recently swollen Wabash to the safety of a Kickapoo village on the other side of the river. Scott's men approached so rapidly that many had not yet crossed when the militiamen swept into the village, quickly killing its few defenders. Forming on the riverbank looking down into the river, a battalion under Lieutenant Colonel James Wilkinson fired a volley that virtually killed all the Indians in five canoes. A later body count recorded thirty dead Indians while the Americans suffered six wounded in the attack. Scott's men destroyed Ouiatenon, including a substantial number of well-built log homes inhabited by Frenchmen. Another column under Colonel Hardin attacked two other small villages and captured fifty-two Indians, mostly women and children. Scott proceeded to burn several other villages before returning to Fort Steuben on June 15. There he turned over forty-two prisoners to the federal government, having previously released sixteen of the weakest.

Scott's expedition succeeded in demonstrating to the Indians that even their remote villages were vulnerable to attack, and with the gathering captives, he induced the Indians to seek a peace treaty. The Indians at Kekionga did not learn of the disaster until mid-June. The warriors returned to their destroyed villages and found that the body of one of their principal chiefs, Wasp, had been skinned. They were as angry with the whites as ever, but in justified fear of further retribution did not aid the Miami Confederacy when St. Clair moved against them in the fall. However, Wilkinson, now a brigadier general of militia, moved against the Wabash villages with about five hundred volunteers in August and burned two or three of them, at a cost of three or four killed or wounded. As a result of his success, he was offered a lieutenant colonel's commission in the regular army, which he accepted.

Since 1800

In the early 1800s, pioneers settled in the area around the fort. The traces of the post that still existed and artifacts left by the Wea, such as beads or a knife blade, were eventually buried under the plows of farmers. No town or village grew up over the site. The almost forgotten vanished settlement received new attention when men digging for gravel discovered parts of a uniform, some utensils, a silver crucifix, and several graves in 1889. Older settlers revealed that they had heard there had been a post slightly below the mouth of Wea Creek. His curiosity aroused, Dr. Richard Wetherill purchased the site and built a model blockhouse to mark the location.

In 1967 Joseph D. Bartlett discovered through an aerial photo that the actual site of the post was about a mile down-river from the blockhouse. An archaeology field school confirmed the location in the following two years by digging up glass gems, gunflints, earthenware shards, and other items. The Tippecanoe County Historical Association purchased the site in 1972 and additional archaeological work was conducted by Michigan State from 1974 through 1979. To date, the archaeological work at Ouiatenon has produced "one of the larges crated collections of eighteenth century European specimens in North America."

Present

Today the Fort Ouiatenon blockhouse is open only on weekends from May through September from 1–5 p.m. There are some artifacts and samples of fur trade items and clothing in the blockhouse. The highlight of the year at the thirty acre park is the Feast of the Hunter's Moon, which has been held every fall for over forty years. This annual event recreates the time period of the 1700s, complete with Native American, French, and military re-enactors. There are programs on five different stages, merchants selling replicas of trade goods from the eighteenth century, foods served representative of the time (such as fry bread), and demonstrations of crafts (for example basket making). There are also hands-on activities (such as candle-dipping), contests (such as tomahawk throwing), costume try-ons, fashion shows, and much more. For information call 765-476-8411.

Fort Wayne

At the present day site of Fort Wayne, Indiana, there have been at least five forts occupied by the French, British and Americans for a span of over one hundred years. In Fort Wayne the St. Joseph River from the north and the St. Mary's River from the south come together to form the Maumee, which flows into Lake Erie. The site, also known as Three Rivers, was recognized early by the French (Robert de La Salle in 1682 or 1683) as the best route to the Mississippi River from Canada. From Quebec or Montreal all the way to Louisiana, the French could travel almost entirely by water. They could either take a ten mile portage from the Maumee down to the Little River, a branch of the Wabash, and hence to the Mississippi; or they could travel up the St. Joseph and portage to the St. Joseph that flows into Lake Michigan and again to the Kankakee, and hence to the Mississippi. While the French may have had a post there earlier, in 1721 Charles Renaud Dubuisson came from Detroit to build a fort, which was complete by May 1722, and called Fort Miamis after the Miami Indians who lived there. (Altogether there were at least six different forts in various locations named Miami or Miamis). This fort was located on the bank of the St. Mary's at the foot of what is presently West Superior Street. It lasted until 1747.

During King George's War, the Huron chief Nicolas with the probable aid of some local Miamis captured the fort along with the eight-man garrison and then burned it. Captain Charles D. Raimond built a new fort in 1750, this time on the east side of the St. Joseph. The area grew in importance as the Miami began to concentrate principally at their village of Kekionga. From this location over 250 Miami departed in 1755 to join the French and inflict a great defeat on General Braddock. However, with the French defeat in North America to the British, the fort came under British occupation in 1760.

Pontiac's Uprising

Ensign Robert Holmes commanded the fort in 1763 with less than twenty men. By that time Sir Jeffery Amherst, commander-in-chief of His Majesty's Forces in North America, had instigated policies of restricting trade only to the forts—prohibiting the supply of ammunition and attempting to halt the flow of liquor—which had alienated the Indians. Pontiac, an Ottawa Chief, concocted a plan to fight the British by capturing all of their forts west of the Allegheny Mountains. Holmes learned from a friendly Indian that war plans were being circulated among the tribes. He had already started making preparations for an outbreak of hostilities after hearing a Frenchman report on May 23 that he had heard cannon fire at Detroit. Holmes had even sent a message of warning to his superior in Detroit, Henry Gladwin. Though he kept his twelve soldiers on extra alert at his fort, he was not prepared for the devious strategy employed by the nearby Miami Indians on May 27.

When Holmes' Miami mistress begged him to bleed her sick mother (as she had seen other white people do), he agreed to accompany her to a cabin about three hundred yards from the fort where her mother lay. Once Holmes left the fort, two concealed warriors shot and killed him in an ambush. Hearing the sound of the guns, the sergeant went outside the fort and was also killed. The Indians then demanded through the mediation of a French trader that the remaining soldiers surrender. The trader relayed the message that the Indians would spare their lives only if they surrendered, otherwise they would be killed without mercy. To emphasize their point, the Indians tossed the severed head of Holmes over the stockade wall. The dejected men then opened the gates, and all save one (who was later adopted into an Indian family) immediately met the same fate as their superiors when the Indians fell upon them.

Indian Occupation

The British never reoccupied the fort after Pontiac's Rebellion and it eventually decayed. Meanwhile the Three Rivers area, which the Indians called Kekionga or Kiskakon for an Ottawa tribe that had inhabited the area, became an important trading center for the British and Indians. To the whites, the area was known as Miami Town because of the concentration of Miami Indians. Within the area were seven Indian villages inhabited by Miami, Shawnee, and Delaware. It was the center of power for the Miami Confederation in the period following Pontiac's Rebellion, through the American Revolution, and during the Indian wars for the Northwest Territory.

For these reasons the area was a target. In the midst of the American Revolution in 1780, a Frenchman named August de la Balme raided

Kekionga with about one hundred men when most of the warriors were absent. Led by Chief Little Turtle, the vengeful Indian warriors soon caught up to La Balme's command and annihilated all but one of them in a night attack. During 1787, Secretary of War Henry Knox recommended that a post be built there to awe the Indians, but nothing came of it. Then in 1790, the expedition led by Josiah Harmar reached the Miami villages, which they abandoned in the face of his superior army of 1,400 men. Harmar's men burnt the villages and all the fields of corn. Under Little Turtle's leadership, the Indians ambushed and defeated detachments of Harmar's army. They again reoccupied the site, only more determined to resist American encroachment on their land. Territorial Governor and General Arthur St. Clair led another expedition in 1791 with the object of establishing a strong fort. However, he never reached his goal. Once again, Little Turtle led a coalition of Indians that stuck St. Clair's army of 1,400 men, inflicting the worst defeat ever suffered by an American army at the hands of the Indians. They routed St. Clair's army, killing, wounding, or capturing about nine hundred men, women, and children.

Wayne's Fort

Finally on August 20, 1794, the American army avenged its defeats when General Anthony Wayne with a well-trained army of 3,500 men defeated the Indian Confederation consisting of Miami, Shawnee, Wyandot, Potawatomi, Ottawa and other tribes in the short but nevertheless decisive Battle of Fallen Timers at the cost of twenty-six killed and eighty-seven wounded. The tribes were no longer led in battle by Little Turtle. Instead, this time Blue Jacket of the Shawnee and Buckongehelas of the Delaware had led the Indians when Little Turtle relinquished leadership shortly after the Indians were defeated in an attack on Fort Recovery. Little Turtle had stated that the Indians should make peace since "we have beaten the enemy twice under different commanders. We cannot expect the same good fortune to attend us always. The Americans are now led by a chief who never sleeps. The nights and days are alike to him, and during all the time that he has been marching on our villages, notwithstanding the watchfulness of our young men, we have never been able to surprise him. Think well of it. There is something whispers me, it would be prudent to listen to his offers of peace."

After defeating the Indian Confederation, Wayne moved toward the site of the Miami villages in early September, arriving there on September 17. Wayne selected a site for the fort that was located just to the north of where Berry Street runs today, between Lafayette and Clay Street, presently marked by a historical boulder. On September 24, Wayne ordered 250 men to begin construction under the supervision of the chief engineer Major Henry Burbeck on a 250-foot square palisade, including two separate blockhouses and another blockhouse in front of the fort. Wayne still feared British hostility and built the fort to withstand artillery. Barracks formed the curtains which were protected by earthworks and a ditch. The men also cleared five hundred acres around the site. According to Lieutenant William Clark (later of the Lewis and Clark expedition), "I think it much to be lamented that the commander-in-chief is determined to make this fort a regular fortification, as a common picketed one would be equally as difficult against the savages." However, Wayne still feared British involvement in the Northwest and built a fort to withstand artillery.

An incident causing some excitement occurred when during the construction they captured an Indian spy hiding in a tree that was being cut down. The Indian later escaped. A violent storm created another memorable incident when the top of a tree fell one night only a few feet from where Wayne was sleeping.

During the construction of the fort, food was in short supply and men attempted to desert even though lurking Indians readily pounced on them. The Indians also killed several of the hundreds of men needed to guard the supply columns destined for the fort. Wayne had to install harsh discipline on the men for fighting, theft, and misconduct. He finally sent 1,500 burdensome militia home a few days before occupying the nearly completed fort on October 19.

FORT WAYNE 1795

Colonel John Francis Hamtramck, whom Wayne had put in command of the six companies and who would remain at the fort, formally named it Fort Wayne on Wayne's orders at a ceremony on October 22. The discharge of fifteen cannon in honor of the fifteen states then in the Union highlighted the occasion. Just five days later, Wayne departed with the rest of the army, never to return to the fort. Wayne wrote Hamtramck, "To your charge and conduct the defense of this important barrier is now committed . . . in full confidence that it will be Maintained to the last extremity & for which purpose it will for the present be endowed with a Garrison of full three hundred men Officers included, composed of Artillery, Infantry & Riflemen." Hamtramck had his hands full with disciplinary problems. He complained to Wayne, "It is with a great degree of mortification that I am obliged to inform your Excellency of the great propensity many of the soldiers have to larceny. I have flogged them till I am tired. The economic allowance of one hundred lashes allowed by government does not appear a sufficient inducement for a rascal to act the part of an honest man."

With the signing of the Treaty of Greenville on August 3, 1795, the Miami, Delaware, Shawnee, Potawatomi, Wyandot, Ottawa, Chippewa, Wea, Piankashaw, Kickapoo, and Kaskaskia ceded 25,000 square miles of land and sixteen reserves inside their territory to the United States. The cost to the United States was $25,000 and a promised annual allowance to the various tribes. Fort Wayne was one of these reserves and included six square miles around the fort. Along with Fort Defiance and Greeneville, Fort Wayne served as a place where Indians surrendered prisoners as required by the terms of the treaty.

Second American Fort

In May 1796, Hamtramck left the fort to take command of Fort Miami from the British.

From 1794, Fort Wayne stood as a remote post difficult to supply at times. In the winter of 1796-97, the garrison faced famine and starvation. In 1799, James Wilkinson, commander of the army, sought for the abandonment of most of the Anthony Wayne built forts, including Fort Wayne. Instead, a new commander, Colonel Thomas Hunt, who had arrived in May 1798, built a new fort in 1800 believed to be about the same size as the first about three hundred feet north of the old stockade. He built six log barracks, a brick magazine and several smaller buildings. This is the fort that essentially would withstand a siege in the War of 1812 after remodeling during the administrations of Captain John Whipple (1803-1807) and captain James Rhea (1810-1812).

By 1798 the U.S. government appointed William Wells as an Indian agent to serve at the agency to be established at Fort Wayne to represent the government to the Indian tribes in the area. Wells also assisted in distributing provisions granted by the Treaty of Greenville to the tribes. The agency officially opened in 1802. Also, during the period from

1802-1812, Fort Wayne served as a site for an Indian trading factory. The trading factories housed goods for distribution to the Indians and served as trading centers. They were also established to gain control over the Indians from the British and to influence the Indians to cede land to pay off debts accumulated at the trading factories. Initially, Fort Wayne was one of the first two of eventually twenty-eight different factories to be established at one place or another prior to the abolishment of the system in 1822. Colonel John Johnston served as the first factor at Fort Wayne from 1802-1811.

Fort Wayne proved to be the most prosperous of all the ten factories or trading houses that conducted business prior to the War of 1812. In little less than the four years before January 1812, the Fort Wayne factory could boast of a profit of $10,502.77. An example of the quantity of furs collected at the fort is illustrated by the list given by Johnston in May and June 1807 for the 110 packs shipped to Detroit: Bear 130; Beaver 47 lbs.; Deer: Does 1,649, Bucks 403; Cat, Fox, and Fisher 248; Mink 24; Muskrat 254; Otter 94; Raccoon 7,894; and Wolf 8. In return the Indians traded for many of the following goods that were sent to the fort: Cotton hose, flannel, broadcloth, wool hats, brass kettles, beaver traps, horn powder flasks, candle holders, claw hammers, soap, candles, saddles, gunpowder, shot, razors, gunflints, medicine, handkerchiefs, looking glasses, awls, coffee, silk, lead, vermillion, chocolate, ivory combs, beads and other items.

In the years that Governor Harrison ruled the Indiana Territory from 1802 through 1810, he extinguished the Indian title to over 29 million acres of land. This greatly incensed many Indians. Under the leadership of Tecumseh and his brother Tenskwatawa, the Prophet, many of them intended to unite in a confederation of tribes to resist any further land acquisitions by the whites and to force the whites to repeal the most recent Treaty of Fort Wayne in 1809, whereby Harrison had obtained 2,900,000 acres. Learning that Tecumseh's followers planned on attacking white settlements under encouragement from British agents, Harrison planned a preemptive strike in the fall of 1811. In October he began marching with over eight hundred men towards the Indian village at Tippecanoe while Tecumseh was traveling down south to gather additional allies. After marching to within a mile of the village, he set up camp. During the night, the Indians attacked and were defeated. Many then scattered back to their own tribes.

Siege of Fort Wayne

In the wake of the Battle of Tippecanoe, the Americans had warning that the Indians under Tecumseh's leadership still were predisposed toward making war on the frontier. In February 1812, the Indian agent William Wells stated that if war broke out between the U.S. and Britain, the Potawatomi would strike both Fort Dearborn and Fort Wayne. Furthermore in March he wrote of Tecumseh that "he has determined to raise all the Indians he can immediately, with an intention, no doubt, to attack our frontiers." On July 6, the inhabitants of Fort Wayne learned that the U.S. had declared war on Britain (on June 17). The increasingly wary commander, Captain James Rhea, gave orders on July 15 to the garrison: "In the future, as soon as a dancing party of Indians comes within fifty yards of the garrison, the guard will parade and stand with their arms until the party leaves. Every soldier will be in readiness to take hold of his arms in case anything should happen, instantly. It is time for all soldiers to be on the lookout."

Shortly after the Fort Dearborn massacre on August 15, Miami Indians friendly to the Americans informed Fort Wayne's eighty-five men garrison of the event. The inhabitants there still had not learned of the fall of Fort Mackinac or of General William Hull's disgraceful surrender of Detroit. Nevertheless, in preparation for the expected blow, they sent most of their women and children to a safe refuge at Piqua, Ohio, one hundred miles from Fort Wayne. Shortly after their departure, between four hundred to five hundred Potawatomi, Shawnee, Miami, and Delaware Indians camped around Fort Wayne. As decided by a council held with the British after the Fort Dearborn Massacre, the Indians planned to wait for a British force under Major Adam Muir bringing artillery to batter down the fort walls. The British had promised their force would arrive within twenty days.

Though the fort could withstand any Indian attack, it was vulnerable to a 6 or 9-pound cannon that could be placed on one of several heights on the south side of the fort. At the time the garrison had only about seventy effectives, with four small pieces of artillery. There were sufficient provisions and water to hold out under siege until relief could arrive.

As had happened in so many like circumstances, the Americans received warning from a member of the enemy. Metea, a Potawatomi chief, revealed the plan to attack the fort to Antoine Bondie, a French trader with an Indian wife, so that they could escape with their lives. Instead of escaping, Bondie informed Benjamin Stickney, the Indian factor at the fort, who in turn informed Captain Rhea. Though Rhea initially discounted the plot, on the night of August 24 or 25 he sent a message to General Worthington and Governor Meigs asserting that he expected the Indians to attack that night. He finished his letter stating, "I think our situation is truly alarming and that our safety depends on assistance we may receive." This desperate message would be the last sent from the fort prior to the beginning of the siege. Meanwhile, Captain Rhea began consuming enough alcohol to escape the reality of the danger around him. Stickney wrote of him, "The commanding officer was drunk nearly all the time."

The situation worsened on the night of the twenty-eighth when Stephen Johnston (brother of the previous fort factor Peter Oliver) and an unknown soldier recently discharged, attempted to leave the fort for Piqua, where Johnston intended to reunite with his wife. About a half mile from the fort, Indians fired on the men, killing Johnston. The other two men raced back safely to the fort. The next day the Indians began plundering and destroying the gardens and the fields surrounding the fort and killing any livestock. They also burnt the rest of the settlement, including the factor's house and those of the traders and families living near the fort. Yet, the garrison did not fire upon the Indians.

The garrison received much encouragement about September 1 when William Oliver and four Shawnees, including John Logan rode into the fort. He let them know that their messages had made it through to Harrison and that he was leading a relief force that should start marching toward the fort in three or four days. One of the lieutenants at the fort later said, "The safe arrival of Oliver at that particular juncture may be considered miraculous, one hour sooner or one hour later, would no doubt have been inevitable destruction both to himself and his escort. It is generally believed by those acquainted with the circumstances, that not one hour, for eight days and nights preceding or following the hour which Mr. Oliver arrived, would have afforded an opportunity of any safety." Soon afterwards Oliver sent the Shawnees back to Harrison to inform him of the fort's condition.

On September 3, Rhea gave his last recorded order proclaiming, "It is earnestly hoped by the commanding officer that for this night everyman will be at his post. Relief is at hand. For on this night, our fame, our honor and everything that is near and dear depends. Be therefore cautious and brave." However, the next day Rhea began to waver in his courage. When the Potawatomi chief Winnemac and others entered the fort to meet with him, Rhea asked if they were going to make war or keep the peace. Winnemac replied: "I don't know what to tell you, but you know that Mackinac is taken, Detroit is in the hands of the British and you must expect to fall next, and probably in a few days." Rhea then invited him to drink some wine with him and asked him to spare his life if the fort was captured, also declaring to him, "My good friend I love you I will fight for you, I will die by your side."

The next morning the Indians stoked Rhea's fear further when warriors hidden near the fort killed two soldiers who ventured outside. The Indians then made one attempt to capture the fort through a ruse. They approached the fort under a flag of truce on September 5 (some accounts give different dates) saying that they now desired to make peace. Stickney only allowed thirteen chiefs to enter and they were supposedly disarmed. After a period of discussion, Chief Winnemac said, "If my father wishes war, I am a man!" He then flashed a knife he had hidden under his blanket in an apparent signal to the rest of the Indians, who hoped to murder the officers and take control of the fort. However, Blondie, who understood Potawatomi, then drew out his own knife and shouted, "I too, am a man." The shouting quickly attracted nearby soldiers, and one of Winnemac's conspirators, who had been looking out the window, signaled a halt to any action. The Indians then immediately departed. Following this incident Lieutenant Daniel Curtis and Lieutenant Phillip Ostrander essentially took over the command of the fort. Curtis later claimed that Rhea was continually drunk for the rest of the siege.

Because he feared that the Indians would soon attack and try to set the fort pickets on fire during the night, Lieutenant Daniel Curtis set up a tripwire with thirty bells about ten inches above the ground and twelve feet away from the pickets to give warning of any intruders. For good measure he had the men water the roofs and fill buckets with water in position for putting out fires. About 8:00 p.m. that evening with a loud noise, the Indians approached the fort and announced to the garrison that they had five hundred men and would soon have over one thousand. They taunted the troops, boasting that in three days time they would take the fort. Curtis later stated: "We answered them that we were ready, and bade them to come on; that we were determined to a man to fight till we should lose our lives before we would yield an inch to them, and then we gave a general shout around the works in true Aborigine style, which they instantly returned, commencing at the same time a general fire." In the ensuing fight, the fort artillery helped to drive off their attack. Firing from both antagonists would continue on and off until September 10. Repeatedly the men put out fires on the buildings started by flaming arrows.

Attempting to intimidate the garrison, the Indians had shaped two logs to appear as artillery when observed from a distance. They approached the fort under a flag of truce and called on the Americans to surrender, for they now possessed artillery sent by the British. If the garrison did not immediately surrender, they would all be massacred the following day. Buckling under the strain, Rhea talked of surrender, especially if the British started firing the artillery that had been captured at Chicago's Fort Dearborn. Ostrander then told him that there had only been a three-pounder at Dearborn and that if any one tried to surrender in those circumstances he would be shot immediately. Afterwards Rhea maintained a silence on the subject. The garrison had learned from William Oliver, who had returned to the fort on September 1, that help was on the way. Therefore the garrison ignored the demand to surrender. Sporadic firing continued until only one other serious attack, on the tenth, just prior to the arrival of a relief force. During the siege the

Indians managed to kill three of the garrison and wound many others. It is estimated that the Indians lost about twenty-five killed or wounded.

Meanwhile, territorial Governor William Henry Harrison had been gathering an army to march to the relief of the fort. Harrison had learned of the siege as early as August 28. He wrote to Secretary of War William Eustis from Cincinnati, "The relief of Fort Wayne will be my first object." On the next day his 2,200 men began their march. On September 2, he reached Piqua where he received information that 140 British and 400 Indians under Tecumseh had left Malden on August 18 intending to assist in the siege of Fort Wayne. After ascertaining from scouts that the British-Indian force had not yet passed the site of Fort Defiance and having received a supply of much needed flints, Harrison left Piqua and proceeded toward Fort Wayne. On September 8, Richard M. Johnson joined him with a force of Kentucky mounted volunteers. The Indians had sent out spies and were aware of Harrison's army. They had reported back to their chiefs that "Kentuck is coming as numerous as the trees." By this time Harrison's army had grown to 3,500 men. Harrison had not heard from the fort since September 3 and feared that the fort may not have been able to resist a siege that long.

On both nights of September 9 and 11, sentinels fired on Indians spying on the army. Harrison wrote the secretary of war on the eleventh, predicting that his army would fight a battle the next day as they approached the fort that was now only seventeen miles distant. He had already forwarded a small detachment ahead to approach the fort, but they could not penetrate the Indians surrounding the fort, though they did defeat a small party of warriors. Nevertheless, Johnny Logan, the friendly Shawnee scout, did manage to reach the fort and inform the garrison that relief was near. Finally on the twelfth, Harrison's army reached the fort at about three o'clock in the afternoon, having seen only one Indian on their march. The garrison had viewed the Indians leaving hastily before Harrison's arrival. They would never again mount any significant attacks in Indiana Territory throughout the remainder of the war. The relief of the siege benefited more than just the garrison; it gave an important psychological uplift to the inhabitants of the Northwest Territory after a succession of disasters at Forts Mackinac, Dearborn, and Detroit.

The morning following Harrison's arrival, Curtis and other officers brought charges of drunkenness against Rhea. He was arrested with the intent of a court martial. However, In consideration of his old age, long service, and young family, Harrison asked for his sword and proposed that he would drop charges for a court martial if Rhea would resign. Rhea accepted and retired in disgrace.

In November, Captain Hugh Moore arrived and took command from Lieutenant Philip Ostrander, who Harrison had left in charge. The next summer Major Joseph Jenkinson succeeded him. The fort served as a center for supplying the American armies in Northern Ohio and Eastern Michigan during the 1813 campaigns. Still another commander, Major John Whistler, assumed command of the fort in May 1814. The next year Whistler asked and received permission from the War Department to rebuild the fort. As author Charles Poinsatte stated, "Thus it fell to the lot of the builder of the first Fort Dearborn to become in turn the builder of the last Fort Wayne." Whistler had also been involved in building the fort under Anthony Wayne in 1794 and Colonel Thomas Hunt in 1800.

Whistler's Fort

Whistler built a smaller fort only 150 feet square with 10 foot high pickets and two-story overhanging blockhouses on the southeast and northwest corners. He constructed officer's quarters, a commissary department, and other buildings on the perimeter to form part of the walls. The roofs of the buildings sloped toward the inside to inhibit an enemy from setting them on fire. Though Whistler bragged that the fort was the most substantial in the West, it was destined to only remain occupied by the army until its formal evacuation on April 19, 1819. Thus what had been the first U.S. built fort in Indiana became the last to be evacuated. Afterwards civil authorities, such as Indian agent Benjamin Stickney, controlled the fort. It served as a location for government agencies (a land office was established in 1822), shelter for settlers, and a center for annuity payments to the Indians of the Old Northwest. Finally in 1852, John Fairfield demolished the multi storied officers quarters, the last part of the fort standing, to clear the land for alternative development of the site.

Present

In the early 1970s, a renewed interest in the historic forts of Fort Wayne was generated by the coming Bicentennial. In 1976 a group known as Historic Fort Wayne, headed by Keith Barker, Lynn Kochlinger, and Charles Walker, gathered the funds to reconstruct a fort based on the extant plans of the fort constructed by John Whistler in 1816. The fort was built on the banks of the St. Mary's River on a four acre site on Spy Run Avenue close to the location of the original. After construction costs of $1.2 million, it opened on June 5, 1976. A bronze statue of Little Turtle was also placed on the west side of the river across from the fort. However, due to falling attendance and the cost of upkeep, the Historical Society, which had been administering the fort, closed its doors. After the Society offered to sell the fort for $1.00 to any group that would keep the fort open, the city agreed to take it over, but allowed the fort to continue deteriorating.

Finally in the spring of 2004, after the Fort Wayne Parks and Recreation Department publicly sought proposals to revitalize the "Old Fort," a group of concerned citizens stepped forward and formed Historic Fort Wayne Inc., a not for profit group, to oversee the fort. Presently, one can only enter the buildings of the fort during special events hosted by the organization from May through October. The Three Rivers Festival held in July each year is a special highlight where the War of 1812 is waged at the fort with demonstrations of how the soldiers would have fought. The admission is free, but donations are collected. Call 260-460-4763, or check the website, www.oldfortwayne.org, to find the schedule for special events.

Battle of Tippecanoe

In 1800 William H. Harrison, who previously served as secretary of the Northwest Territory, was appointed governor of Indiana Territory by President John Adams. The states of Illinois, Indiana, Wisconsin and portions of Michigan and Minnesota formed the territory and contained a white population of about five thousand. Harrison established the territorial government in Vincennes. In various treaties from 1802 through 1809 Harrison obtained a total of over 29 million acres of Indian land for the United States. In the most recent, the 1809 Treaty of Fort Wayne, under instruction from President James Madison, he paid $8,200 down and annuities amounting to $2,350 to the chiefs of the Delaware, Potawatomi, Miami, and Eel River tribes for 2.9 million acres. Though this greatly increased his popularity with white settlers who were continually pouring into the young territory, it only increased the animosity of the native population.

Due to the loss of their land, the lessening of game, and the debilitating effect of white influence on their culture—especially through the consumption of alcohol—many Indians began to follow Tenskwatawa ("The Loud Voice"), the Shawnee Prophet who preached a return to traditional Indian ways. Tenskwatawa, formerly known as Lalawethika, a younger brother to Tecumseh ("The Wildcat springing on its Prey"), assumed the new name in 1805 when he claimed to have had visions, talked to the Master of Life, and visited Heaven and Hell. He began preaching a new religion urging the Indians to give up alcohol, throw away their medicine bags, live with only one wife, wear only Indian dress, and dispose of European introduced animals (except for the too valuable horse). He taught that the Indians should not live near the whites, that they would be supernaturally overthrown, and meanwhile the Indians should not sell anymore land without unanimous consent among the tribes. He said that the Great Serpent, ruler of the powers of evil in the universe, had created the Americans. He also advocated getting rid of old leaders and incited the murder of some Delaware chiefs who stood against him. Together with his brother, the warrior Tecumseh, he established a community at Greenville, Ohio, in 1806-1807.

Most frontiersmen believed the British were instigating the Indians to war against the Americans. Harrison knew better. An informed intelligence source had written to him: "although I am decidedly of the opinion that the tendency of the British measures is hostility to us, candor obliges me to inform you that, from two Indians of different tribes, I have received information that the British Agent absolutely dissuaded them from going to war against the United States." In any case, whites were fearful that the Prophet was inciting violence toward them. They condemned the Prophet and his followers and clamored for his removal.

Under pressure from the white population, Tecumseh and Tenskwatawa, neither of whom was a chief by birthright, moved to Delaware-donated land in Indiana to continue their work of establishing an Indian confederation that with unity of purpose would resist any further white encroachment. They established Prophetstown, known to the Indians as Keh-tip-a quo-wonk, in 1808 on the north bank of the Wabash a little below the mouth of the Tippecanoe. There they gathered and trained Indians from many tribes. As many as one thousand warriors and three hundred women and children lived there in dwellings built in rows with lanes or streets between them. The Prophet did not fail to remind them of white injustice. The white government deducted money from their annuities whenever horses were stolen from any whites; however, white men could openly murder an Indian and get away with it. In the history of the Indiana Territory, no white man was ever convicted of the murder of an Indian, even when the evidence was undeniable.

Tecumseh particularly resented the recent 1809 Treaty at Fort Wayne. He had already stated that the tribes could not sell land without the unanimous consent of all. He threatened to kill any of the chiefs who signed the treaty and any surveyors attempting to mark off the land. When this was reported to Harrison, he sent a message to the Prophet, who he still believed was leading the Indian opposition against his land acquisitions, stating:

> I know your warriors are brave, but ours are not less so. What can a few brave warriors do against the innumerable warriors of the Seventeen Fires? Our bluecoats are more numerous than you can count; our hunters are like the leaves of the forest, or the grains of sand on the Wabash. Do not think that the red-coats can protect you; they are not able to protect themselves. They do not think of going to war with us. If they did, you would in a few moons see our flag wave over all the forts of Canada.

Harrison then invited the Prophet to come to Vincennes to discuss any complaints he had about the Treaty of Fort Wayne. He told the Prophet that he had the power to right any wrongs that had been committed. Instead of the Prophet, Tecumseh and about seventy-five warriors arrived at Vincennes in August 1810 to meet with Harrison.

Tecumseh met with Harrison in the summers of 1810 and 1811. In the meetings he warned him that the Indians would resist any attempts to survey the land and that he wanted the United States to return the land, or there would be war. He told Harrison that he was forming a confederacy among the tribes to prevent any single tribe from selling land without consent of the others. He said that he would rather be an ally of the Seventeen Fires (United States) than to be drawn into a war against them. However, if they would not make another treaty with him, he would be forced to join with the British. The Governor said he would inform the President of Tecumseh's position. Tecumseh replied, "Well, as the great chief is to determine the matter, I hope the Great Spirit will put sense enough into his head to induce him to give up this land; it is true he is so far off, he will not be injured by war; he may sit still in his town and drink his wine, while you and I will have to fight it out." From the tone of these meetings, Harrison likely believed that war was inevitable.

Following these meetings, Indian depredations continued on the frontier with the murder of several whites. Harrison had sent various Frenchmen to spy on the Prophet to remain informed on his plans and activities. They reported to him that that the Prophet had confiscated more than his share at the annual distribution of the salt annuity (granted by treaty), remarking at the same time that the two thousand Indians Tecumseh was bringing would require the use of it. An Ioway Indian visiting St. Louis had started a new wave of fear throughout the frontier. He had alluded to Indian plans when he let it slip out that "the time is drawing near when the murder is to begin, and all the Indians that will not join are to die with the whites."

Harrison continually heard from friendly Indians of the hostile intentions of the two brothers and Tecumseh's travels to gain additional allies. In addition, he learned that many Indians had departed from the center of the Indian Confederation, the village at Tippecanoe, because the Prophet was inciting them to participate in a massacre at Vincennes and to surprise and massacre the garrisons at Chicago, Fort Wayne, Detroit, and St. Louis. He was also informed that the Sauks and Foxes had joined the alliance. In one incident a small party of Indians, probably Potawatomi, stole some horses and then killed the three men who pursued them. Realizing his own weakness, Harrison sent a call for help to Secretary of War William Eustis and to the governors of nearby states. In response he received nine companies of the Fourth Regiment U.S. Infantry led by Colonel John Parker Boyd.

He then began contemplating plans to break up the Indian Confederation and received permission from the secretary of war to take action against it. As governor, Harrison would lead any army marching against the Indians. When nineteen years old, he had joined the army as an ensign, shortly after the defeat of St. Clair's army by the Miami Confederation headed by Little Turtle. He soon earned promotion to lieutenant and in 1793 was appointed the second aid-de-camp to the commander-in-chief of the army, General Anthony Wayne. In the Battle of Fallen Timbers, he formed the left wing of the troops (Tecumseh also participated in opposing Wayne's army). At the age of twenty-three he was given the command of Fort Washington. Thus he had proven his competence in the army, had battle experience, and had received instruction from the most successful general in the Northwest, Anthony Wayne. When he proceeded on a campaign against the Indians, he knew what was required to wage a successful campaign in regard to equipment, transportation, men, tactics, and leadership.

Fully aware of Tecumseh's leadership in the Indian movement, Harrison wrote a letter to him accusing him of planning a war. He wanted Tecumseh to come to Vincennes to explain his actions. Tecumseh came to Vincennes in August 1811 with over three hundred armed warriors to explain his actions. In a tense atmosphere, both men voiced their complaints without resolving any differences. Tecumseh made the mistake of informing Harrison that he was journeying to the south to complete his confederacy and would settle everything when he returned. He would even see the U.S. president.

Determined to crush Indian resistance while Tecumseh was away on a recruiting mission among the Southern Creek, Choctaw, and Cherokee tribes, Harrison let it be known that he was getting ready to march against Prophetstown. He warned the tribes to withdraw their men from the village.

When Tenskwatawa and his assistants learned of this, they sent a delegation of Kickapoos to try to conciliate Harrison. Harrison wanted the recently stolen horses returned, and the murders turned in. The Indians could not meet his terms. Harrison then began marching from Vincennes toward Prophetstown 180 miles away on September 26, 1811, at the head of an army of 1,000 men. About one third of Harrison's army were regulars under Colonel John Parker Boyd; the rest consisted of 400 Indiana militia under Lieutenant-Colonel Joseph Bartholomew, 120 mounted Kentucky volunteers under Joseph Hamilton Daviess (a famous and popular lawyer in his state who as a U.S. Attorney had prosecuted Aaron Burr in 1806), and 80 mounted riflemen under Captain Spier Spencer. The regulars wore brass-buttoned tail coats and stove-pipe hats while the citizen soldiers displayed their deerskin jackets and bearskin caps. Just north of present day Terre Haute, Indiana, Harrison halted the army for about three weeks and built a fort. According to Isaac Naylor (one of the soldiers in the army who kept a diary), Joseph Daviess represented the unanimous will of the officers by requesting that the fort be named after their commander. Harrison completed the stockade fort, including blockhouses on three of the angles, over about an acre of ground on a bluff approximately thirty to forty feet above the Wabash on October 28. The fort was to serve as a storehouse for supplies and a refuge in the event the campaign suffered a disaster or defeat. During the fort construction, Indians fired on and wounded one sentry. After this incident Harrison considered himself in a state of war with the Prophet.

Leaving a small force behind under Lieutenant Colonel James Miller, Harrison left on the twenty-ninth and continued the march toward Prophetstown near the junction of the Tippecanoe and Wabash Rivers. He again stopped briefly on November 2 to build a twenty-five square foot blockhouse about three miles below the Vermilion River on the west side of the Wabash to provide a guard for the supply boats.

While on the march, Harrison received authority from the secretary of war to disperse the Indians from Prophetstown. The Indians had made no successful attempt for a full scale attack on the army during the march toward them despite the existence of several good ambush sites. Harrison's good fortune in avoiding an attack can be attributed to the skill of his scout Zachariah Cicott II, who helped him avoid an ambush near Big Pine Creek on his way to Prophetstown. Cicott also has been credited by some to have gone south a year before Tecumseh's recruiting mission to the southern tribes and persuaded many to refrain from joining Tecumseh's confederacy. However, the Indians did fire on a boat carrying corn for the army about four miles above Fort Harrison, killing one of the crew in the attack. Waubansee, a Potawatomi chief, had leapt onto the boat and killed the boatman while his crew pulled the boat upriver with a rope on the opposite bank. Many of the Indians fled as Harrison's army approached Prophetstown.

Harrison's army neared Prophetstown on the afternoon of November 6. There he sent out the head of his scouts, Captain Touissant Dubois, to meet with the Prophet, but he was ignored. Harrison's army then advanced in attack formation until they were within 150 yards from the outskirts of the town, where Harrison observed Indians scurrying behind log breastworks. As recorded by Isaac Naylor, "When the army arrived in view of Prophetstown an Indian was seen coming toward General Harrison, with a white flag suspended on a pole. Here the army halted, and a parley was had between General Harrison and an Indian delegation who assured the general that they desired peace and friendship between them and the United States." They told him that a peace delegation had gone down the east bank of the Wabash, but had missed him because his army was on the west side. Chief White Horse, one of the Prophet's principal counselors, whom Harrison knew, and the others made an agreement to prevent all hostilities before a meeting between Harrison and the Prophet the next day. Harrison told the Indians that he would not attack if they would comply with his demands. Harrison's army then made camp less than a mile from the Indian village at a site chosen by Major Marston Clark and Walter Taylor after listening to Indian suggestions. Harrison did not believe the Indians contemplated an attack since they had foregone excellent opportunities during his march.

The camp was situated near present-day Battleground, Indiana, on high ground next to Burnett's Creek. It covered about ten acres of land in the shape of an irregular Parallelogram. The rear of the camp, guarded by militia, ran for about three hundred yards facing the creek. On the northern side or left flank, Samuel Wells placed his Kentucky riflemen. The regulars defended the three hundred yards facing the prairie, and Spencer's riflemen stood on the eighty yards composing the right flank. The baggage, horses and cattle, and command tents occupied the center of the camp, as did the cavalry, which were to act as a reserve. While some of Harrison's men felt disappointment, believing there would no longer be a battle, Colonel Jo Daviess was heard to say that without a doubt he believed the Indians would attack before the morning. The men did not build a barricade of logs because there had only been enough axes to cut firewood; however, they were ordered to sleep on their arms and in place to immediately fall into their lines if necessary. The night was dark and cloudy with a drizzling rain; the moon rose late. Taking precautions against attack, Harrison placed about 108 guards and sentinels under Captain James Bigger and three lieutenants far enough outside the camp perimeter to give sufficient notice of an attack. The watchword for the men that night was "wide awake, wide awake."

The Battle

The next day did not unfold as generally expected. According to Shabonee, a Potawatomi chief and grand nephew of Pontiac, during the night two white men persuaded the Prophet to attack Harrison's army. From a captured Negro wagon driver named Ben, the Prophet learned that Harrison's army did not have any cannon with them and that Harrison intended to attack the next day. The Prophet decided to ignore Tecumseh's command to avoid battle and to attack first. He bolstered the courage of the approximately five hundred to six hundred Indians present, telling them that victory was theirs and that the white man's bullets would not harm them—the gunpowder had already changed into sand and the bullets to mud. He also told them that he had received assurance from the Master of Life that if they struck before the next sunrise the darkness would hide them, and they would achieve victory.

The Indians, primarily Winnebago and Kickapoo with contingents of Shawnee, Wyandot, Potawatomi, and Piankeshaw, moved in positions around the quadrangle shaped camp in the hours before dawn. According to various sources, Indian leadership has been attributed to Mengotowa of the Kickapoo, Waweapakoosa of the Winnebago, and Shabbona, Waubonsee, Winnamac of the Potawatomi, along with White Loon and Stone Eater. The Kickapoos were to fire on one side of the camp and the Winnebagos the other. The Indian force of between four hundred to five hundred men were to creep on their bellies to get as close as possible before assaulting Harrison's army of almost a thousand men. They were attempting to sneak into camp to first kill Harrison, whom they had been observing throughout the march and had been given the opportunity to shoot many times. The Prophet had foretold the disintegration of the army if they could first kill Harrison. However, shortly before 4:00 a.m., their plans were swept aside. First, two pickets, Private William Brigham and William Brown, heard an arrow swish past them, and they turned to run back to camp. Then Corporal Stephen Mars of Geiger's Kentucky Volunteers, a sharp eyed sentry, spotted an Indian and shot him. Mars started back towards camp but was killed before he could enter the lines. The wounded Indian cried out. Immediately the others rose up and began yelling expecting the soldiers to run away.

The troops responded quickly to the yells, which only served to alert them to the danger. If the attack had started just four minutes later, they would already have been in their positions in a single rank around the camp perimeter—Harrison was just in the process of putting on his boots and preparing to give the order to arouse the men when the attack started. Nevertheless, the Indians quickly hit Captain Barton's company and Captain Geiger's company on the left angle of the rear line first. Naylor stated that the Indians were already charging the line less than a minute after he heard the first two rifle shots. Inside the camp the men were targets in the light of the camp fires which had been left burning since many of the men did not have blankets or tents. Early in the battle, Indian sharpshooters took advantage and inflicted casualties before the soldiers extinguished the fires.

A few Indians penetrated the lines and were quickly killed in the center of the camp. One was killed while attempting to tomahawk Captain Geiger in the back of his tent, where he had gone to fetch a new weapon for a soldier who had lost his gun. Indians had their sights on Harrison who they knew rode a gray mare. Harrison had mounted a horse at the first sounds of battle. His own horse had broken its tether and could not be found. Instead, Harrison had mounted a bay. His aide, Abraham Owen had rushed out to join Harrison. After jumping on his own light colored horse, he was immediately fired on from ambush and killed. Harrison stated afterwards that he thought the Indians were trying to kill him because they had apparently been waiting for him to mount his gray horse. Harrison survived the assassination attempt but did suffer a graze to his head when a bullet passed through his hat.

Harrison stated that his men responded quickly as veterans, though "nineteen-twentieths" of them had never been in an Indian battle before. His first response was to ride quickly toward the rear northeast angle that received the first Indian charge. Seeing that the Indians were severely punishing Barton's company—thirteen of his raw recruits had already fled toward the center of the camp—he quickly reinforced them with Cook's company and Wentworth's company (now under Lieutenant Peters). He then busied himself rushing to and fro from one part of the perimeter to the other, sending reinforcements where needed most. The rest of the perimeter had not been under immediate attack since the Indians had not moved into their positions, having been forced into battle before final preparations by the firing of the sentry. Harrison later stated, "My great object was to keep the lines entire, to prevent the enemy from breaking into the camp until daylight should enable me to make a general and effectual charge."

A grove of oak trees sheltered the Indians on both flanks. The left flank (the southeast angle) almost immediately caught Harrison's attention after he relieved Barton. Stationed there were the companies of Baen, Snelling, and Prescott, of the Fourth Regiment. There Colonel Daviess sought permission form Harrison to charge the Indians to remove them from their shelter. Finally, after three times Harrison allowed him to use his own discretion. Daviess, dressed in a white coat, charged with only eight men and was shot down almost instantly as the Indians fell on the flanks of his small force (he died of his wounds thirty-six hours later). Captain Josiah Snelling then charged with his company and dispersed the Indians from the grove. Next, Harrison rode over to the right flank and the right of the rear line where Captain Spier Spencer's mounted riflemen and those of Warrick's company were posted. He arrived there and asked where Spencer was. Ensign John Tipton answered him, "Dead." Harrison then asked, "Where are the lieutenants." Again Tipton replied, "Dead." Finally, he inquired, "Where is the ensign?" Tipton replied, "I am here." Harrison ordered him to hold his position and promised to relieve him right away. He immediately sent him Robb's company of regulars. For his cool conduct and heroism, Harrison commission Tipton a captain of his company as his reward. Harrison's men fought off at least three Indian charges pouring a devastating fire at them with cartridges filled with twelve-buckshot in each one. Concentrating at both ends of the camp using the oak trees for cover they rushed toward the camp in groups. The Indians fought using a rare tactic for them: one group would fire and retreat to load while the other group rushed forward.

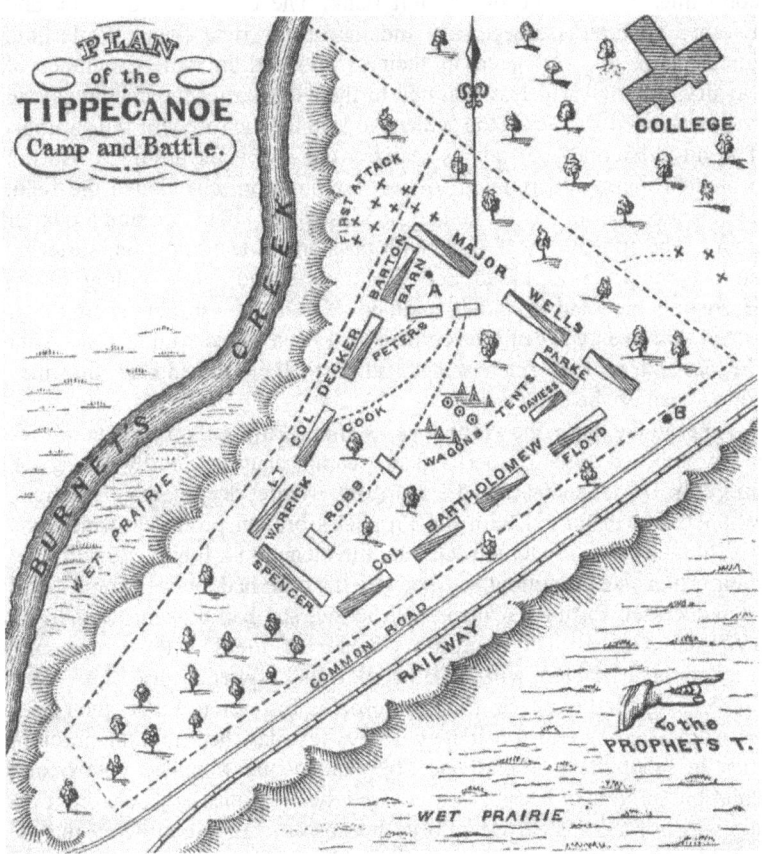

Image credit: Tippecanoe County Historical Association

As Harrison's second in command, Colonel Boyd commanded the infantry during the battle. Boyd had begun his army career as an Ensign in 1786. He resigned in 1788, traveled to India, and fought with the British as they conquered the country. He organized his own army of mercenaries in the early 1800s gathered from the best horsemen India had to offer. He owned all of the equipment, horses, cannon (which he transported on the backs of elephants), and weapons. By renting his army to various princes of India, he became a wealthy man before returning to the United States in 1808. During Tippecanoe he rallied the men with the words, "Huzza! My sons of gold, a few more fires and victory will be ours." In the years after the battle, Harrison's political enemies would attribute the victory to Boyd instead of Harrison.

With daybreak Harrison prepared to order charges from both sides of the perimeter. Major Samuel Wells, unaware of Harrison's plans, led four companies in a charge on the left flank. The companies of Cook and Larabee afterwards charged the Indians on the right flank. While both forces were uncoordinated in their efforts and limited in number of cavalry, they nevertheless returned to their lines after the charge having had succeeded in forcing the Indians to flee for the safety of the swamps. The now demoralized Indians realized the Prophet's promises had not protected them, and running low on ammunition, abandoned the field. Thus ended the bloody battle that had lasted for about two and a quarter hours. The Indians had fought with passionate determination, suffering an estimated 25-50 killed and 70-80 wounded while killing 68 of Harrison's men and wounding another 120. One newspaper account later stated that twenty-six of the sentinels had been killed with arrows. After the battle Harrison's men scalped almost all of the Indians that they found dead on the battlefield.

During the battle the Prophet had stationed himself on a ledge of rock a few hundred yards from Harrison's camp, chanting loudly during the entire battle to encourage the warriors. While fleeing the battlefield, Winnebagos disgusted with the Prophet's broken promises came upon him at the rock (Prophet's Rock) and threatened to kill him. He deflected their criticism by claiming that because his wife had touched some of his sacred vessels during her menstrual period, she had broken the spell. In 1929 the General De Lafayette Chapter of the D.A.R. permanently marked the location of what became know as Prophet's Rock

Fearing another attack, Harrison ordered his men to fortify their lines with breastworks four feet in height. The next day, he sent out a group of men to scout the surroundings. They found one wounded Potawatomi chief on the field of battle. They advised the chief that he would die if his leg was not amputated. He refused because of the Indian belief that he would need all of his limbs to be a good hunter in the after life. Harrison left him with an old squaw in the now deserted town. He was to deliver a message (which he did before he died) to the other Indians that if they would leave the Prophet, Harrison would forgive them.

Harrison's men found new equipment and supplies from the British in the town. The army then burned Prophetstown and over five thousand bushels of corn and beans, including food caches that were hidden in the nearby woods. With rumors flying that Tecumseh was coming with one thousand warriors, and being low on food supplies since the Indians had either killed or driven off their forty head of cattle, they buried their dead in mass graves two feet high with five to ten men in each grave, made the wounded as comfortable as they possibly could, and started back toward Vincennes on November 9. According to Isaac Naylor, they were issued rations for two days the morning following the battle and did not receive any additional rations for six days. Harrison took Spier Spencer's fourteen-year-old son, who had accompanied his father, under his personal care.

The battlefield result may have been very different if the Indians had managed to kill Harrison early in the battle. That they did not succeed was not for lack of trying. Apparently the Prophet had sent Ben, the captured Negro, back into Harrison's camp the night before the battle. After he had been missing, he appeared near the general's marquee, where he was apprehended and charged with desertion and the intent to murder the general. He could not give a plausible explanation when interrogated why he was looking for the general. He only escaped a death sentence when Harrison mercifully granted him clemency, apparently swayed by Ben's imploring eyes while confined to stocks.

Aftermath

Harrison proclaimed a victory on the field of battle since the Indians had fled. However, the Indians moved back to the town after Harrison's army left. When Tecumseh returned the next month, he banished the prophet, who never regained his previous influence, though he collected a pension from the British Government until 1826 and lived until 1836. In the ensuing months, many Indians abandoned the confederacy and returned to their own villages. Yet, many others reacted with fury and continued raiding and killing whites, forcing many of them to abandon their farms. The battle did not reduce the danger to the frontier settlements. Harrison even sent his wife and children away to a safer haven in Kentucky and constructed an underground escape tunnel from his home, Grouseland, on the outskirts of Vincennes.

As for Tecumseh, the bitterness of the defeat at Prophetstown increased his hatred of the whites to a new level. He later said, "I stood upon the ashes of my own home, where my own wigwam had sent up its fires to the Great Spirit, and there I summoned the spirits of the braves who had fallen in their vain attempts to protect their homes from the grasping invader, and as I snuffed up the smell of their blood from the ground I swore once more eternal hatred—the hatred of an avenger." His recruiting drive in the south had not been very successful. Yet, when war began between the British and Americans in June 1812 he joined the British in the hope of acquiring Indian land back from the Americans. In the course of the war, he participated in numerous battles, including actions against General William Hull's army around Detroit and the two sieges of Fort Meigs. He died as a warrior fighting against his enemies in October 1813 at the Battle of the Thames in Ontario, Canada, after convincing General Henry Proctor to make a stand against his old nemesis, General William Henry Harrison. The 260 Delaware, Shawnee, Wyandot and Iroquois warriors who marched with Harrison's army in pursuit of the British and Tecumseh's warriors illustrated the failure of Tecumseh's ambitious plan to unite the Indians into a confederation.

Samuel Hopkins

A year after the Battle of Tippecanoe, General Samuel Hopkins fought a skirmish a few miles east of the battlefield in what has been referred to as the Second Battle of Tippecanoe. Hopkins had led 1,200 men out of Fort Harrison on November 11, including three regiments of Kentucky militia, Zachary Taylor's company of regulars, a company of Rangers, and some scouts. His men destroyed Prophetstown's forty huts, a Winnebago town, and a Kickapoo town of 160 lodges. They also burned and cut down the crops, all done without meeting any Indian resistance. Since they were not strong enough to directly face Hopkins' army, the Indians resorted to their preferred tactic of ambush. Tecumseh's brother, Kumskaukau and some friends shot and killed a member of a scouting party. The next day, while fulfilling the task to bury the fallen scout, a detachment of sixty horsemen commanded by Lieutenant-Colonels John Miller and Philip Wilcox fell for the old trick of chasing an Indian decoy. They rode straight into a hail of bullets from three sides, losing sixteen men killed and three wounded before making a retreat. With the weather turning harsh and his men lacking winter clothing, Hopkins decided to return to Fort Harrison. He considered that the mission had been a success in light of the damage he had inflicted on the Indians.

Battlefield to Park

Ensign John Tipton, then twenty-five, had performed as a veteran during the Battle of Tippecanoe when he assumed the command of his company (Harrison County Yellow Jackets) after Captain Spier Spencer and Lieutenant McMahan were killed. Ten years later he found himself once again on the field of the battle while engaged in surveying. The neglected condition of the battlefield helped motivate him to purchase the site as part of a 200-acre tract in 1829. The state then purchased the sixteen and a half acre battlefield site from Tipton, now a United States senator, in 1834. It was formally presented to the state of Indiana on November 7, 1836, the twenty-fifth anniversary of the battle. The battle had been thought of as so significant that early in Indiana's history newly organized counties were named for outstanding men who had participated in it. The counties so named are as follows: Bartholomew, Daviess, Dubois, Owen, Parke, Spencer, Tipton, Warrick, White, and Tippecanoe (Illinois also named a county after Jo Daviess). In May 1840, about thirty thousand people gathered there for the launching of William

Henry Harrison's campaign as the Whig candidate for the ninth president of the United States. Running with the slogan "Tippecanoe and Tyler too" Harrison won the election only to die in office a month later.

The state did not even protect the site with a wooden fence until the early 1850s after a resolution was introduced by John Pettit, a member from Tippecanoe County, at the Indiana Constitutional Convention in 1850-51. The resolution that passed stated: "It shall be the duty of the General Assembly to provide for the permanent inclosure and preservation of the Tippecanoe Battle-ground." Though the fence was built, a resolution to build a monument failed to pass. In 1873 an iron fence replaced the wooden fence. Finally as a result of fifteen years of effort by the Tippecanoe Monument Association formed in 1892, bills were passed by both the state and national governments to erect a monument. At a cost of $24,500 an eighty-five foot marble obelisk monument was dedicated on November 7, 1908, on the ninety-seventh anniversary of the battle. Smaller monuments were also placed to mark the locations where officers fell in battle.

Present

Today Tippecanoe Battlefield Memorial Park contains over one hundred acres of land. The responsibility for programs and upkeep now belong the Tippecanoe County Parks & Recreation Department and the Tippecanoe County Historical Association. Annual historic celebrations are conducted. In addition a museum is operated that displays artifacts from the battle and explains the battle and the cultures of the early pioneers and Indians.

The center is open 10:00 a.m. – 5:00 p.m. daily, from March through November, and 10:00 a.m. – 4:00 p.m. December through February, except Thanksgiving, Christmas, and New Years' day. Call 765-476-8411 for more information.

(See Appendix III for a list of causalities)

Fort Harrison

Almost a year after the Battle of Tippecanoe, in early September 1812, a war party of Kickapoo, Miami, Shawnee, and Winnebago departed Prophetstown to attack weakly defended Fort Harrison. Captain Zachary Taylor, who had assumed command in June, defended the post with fifty-five regulars of the Seventh Regiment of U.S. Infantry and some civilians including nine women and children who had fled their farms for the safety of the fort. Fortunately for the garrison, the Indians revealed their presence by firing on and killing two civilians (one named

John Guppy, the other unknown) out in the fields cutting hay less than a quarter mile from the fort on the evening of September 3. In an attempt to allay suspicions, the Indians sent a delegation of about thirty chiefs, old men, women, and children, under a white flag the next day to talk peace and to seek provisions. Taylor had already heard of Indian hostilities and was not fooled by their pretensions. He maintained an alert guard and distributed sixteen rounds of ammunition to each of the ten to fifteen sentinels that night. At the time only sixteen of his men were healthy. Surgeon's Mate Dr. William A. Clarke kept the remainder under his care.

The Indians, who usually attack an hour or two before daylight (e.g. the Battle of Tippecanoe), surprised the garrison. On what was a dark night, they crept up to the fort at about 11:00 p.m. and started a fire through a hole in a lower portion of a blockhouse. According to legend the Indians evaded detection by carrying the coals in a kettle covered with a blanket. Discovered by a sentry, who discharged his weapon to alert the garrison, the fire spread quickly and enveloped the upper story and roof while Taylor's men fought desperately against the 400 to 450 warriors they faced. At the same time the doctor led a party to pull shingles off the roof connecting the blockhouse to the guardhouse to keep the fire from spreading. While exposed to gun fire, one man was killed this way. The women assisted the men by carrying buckets of water. One heroic woman, Julia Lambert, had herself lowered into the well after the defenders noticed that the bucket came up only partially full. After filling buckets with a gourd, the water in the well began to rise. This event was later proclaimed a miracle. Nonetheless, despite their best efforts, the fire spread quickly with assistance from the stored barrels of whiskey. The fire destroyed the blockhouse and consumed most of their provisions, including 150 barrels of flour, pork, salt, and 25,316 rations of whiskey.

According to Taylor it had been difficult to rally the men. "Most of the men immediately gave themselves up for lost, and I had the greatest difficulty in getting my orders executed." He also lost two defenders at the start of the battle when they jumped the pickets to flee the fort (one returned later with a severely broken arm). Once the men began fighting, the fire in their resolve stiffened and they fought bravely. One courageous man, William Cowen, while firing from a bastion, laughed and shouted to his companions "I killed an Indian that time." In his excitement he neglected to hide behind the ramparts and was immediately shot dead. The defenders managed to build a temporary breastwork twenty feet in length from pickets torn down from the guardhouse to fill the gap created by the burnt down blockhouse. Their spirited defense and improved marksmanship with the arrival of daylight dissuaded the Indians from making a costly frontal assault. Failing to penetrate the defenses or burn the defenders out, the Indians resorted to a starvation strategy. They drove off all the livestock outside the fort and prepared defenses to intercept and attack any relief force bound for the fort. Altogether the defenders lost seven killed and three wounded, Indian losses are unknown.

Still under siege by Miamis and Weas (identified by a Frenchman who understood their language), Taylor sent out two messengers on the tenth by canoe, but they had to abort their mission because they could not penetrate the Indians guarding the river. The Indians had built fires on both sides of the river and had a canoe ready to intercept anyone trying to pass. Waiting another three days, Taylor sent out a sergeant and one other man by land. Edward Gilbert relates that according to popular legend, a civilian in the fort named Peter Mallory carried a message. In any case, the message reached Vincennes on September 16. Colonel William Russell led a column of around 1,200 mounted men consisting of Colonel Wilcox's Regiment of Kentucky Volunteers, three companies of rangers, and two regiments of Indiana militia from Vincennes—relieving the fort after thirteen days of siege. He brought much needed provisions and left a regiment for reinforcement. During his march the Indians attacked the escort for one of his supply wagons, and killed seven men. Essentially that ended the danger that the fort would fall to the Indians. However, Indians continued to harass the supply line.

For his heroic defense, Taylor received the first brevet promotion (to major) by the United States Government. Interestingly, both William Henry Harrison and Zachary Taylor served at the fort—both later elected President. Both also died in office and were succeeded by a Vice President—Harrison by John Tyler and Taylor by Millard Filmore.

Present

In 1848 at the occasion of a Grand Barbecue held at Fort Harrison during Zachary Taylor's campaign for president, two men were inspired to preserve the fort's features. James Modesitt, whose father had been in the fort while it was still maintained, and Luther G. Hager consulted with other citizens who "knew it like a book" and made a print to illustrate the original appearance of the fort. They then took photographs and sold them. That is how we know today what the fort once looked like. The original fort had shed roofs slanting to the inside; however, when the roofs needed repair, workers replaced them with hip roofs. A historical marker in Vigo County, Indiana, about three miles north of Terre Haute at the intersection of Fort Harrison Road and U.S. 41, commemorates the fort and siege. The actual fort site lies nearby, on land now occupied by the Elk's Fort Harrison Country Club.

(See Appendix III for a list of persons who served at Fort Harrison)

Fort Michilimackinac

The first of three forts to be built at the straits of Mackinac was built on the north side at St. Ignace, where Father Jacques Marquette had established a mission about 1670. In 1681 the French government sent M. de Villeraye with a detachment of soldiers to establish a post there. In 1690 Governor Louis de Buade, Comte de Palluau et de Frontenac, sent 150 troops under Louis de Louvitny to St. Ignace. They constructed Fort de Buade, named for the governor, to control the fur trade (historians have also referred to this fort as ancient Michilimackinac). This first fort made of stakes has been described in the following manner:

> Those in the outside row are thick as a man's thigh and about thirty feet high. The second row, inside, is quite a foot from the first, which is bent over onto it, and is to support and prop it up. The third row is four feet from the second and consists of stakes three and one half feet in diameter standing fifteen or sixteen feet out of the ground. Now in that third row they have no space at all between the stakes; on the contrary, they set them as close together as they can, making loop holes at intervals. As to the first two rows, there is a space of about six inches between the stakes, and thus the first and second rows do not prevent them from seeing the enemy; there are no bastions, and the fort is strictly speaking, only an enclosure.

Because of the debilitating effects of brandy on the Indians the local Jesuits persuaded the Crown to order an abandonment of the fort. At this time British traders had already begun to penetrate into the Ohio region and beyond. Thus in 1701, in order to block the further spreading of British influence, the commander of the fort since 1694, Antoine de la Mothe Cadillac, was ordered to Detroit to build a fort there.

About 1715 the French once again established a fort in the straits, this time on the south side of the strait at the present site of Michilimackinac

State Tourist Park about a mile west of the present Mackinaw City. Under orders from Governor Philippe de Regaud Vaudreuil, Constant Le Marchand de Lignery arrived with a small company of soldiers and workmen and constructed a square log palisade with sharpened points. Blockhouses were built and six small iron cannon were mounted on bastion platforms. There were also two gates, one on the south side for the land entrance and one on the north called the water gate, for entrance from the lake. By 1722, thirty families of officers and soldiers lived in the fort and thirty more families of traders lived outside the walls. The soldiers served for terms of three years, and many resigned when their terms expired. Nevertheless some stayed; by 1750 one soldier had resided there twenty years and another thirty years. Soon after the fort was built, a mission was established there, and in 1743 the Church of Ste. Anne was built.

Image credit: Mackinac State Historic Parks Collection

Several times troops and inhabitants at Michilimackinac were called upon for various French expeditions against Indians. In 1716, Louis de la Porte Louvigny recruited men there for an expedition against the Fox in Wisconsin, who in the face of a superior army agreed to halt hostilities against the French. In 1728, another expedition of 1,200 men departed the fort again on a foray against the Fox. Under Lignery the French again returned without defeating them. Men from Michilimackinac joined Antoine Coulon de Villiers, commandant at Green Bay in 1733, to attempt to exterminate the Fox. Once more unsuccessful, Villiers lost his life in an attack on the Fox stronghold. Under Michilimackinac commandant Pierre-Joseph Celoron de Blainville, men from the fort traveled all the way to present day Mississippi in 1739 in a campaign against the Chickasaw, which resulted in a short lived peace with that tribe.

The fort known as Michilimackinac or Old Mackinaw became a center for trade and a depot for trade goods. As many as sixty Indian slaves were also sold in a year there by the mid-eighteenth century after they were purchased from the Crees and Assiniboines. Since many of the purchased Indians were Pawnee, the word Panis was used generically for a slave.

With the start of King George's War in 1744, fear of British incited Indian attack prompted the soldiers to erect a new stockade around the fort. When the French learned that the Ottawa and Chippewa Indians planned to attack the fort, they banned them from entering. The garrison was not large. In 1749 only twenty soldiers garrisoned the fort shared with ten families that resided there. Many of the Indians began to turn away from the French and toward the English by the late 1740s because the English sold goods of high quality for a cheaper price and gave more in trade. For example, the French gave a pint of powder for a buckskin, while the English gave a quart. The Indians even began to kill isolated Frenchmen. In 1749 Celoron de Blainville with two hundred troops traveled through the Ohio region to awe the Indians into reaffirming their alliance with France and to bolster the French claim to the Ohio Valley. In his report he stated, "All I can say is that the nations of these localities are very badly disposed toward the French and are entirely devoted to the English. I do not know in what way they could be brought back."

Frenchman Charles Langlade made a huge difference in bringing the Indians back into the French fold. In 1729 Langlade was born to an Ottawa mother, sister of the chief Nissawaquet. The Chippewas insisted that he be a part of many expeditions against their enemies as he was a good luck talisman. He was first brought on a campaign against the Chickasaws when he was only ten years old. Langlade would have a great impact on events in the region and far away places in the years ahead. He started his rise to fame in the spring of 1752, when he led 250 Ottawa, Chippewa, and a dozen French soldiers in a surprise attack on the village of Pickawillany, under the Miami chief "Old Britain," where the British had set up a trading post. In the attack Langlade's men killed twenty Indians and captured five English traders. Additionally, his Indian allies allegedly boiled and ate Old Britain. The next summer the French summoned the tribes for a council at Mackinac. There they gave gifts to over 1,200 warriors and persuaded them to commit to fighting against the

English. In giving their renewed allegiance to the French, the Indians accused the English of cheating and deceiving them.

French and Indian War

In anticipation of a continuing struggle with the British over Ohio lands, the French held a huge council at Michilimackinac in 1753. A gathering of 1,200 Indians from 16 tribes listened to Commandant Louis Lienard de Beaujeu as he implored them to remain allied with the French to fight the English. Upon receiving many presents they agreed. During the French and Indian War, Michilimackinac was a rendezvous for Indians bound east to assist the French in fighting the British. Frequently war parties were led by Charles Langlade. Langlade led forces that participated in Braddock's defeat, Montcalm's siege and capture of Fort William Henry, a battle with Rogers' Rangers at Lake Champlain in which Rogers was wounded, and finally in the defense of Quebec against British General James Wolfe. Langlade later said that he had participated in ninety-nine battles in his life and wished he had fought in one more.

Following the French surrender in Canada, Captain Henry Balfour brought the Eightieth Regiment, Gage's Light Infantry, and other British regulars to Fort Michilimackinac, marching through the fort gates on September 28, 1761. In council with the local Indians, he obtained acquiescence to remain at the fort. He then moved on to occupy additional forts at Sault Ste. Marie, Green Bay, and St. Joseph (Niles, Michigan). He left Lieutenant William Leslie in command with twenty-eight men.

In reality the Indians were still loyal to the French, disliked the British, and were hoping the French would return to power. Captain Beaujeau had departed in October 1760 with four officers, two cadets, forty-eight soldiers and seventy-eight militia, leaving Charles Langlade in charge of the fort. The first traders came in late summer of 1761 before the British troops arrived. A good illustration of the Indian attitude toward the English is exemplified by their reception of these first fortune-seeking British traders to arrive at Michilimackinac. Among them was young Alexander Henry, only twenty years old. A group of Ojibwa (Chippewa) Indians visited Henry. As Henry later related, Chief Minavavana spoke the following words to him:

> Englishman, you know that the French king is our father. He promised to be such; and we, in return promised to be his children. This promise we have kept. Englishman, it is you that have made war with this our father. You are his enemy; and how then could you have the boldness to venture among us, his children? You know that his enemies are ours. Englishman, we are informed that our father, the

King of France, is old and infirm; and that, being fatigued with making war upon your nation, he is fallen asleep. During his sleep, you have taken advantage of him, and possessed yourselves of Canada. But his nap is almost at an end. I think I hear him already stirring, and inquiring for his children, the Indians; and when he does awake, what must become of you? He will destroy you utterly.

Englishman, our Father, the King of France, employed our young men to make war upon your nation. In this warfare, many of them have been killed; and it is our custom to retaliate until such time as the spirits of the slain are satisfied. But the spirits of the slain are to be satisfied in either of two ways; the first is by the spilling of the blood of the nation by which they fell; the other, by covering the bodies of the dead and thus allaying the resentments of their relations. This is done by making presents.

Englishman, your king has never sent us any presents, nor entered into any treaty with us; wherefore he and we are still at war; and, until he does these things, we must consider that we have no other father nor friend, among the white men, than the King of France; but for you, we have taken into consideration that you have ventured your life among us in the expectation that we should not molest you.

The Indians then smoked a pipe with Henry as a token of friendship.

Shortly after the Chippewa had departed, a party of Ottawa Indians arrived. They demanded in a council that the traders release all of their goods to them on credit, which they would pay for the following summer when they returned from their winter hunting. The traders were warned that if they refused these terms they would be killed. They would have to give their answer the following morning. Henry and about thirty other traders fortified his cabin and waited for an attack. The Ottawa failed to enlist the Frenchmen to assist them, and knowing that British troops would soon arrive, they departed after threatening an attack for two nights.

Fortunately for Henry's future safety, a Chippewa chief named Wawatam befriended him the next year. One day Wawatam entered Henry's trading house and told him that he had a vision when he was around fourteen years of age in which the Great Spirit revealed to him that he would meet a white man when he was much older, and that he should adopt the man as a son. He informed Henry that he was the one that the spirit had prompted him to adopt. He then bestowed presents of dried meat, furs, and sugar to Henry. Henry graciously accepted the offer but soon forgot about it. In May of 1763, Wawatam again visited Henry and attempted to persuade him to accompany him to Sault Ste. Marie. He also subtly warned Henry of danger from an unusually large number of drunken Indians that would be at the fort. Henry disregarded the warning, stating that he could not leave. Wawatam departed in tears.

Pontiac's War

Captain George Etherington, commander of thirty-five men at Fort Michilimackinac paid the consequence of ignoring warnings of possible Indian trouble. He shrugged off the warnings from traders about the increasing number of Indians around his fort and took no extra security measures. Charles Langlade tried to warn him twice about hostile Indian intentions, but when the Indians denied it, the captain said to Langlade, "I am tired of hearing the stories you are so often telling to me. They are the foolish stories of old women, and unworthy of belief. The Indians are well satisfied with the English, and have no hostile designs against them. I hope, therefore, that you will no longer advise me on the subject." Langlade replied, "Very will Captain Etherington, I will not trouble you any more with my so-called women's stories; but you will ere long regret not having listened to my advice." Though as many as four hundred Indians had gathered around the fort, they brought furs in to trade and had not indicated anything out of the ordinary in their behavior. Thus, on June 2 Etherington allowed squaws to mill around the fort and some of his soldiers to go outside to watch a game of baggattaway (modern lacrosse), which the local Chippewas under Chief Minavavana were playing against visiting Sauks.

To play baggattaway, the Indians set two posts in the ground about a mile apart. Each player uses a curved bat of about four feet with a racket on the end to hit a ball. The two teams start in the middle of the field and attempt to throw the ball to the opponent's post. The Indians had set up the playing field directly in front of the fort, so the garrison could enjoy watching the game.

Before Etherington knew it, the Indians had run through the gate past the sentries in pursuit of the ball, which had purposefully been thrown over the fort's walls to give the Indians the excuse they needed to enter the fort. Once inside, they dropped their bats and grabbed knives and tomahawks from the squaws who had concealed them under their clothing. The Indians immediately seized Etherington and Lieutenant William Leslie and attacked the surprised garrison, killing twenty and capturing a dozen. One officer, Lieutenant John Jamet, bravely resisted for awhile with his sword before the Indians swarmed over him and cut off his head.

Meanwhile Alexander Henry had been inside his house writing letters that he wanted to send out to Montreal the next day. Another trader, Mr. Tracy had just called on him to come to the beach and inquire about the news, since a canoe had just arrived from Detroit. Henry told him that he would follow in a few minutes, as soon as he finished the letters. Just moments after Tracy walked out the door, Henry heard Indian war cries. He moved to the window and saw to his horror that the Indians were slaughtering the garrison while the French inhabitants just stood by and watched. In his own words he later wrote, "Going instantly to my window I saw a crowd of Indians within the fort furiously cutting down and scalping every Englishman they found."

The sudden attack played out so swiftly that no organized resistance developed. Seeing that his own resistance would be futile, Henry sought refuge in Charles Langlade's house next door. There an Indian slave escorted him upstairs to the garret (an attic room under the pitched roof) and helped to hide him in a pile of birchbark pails. She then left him, locking the door behind her. Shortly a group of Indians came upstairs looking for him, but did not discover him though they were so close that Henry could have reached out and touched them. His luck ran out the next day when they returned and pulled him from his hiding place. The Indian who had dragged him from the garret forced him to trade clothes since he planned on killing him and did not want to spill blood on what were to be his new clothes. Henry was only saved from certain death when a former Indian friend, Wenniway, intervened.

Image credit: Mackinac State Historic Parks Collection

Soon the Indians placed Henry with the other prisoners. He discovered that about seventy soldiers had been killed and that about twenty soldiers and other Englishmen were still alive. The men contemplated a plan to regain the fort while most of the Indians were drunk; however, a Jesuit missionary, Father du Jaunay, dissuaded them, since they could expect little help from the almost three hundred Canadians who were there at the time.

Wawatam then came to Henry's rescue, saving him from certain death, after several days of anxious captivity. He purchased Henry from Wenniway for the price of an armful of blankets, shirts, and other implements. Henry then lived with Wawatam and his family through the winter and into the next year. During this period his life still was in danger. He dressed like an Indian so as not to present himself a tempting target for any visiting Indians. At one time he saw the Indians drag seven Englishmen to fires to be burned. He saw them behead one of them and hack the body into four parts, which were then thrown into a kettle. Wawatam also participated in the feast and had returned to his lodging with a dish containing a human hand. He explained to Henry that the Chippewa customarily held a war feast of their slain enemies to gain their strength and courage. Henry eventually made his escape on a trading canoe and later became a Montreal merchant. He also wrote down the only detailed report that we have of the massacre.

The Chippewas had learned of Pontiac's plan to drive the British from the country and had devised the scheme without consulting the local Ottawas. Due to Chippewa negligence or their desire to keep all of the loot in the fort for themselves, Etherington and most of the remaining survivors probably owed their lives. Once the Ottawas heard of the fort's fall they came and apprehended all of the prisoners for themselves. After a conference with the Chippewas, they gave up four of the soldiers and returned to their own village with two traders, eleven soldiers, and the two officers. Later in July the Ottawas traveled to Montreal with the prisoners and turned them over for payment.

In 1764 as Pontiac's Rebellion was dying out, Captain William Howard reoccupied the fort with two companies of regulars and an artillery force. Before his reoccupation the fort had stood vacant for a year. Major Robert Rogers of Roger's Rangers fame from the French & Indian War succeeded Howard in August 1766. Rogers lost no time on undertaking to fulfill a long time dream of many explorers. He sent one of his old ranger buddies, Captain James Tute, on an expedition that same fall to discover the fabled North West Passage (a water route from the Atlantic to the Pacific Ocean). Unfortunately, Tute's party only made it to the northwestern shore of Lake Superior before they had to return because of a shortage of food.

Superintendent William Johnson had ordered Rogers to restrict trading only to government posts so that the traders could be watched. This way they could not cheat the Indians and the likelihood of fighting could be lessened. Apparently Rogers believed that his distance from any authority allowed him to run the fort as he saw fit. He ignored this rule and further instructions from Johnson to limit his expenses on presents to the Indians when entertaining them and attempting to win their friendship at a great conference held at the Fort in the spring of 1767. Rogers distributed presents to the Indians from goods he obtained from the traders on credit. When the government refused to pay him for his expenses, Rogers sought funds to clear his debts by disobeying the rules prohibiting the sale of rum to the Indians. Meanwhile William Johnson sent out a commissary of Indian affairs, Lieutenant Benjamin Roberts, to keep a watch on Rogers' activities. Roberts called Rogers a traitor and accused him of treason after discovering his rum sales and hearing rumors that Rogers planned on looting British forts and joining the French on the Mississippi. General Gage and Sir William Johnson ordered Roger's removal from command and confined him to prison. Allegations that Rogers was attempting to gain assistance to escape prompted his removal from Fort Michilimackinac. The once famous Ranger was brought in chains to Detroit and then shipped to Montreal to face charges of mutiny. Lack of evidence allowed him to escape a conviction, and he sailed to England in 1770. After serving some time in debtor's prison, he was released. He later would fight against the Americans during the American Revolution.

Image credit: Mackinac State Historic Parks Collection

American Revolution

In the years after the French and Indian War, the fort continued to be a major trading center. Many traders lived in the village near the fort, which consisted of almost one hundred buildings. In the fort itself, which enclosed three and a half acres, and in which many of the buildings were privately owned, improvements were made. In 1769 a new barracks, divided into four rooms of twenty square feet each, was erected. The barracks housed seventy-two men. The men worked hard throughout the year just to heat the rooms in the winter. They had to obtain fire wood from as far as thirty miles away, since any wood in the vicinity of the fort had already been cut down during the previous sixty plus years of the fort's previous occupation. It took as much as seventeen and half cords of firewood to keep one room warm during the winter. The men lived on a basic diet of flour, beef or salt pork, peas and oatmeal—supplemented by fresh vegetables in season and fish or wild game. In addition to their rum ration, they drank a beer brewed from spruce needles to ward off scurvy.

Just prior to the outbreak of the American Revolution, in 1774 soldiers from the fort were transferred to the East and fought in the battles at Lexington and Concord. In July of that year, Major Arent Schuyler De Peyster assumed commanded at Michilimackinac. He soon learned that Delaware and Shawnee were seeking allies to fight the Virginians who were beginning to penetrate the Ohio country. Soon war broke out and the Americans under General Richard Montgomery captured Montreal, threatening to cut off trade to the Great Lakes region. However, Congress allowed the Montreal merchants to continue. De Peyster, who upon taking command had immediately realized the need to make strenuous efforts to maintain the loyalty of the Indians through trade, was relieved. He had seen how much merchandise was traded in the region. For instance, in 1774 trade goods included 32,000 pounds of gunpowder, 37,000 pounds of ball and shot, 800 trade muskets, 800 barrels and kegs of various liquors, 48 bales of kettles, 40 cases of axes, and various other items. He made sure that during the five year period of his command that he kept the Indians well supplied with rum, brandy, muskets, and gunpowder in exchange for furs. For example, in 1778, 1,500 muskets, 28 tons of gunpowder, and 2,100 kegs of rum and brandy were brought to the fort.

During the war De Peyster, who was related to American General, Philip Schuyler in New York, sent out war parties to aid the British effort in the east. In 1776 he sent Charles Langlade with a party of Menominee to Montreal; however, Governor Guy Carleton no longer needed their services that year and sent them back with presents. In response to Carleton's orders, Langlade brought two hundred Indians the next year in

July to join Burgoyne's campaign. Relations between the British and Indians soured when Indians did not obey orders and killed loyalist Jane McCrae. They left with Langlade in August. In 1778 De Peyster sent another 550 Indians east to fight. War parties organized from the fort also participated in defending St. Joseph (Niles, Michigan) in 1779, attacking St. Louis—then under the Spanish—in 1780, and in defeating Daniel Boone at Blue Licks, Kentucky, in 1782.

When De Peyster learned of George Rogers Clark's success in capturing Kaskaskia, Cahokia, and Fort Sackville at Vincennes, Indiana, in 1779, he feared Clark might advance further to Detroit and then on to Michilimackinac. Thus he sought to strengthen the fort's defenses. He reinforced the pickets, erected a firing platform and a stockade around the barracks, and attempted to reduce the sand hills near the fort. He also purchased two houses near the fort walls and demolished them so they would not provide shelter for a hostile force.

Meanwhile the newly installed lieutenant governor and superintendent of the post, Patrick Sinclair, arrived in October 1779. Almost immediately he concluded that the fort could not be defended if the Americans sailed up Lake Michigan and brought cannon against it. It was so close to the water that strong west winds drove waves against the palisade and sprayed water inside the fort. Within four days of his arrival, he chose a location better situated for defense on the south end of Mackinac Island. First he did what he could to strengthen the fort by reinforcing the palisades and constructing a sixteen square foot blockhouse to command the approach behind the sand hills to the south of the fort. Then without waiting for approval from Frederick Haldimand, governor of Quebec, he sent a corporal, four privates, a carpenter, and some trader's servants to the island to start clearing land and to build a wharf and a blockhouse. During the winter of 1779-1780 he also had his men dismantle the barracks, guardhouse, and King's storehouse within the fort and pull them across the ice to be reassembled in the new fort. To encourage the civilians to move with the soldiers to the new fort, in February he dismantled the church of St. Anne and the priest's house and moved them to the new trader's village by the fort. To supplement the food supply necessary for the hard working garrison that winter, Sinclair directed a Sergeant and six privates to work as fishermen. He later estimated that just three expert fishermen with proper gear would be able to haul in a hundred thousand pounds of fish during the winter.

In May Sinclair faced a new challenge when Captain John Mompesson arrived with a sergeant, a corporal, and twenty privates. Mompesson claimed that he was in command since he had been commissioned a captain before Sinclair. The confusion was cleared up when word from Haldimand affirmed that Sinclair was in command. Most officers were from the wealthy class, and like other officers of the period, Sinclair had to purchase his commission. In 1780 he purchased his commission as Captain in the Eighty-Fourth Foot (Infantry). He also received approval for constructing a new fort. Since Haldimand did not send an engineer as Sinclair assumed he would, it was left to Sinclair to design the fort himself. His men erected a ten foot high stockade with iron spikes on top of the cedar pickets and built blockhouses on the corners. These blockhouses served as their quarters for the first winter. That summer the traders at Michilimackinac took down their homes and built new homes on the island. In midsummer the King's Eighth Regiment hauled down the flag from Fort Michilimackinac for the last time. For many years they celebrated July 15 as the anniversary of the removal.

Within a few years after the American Revolution ended, windblown sand was already at work covering up the few deteriorating buildings and rotting palisades that remained. When present day Mackinaw City was platted in 1857, the fort site became a public park. The state accepted the land from Mackinaw City in 1904 and in 1909 the state created the thirty-seven acre Michilimackinac State Park, the second after Mackinac Island State Park. In 1932 while leveling a site for use as a tent and trailer campground, the custodian of the Michilimackinac Tourist Park discovered remains of the old fort. His plow had turned up rotting post ends from the walls. His discovery resulted in the reconstruction of the stockade by the state of Michigan in the 1930s. Under the care of the Mackinac Island State Park Commission, professional archaeological excavations were begun in 1959. Continuing every summer to the present, the diggings are the longest ongoing archaeological excavations in the country. Today over one million artifacts have been recovered and approximately 65% of the fort has been excavated. Reconstruction of the fort, the most accurate so far, began again in 1960.

Presently every Memorial Day Weekend, in what is called the Fort Michilimackinac Pageant, over four hundred re-enactors representing the Indians, soldiers, voyageurs, and villagers of the period re-enact the 1763 Indian attack on the fort. During the summer months there are daily re-enactments of various events. The Fort is reconstructed to the 1770s plan with thirteen buildings reconstructed. British military life of the period is portrayed as is that of the French civilians living at the fort in the late 1700s. Costumed interpreters portray daily life, including cooking, children's activities, and a French wedding at St. Anne's Church with music and dancing. Guided tours are also conducted. Two permanent exhibits are on display at the fort. In the Soldiers' Barracks, the Redcoats on the Frontier exhibit artifacts of British military life. The exhibit also includes a mess room and a Discovery Room for younger visitors where questions are answered on what enlisted life was like for a soldier. In addition there is an underground exhibit gallery under the northwest rowhouse that tells the story of the archaeological investigations conducted at the fort since 1959 and displays some of the most prominent artifacts yet discovered.

Image credit: Mackinac State Historic Parks Collection

For anyone interested in serious research, an appointment can be made (two weeks notice required) to visit the Petersen Center Library in Mackinaw City. In this non-circulating library, one can delve into books, research files, photos, maps, and microfilm on Mackinac history.

The summer daily schedule for the fort includes Musket Firing, Children's Games, Walking Tour, Cannon Firing, Baggattaway Game, and a French Colonial Wedding and Dance. For hours and admission prices check online in advance.

The Fort is open seven days a week in the season from May through October. The hours are as follows:

May 6 – June 6	9:00 a.m. to 4:30 p.m.
June 7 – August 23	9:00 a.m. to 7:00 p.m.
August 24 – October 12	9:30 a.m. to 4:30 p.m.

Phone number: 231-436-4100

Image credit: Mackinac State Historic Parks Collection

1. Native American Encampment
2. Water Gate
3. Cannon Firing Demonstration
4. King's Storehouse
5. Commanding Officer's House
6. Parade Ground
7. Military Latrine
8. Northwest Rowhouse
9. Guardhouse
10. Blacksmith Shop
11. Priest's House
12. Church of Ste. Anne
13. Soldiers Barracks
14. Southwest Rowhouse
15. French Fireplace
16. Solomon/Levy and British Officer's Houses
17. Powder Magazine, original remains
18. Chevalier
19. Land Gate
20. Barnyard and Corrals
21. Restrooms
22. Archaeology in Progress

Fort Mackinac

Almost immediately after his arrival at Michilimackinac in October 1779 the newly installed lieutenant governor and superintendent of the post, Patrick Sinclair, concluded that the fort could not be defended if the Americans sailed up Lake Michigan and brought cannon against it. He quickly selected a location better situated for defense on the south end of Mackinac Island with a fine harbor nearby. Without waiting for approval from Frederick Haldimand, governor of Quebec, he sent his men to the island to start clearing four acres at the top of a steep hill about 150 feet above the water of the harbor during the winter of 1779-1780. His men then dismantled the barracks, guardhouse, and King's storehouse from the old fort and moved them over the ice to be reassembled. The traders at Michilimackinac followed suit in the summer, taking down their old homes and building new ones on the island. In midsummer the old fort flag was lowered for the last time.

Local Chippewa chiefs, Kitchi Negon or Grand Sable, Magousseihigan, and Pouanas Kousse deeded the island, (Turtle Island to the Indians) to the British on May 12, 1781, for £5,000 in New York currency, or about $3 an acre for the two by three mile island. A little later Sinclair heard rumors that some of the Indians were remorseful over the sale of the island and they were threatening to reclaim it. He quickly sent a message to Detroit requesting aid. The arrival of the brig *Dunmore* with artillery for the fort put an end to any threat. Sinclair requested to name the new fort after Haldimand, but the governor insisted that it be named Mackinac. For many years afterwards, the names Mackinac and Michilimackinac were both used in reference to the new fort.

During the next several years, Sinclair's men worked on construction of the fort, building a barracks, guardhouse, stone powder magazine, King's storehouse, the foundation of the officer's quarters, and a well—all within the fort walls. Sinclair resigned in 1782 while under investigation for the huge expenses he had incurred in building the fort and pacifying the Indians with presents. The fort had become a major trading center and Sinclair distributed blankets, calico shirts, mirrors, knives, hatchets, guns, powder, shot, kettles, thousands of gallons of rum, and other gifts to the Indians. Due to his lavish spending on the Indians, Sinclair landed in London's debtor prison when he returned to England. Captain Daniel Robertson succeeded Sinclair, and he completed the construction of the fort using both stone and wood for the walls and buildings. By the time of his death in 1787, it was one of the strongest forts in North America. While drunk, Robertson fell to his death off a cliff on the southeast part of the island; the site has been known erroneously as "Robinson's Folly" ever since.

Image credit: Mackinac State Historic Parks Collection

During the period that the British occupied the fort, the soldiers wore clothing dictated by the Warrant of 1768, which set down standards for army clothing. An infantryman would have worn a long, dull-red, double-breasted coat. The lapels of the coat were buttoned back, and the coat hung open in the front to show the color of the facings, which identified the regiment. The facings could be one of a various shade of black, white, buff, green, red, yellow, green, orange or the blue of the "Royal" regiments. The regimental number was inscribed on the pewter buttons. The men wore white waistcoats and breeches (except the buff units) and black linen gaiters over their stockings. They also wore a pair of white leather cross belts, which supported a cartridge box on the right side and a bayonet on the left side. Their hats were similar to tri-corns, but flatter with white tape trimming the edges of the three turned up sides.

An infantryman carried a .75 caliber, smoothbore flintlock musket weighing about twelve pounds known as the "Brown Bess." It was loaded from the muzzle and prepared with a paper cartridge. At best a well trained soldier could fire the weapon four times in a minute, though very inaccurately at any range over one hundred yards. A good marksman could only begin to accurately hit man-sized targets when the range was reduced between sixty to eighty yards.

American Acquisition

Technically the British had ceded Fort Mackinac to the United States in the 1783 Treaty of Paris that concluded the American Revolution; however, they did not give it up until 1796. That same year, President Washington sent Baron von Steuben to Governor Haldimand to make arrangements for the handing over of the British held forts in American territory, but Haldimand put him off, stating that London had not instructed him to turn the forts over to the Americans. The newly formed United States was weak and the British wanted to maintain the benefits of the fur trade in the region. They used the excuse that the United States had reneged on its promises to reimburse Loyalists who were forced to leave the country. Thus the British continued their continued occupation of forts at Mackinac, Detroit, Niagara, and Oswego. In 1784 Haldiman received instructions to maintain the forts in British control. It was not until Jay's Treaty signed in 1794 that the British finally agreed to evacuate Mackinac and the other frontier posts they had retained on United States territory.

Ultimately, Major Henry Burbeck with a company of infantry and a company of artillery and engineers took possession of Fort Mackinac for the United States on October 2, 1796. A few years later one inspector would describe the fort:

> Our fort at Michilimackinac [Read Mackinac] from every consideration is one of the most important posts we hold in our western frontier. It... is an irregular work partly built with a strong wall and partly with pickets; and the parade ground within it is from 100 to 125 feet above the surface of the water. It contains a well of never failing water, a bomb proof used as a magazine, one stone barracks for the use of the officers, equal if not superior to any building of the kind in the United States; a good guard house and barracks for the solders and convenient storehouses. This post is strong both by nature and art, and the possession of it has great influence with the Indians in favor of the United States.

However, this great influence hardly affected the fur trade, which the British still largely retained at their new post on St Joseph Island in the lower St. Mary's River about forty miles from Mackinac.

War of 1812

Congress declared war on Great Britain on June 18, 1812, but Lieutenant Porter Hanks, then in command at Fort Mackinac, did not learn that there was a war until July 17 when he found the muzzle of a cannon pointed at his fort. On that day Captain Charles Roberts landed a force of 47 regulars of the Tenth Royal Veteran Battalion, 150 voyageurs, and several hundred Indians—including 100 Sioux, Menominee, and Winnebago, and about 300 Chippewa and Ottawa—on the northwest part of the island in the early morning. Roberts had learned of the state of war on July 8 from British General Isaac Brock, commander of Upper Canada. He immediately made preparations to take the offensive and attack the American fort at Mackinac. Upon receiving permission from General Brock to use his own judgment, he loaded powder, shot, and two iron cannon aboard the schooner *Caledonia*. With several bateaux and canoes full of Indians accompanying him, he started toward Mackinac on July 16.

During the voyage across the water of Lake Huron, he intercepted Michael Dousman. Hanks had sent Dousman to spy on the British after hearing that many warriors were gathering at St. Joseph Island. From Dousman, Roberts learned that the Americans were unaware of the declaration of war. Roberts then paroled Dousman, who was a friend to some of the British members of the expedition; on the condition he would not warn the garrison of the British presence. Instead, Dousman was to warn the villagers to take shelter so they would be safe from marauding Indians, who were always difficult to control.

Robert's landed on the northwest shore of the island about two miles away from the fort. His Canadian troops dragged one of the British 6-pounders through the woods to the top of a hill behind the fort. About two hours before dawn, his men had placed the cannon in a position from which Roberts could virtually destroy the fort below. Hanks had received warning in the night from an army surgeon who lived in the village below the fort. He mustered his men and prepared for an attack. Roberts then fired the cannon once and sent three prisoners—Ambrose Davenport, Samuel Abbot, and John Dousman—to deliver his terms demanding Hanks to surrender. Told that there were one thousand men ready to assail his fort, and in command of sixty-one men, of which only fifty-seven were fit for duty, Hanks knew the odds were against him. After a conference between Hanks and his officers, it was agreed that resistance was futile. They agreed to the following terms of surrender submitted by Roberts:

I. The Fort at Michilimackinac shall immediately be surrendered to the British forces.
II. The garrison shall march out with the honors of war, and shall be sent to the United States of America by His Britannic Majesty, not to serve in this war until regularly exchanged; and for the due performance of this article the officers pledge their word and honor.
III. All the merchant vessels in the harbor, with their cargoes, shall be in possession of their respective owners.
IV. Private property shall be held sacred as far as in my power.
V. All citizens of the United States of America who shall not take the oath of allegiance to His Britannic Majesty shall depart with their property from this Island in one month from the date hereof.

Ironically the British recaptured a number of cannon that the Americans had captured from them at the Battle of Yorktown in the Revolutionary War. Upon surrender most of the garrison's men were paroled on the condition that they would not serve in the army for the remainder of the war. However, three men were accused of desertion from the British army, and twenty were conscripted into the British army since they were judged to be former British subjects. Roberts paroled Hanks to Detroit where a canon ball killed him during the British attack before a court of inquiry could judge his conduct in surrendering Mackinac without a fight.

Amazingly, and rare for the circumstances, the British were able to keep the Indians from destroying any property or harming any of the prisoners. Roberts rewarded them with a feast and loot from the fort and government trading house, including enough whiskey to get them all drunk. Most importantly, the victory prompted many of the wavering Indians to cast their allegiance to the British and to fight against the Americans. General Hull at Detroit wrote, "After the surrender of Michilimackinac, almost every tribe and nation of Indians, excepting a part of the Miamis and Delawares, north from beyond Lake superior, west from beyond the Mississippi, south from the Ohio and Wabash, and east from every part of Upper Canada and from all the intermediate country, joined in open hostility, under the British standard, against the army I commanded." The Indians allied to the British would be a major factor in Hull's decision to surrender his two thousand man army to Colonel Henry Proctor.

In September 1813 little more than a year after Roberts captured Mackinac, he resigned because of poor health. The new commander, Captain Richard Bullock, quickly learned that he faced a grave threat. On September 10, the Americans under Captain Oliver Hazard Perry had won an important strategic victory, winning control of Lake Erie with the defeat of a British fleet of greater fire power under Captain Robert Barclay. Perry's victory enabled William Henry Harrison, no longer fearful that his supply lines would be cut off, to move his army against the British in Detroit. Fearful that his own supply line was now threatened by American naval control of Lake Erie, Proctor retreated into Ontario. Tecumseh, the leader of Britain's Indian, allies clamored for Proctor to make a stand against the Americans or risk losing all remaining Indian support. On October 5 Harrison's pursuit ended when he defeated the British army at the Battle of the Thames. In a decisive battle lasting just minutes, the British line broke and fled after firing only a few volleys. Harrison's troops killed Tecumseh, thus dealing a mortal blow to the Indian alliance. Proctor escaped with only a small force that could no longer threaten the Americans.

Soon after the battle, Harrison attempted to transport his troops to Mackinac on Perry's ships, but the ships ran aground in the St. Clair River. He then cancelled the campaign due to the lateness of the season. Fortunately for the British garrison at Mackinac, one supply ship, the schooner *Nancy*, slipped through just in front of Perry's fleet. However, even with the supplies from the schooner, the garrison faced a hungry winter. Starvation was avoided by the purchase of food from the inhabitants of the surrounding area.

With the knowledge that the Americans would mount an attack the following year, British officials made every effort to strengthen the fort. From Georgian Bay, Lieutenant-Colonel Robert McDouall led a relief force to the fort where he took over command. Many Indians also came to the island to support the British. McDouall strengthened the fort walls, and to guard against an attack from the land side, built a new blockhouse on the heights behind the fort, on the highest point on the island. The blockhouse had an underground magazine, and was surrounded by a stockade with an earth embankment. McDouall named it Fort George in honor of the current king, George III. While waiting for the inevitable American attack, McDouall learned that the Americans were building a fort at Prairie du Chien on the Mississippi River. To maintain Indian support and to remove this threat, he sent a force of Indians and militia under William McKay to attack the new American fort. When word came that this force had defeated the Americans on July 20, it bolstered the morale of his garrison. Upon the heels of this good news came the American fleet, which was sighted on July 26. A combined army-navy expedition under 22-year-old Lieutenant Colonel George Croghan—the hero of the defense of Fort Stephenson—and Commodore Arthur Sinclair with 760 troops were about to test the fort's defenses.

To their embarrassment on the next day, the Americans aboard the *Lawrence* and *Niagara* discovered that they could not elevate their 32-pound cannon high enough to reach the fort. Instead the shells fell harmlessly in the gardens below. Croghan then decided to try to capture the fort from behind on the land side, as the British had done to the Americans two years earlier. After bombarding the area, the Americans commanded by Major Andrew Hunter Holmes landed at the same place the British had earlier and started moving through the woods toward the fort. Anticipating this move McDaoull had placed his men directly in the line of their advance at the end of an open field. The Americans tried to flank the right of the British line but Indians, especially a band of Menominee, resisted stubbornly. Croghan then ordered Holmes to make a frontal attack on the British line. When the Americans approached, McDouall's force of 140 soldiers and 350 Indians with an artillery battery in the center of the line met them with a withering fire. After only a few minutes of intense fighting in which they lost several officers, the Americans retreated under fire back to their ships. Altogether they lost thirteen killed and fifty-one wounded. Among the dead was Major Holmes. In the lopsided battle, no one was killed on the British side.

Image credit: Mackinac State Historic Parks Collection

Unsuccessful in a direct assault, Croghan headed the expedition to Georgian Bay to blockade supplies from reaching Fort Mackinac. Under threat of capture, the British destroyed their schooner *Nancy* on the

Nottawasaga River to keep it from falling into American hands. Croghan then took the fleet back to Detroit, leaving two small schooners, *Scorpion* and *Tigress*, near St. Joseph Island to prevent supplies from reaching the fort from Georgian Bay.

The American blockade succeeded in reducing the British food supply on the island, but in desperation an enterprising British lieutenant, Miller Worsley, managed to outwit the Americans and end the blockade. From Nottawasaga Bay he evaded detection and paddled a canoe with twenty men to Mackinac. There he assembled a mini fleet of four bateaux with one hundred troops and a group of canoes filled with two hundred Indians. Voyaging back to St. Joseph he slipped up to the *Tigress* in the dark. The vessel's crew of thirty only fired once before Worsley's men boarded and captured the *Tigress* at the cost of two men in a brief fight. Unknowingly Lieutenant Daniel Turner brought the *Scorpion* near to the *Tigress*. Before he comprehended what was happening, Worsley had fired cannon from close range and sent boarding parties onto the ship. With the capture of the two ships, the British had regained control of Lake Huron and were able to supply Fort Mackinac. While the fort remained in British possession for the duration of the war, afterwards the Treaty of Ghent handed Mackinac back to the Americans, much to the dismay of McDouall. McDouall wrote, "Our negotiators, as usual, have been egregiously duped. As usual they have shown themselves profoundly ignorant of the concerns of this part of the empire. I am penetrated with grief by the restoration of this fine island fortress built by nature for herself.'"

The Nineteenth Century

Not until July 18, 1815, when Colonel Anthony Butler arrived to take command, did American troops once again occupy the fort. Butler departed soon thereafter and left in command Captain Willoughby Morgan, who had been wounded in the American attack in August 1814. Morgan changed the name of Fort George to Fort Holmes in honor of Major Holmes, who had died in the 1814 attack. Subsequently, the Americans later destroyed Fort George with artillery fire. Following the war, John Jacob Astor established his northern capital for his American Fur Company at Mackinac. After pushing Congress to pass a law prohibiting foreigners from engaging in the fur trade and buying out the Montreal trading companies, his company would soon monopolize the fur industry in the United States. During the 1820s millions of dollars of fur were shipped east from Mackinac Island. Astor would die in 1848 the richest man in America.

In 1820 Dr. William Beaumont arrived at the fort to be its surgeon. There he would achieve fame partially as the result of an accident—in this case, a young nineteen-year-old Canadian voyageur's self inflicted wound from the firing of a shotgun. The gun blast tore away part of the sixth rib, part of the lower lung, and the left end of his stomach. In June 1821, Beaumont treated the man, Alex Sanata (spelled phonetically) known ever after as Alexis St. Martin. After applying dressings to the walls of the blown open stomach, he stated that he did not believe St. Martin would live another thirty-six hours. Defying prediction St. Martin lived on with a wound that would not completely close. Within a few years Beaumont realized the opportunity he had to study the digestive process as he could lift a flap covering the opening and peer into St. Martin's stomach. He took St. Martin into his family to make detailed observations. He would insert various foods attached with strings and pull them out at intervals, noting the changes due to chemical reaction. Also he would record temperatures and even remove gastric juices. He did experiments periodically over eight years when St. Martin was present.

The army transferred Beaumont to Fort Niagara in the summer of 1825, and St. Martin went with him. That winter St. Martin disappeared without even saying goodbye. While at Green Bay in 1827, Beaumont reestablished contact with St. Martin. Finally, in 1829 St. Martin agreed to come with his family for payment of $300 a year and board with the doctor at Fort Crawford so further experiments could be conducted. The U.S. army enrolled him as a sergeant for $150.00 a year plus board and lodging in 1832. In 1833 Beaumont published *Experiments and Observations on the Gastric Juice and the Physiology of Digestion* based on 238 detailed recorded observations, thus greatly increasing scientific knowledge for the medical profession. The book was later published in England, France, and Germany. In 1834 St. Martin departed never again to be seen by Beaumont. Ironically St. Martin outlived Beaumont by twenty-seven years. Beaumont died in 1853 when he accidentally slipped on ice and hit his head on a step.

Building continued on the fort. In 1835 construction of quarters for the commanding officer was begun. After the Treaty of 1836, an Indian dormitory was built at the fort so the Indians would have a place to obtain their annual payments. They came every year from 1838 through 1846. A two-story barracks was built in 1855. Some of the buildings inside the fort were not completed until 1885. Throughout its history the fort was plagued by fire. Perhaps this explains why one of the responsibilities of the men on guard duty was to make sure the fire buckets were always filled with water. In 1783 the old guard house burned; in 1819 the roof of a blockhouse burned; the post hospital burned in 1827 before it was completed; the barracks burned down in 1855; and in 1858 the new barracks burned.

Several times the fort was abandoned when its soldiers were needed elsewhere to do battle against America's foes. Fort Mackinac's troops departed during the Second Seminole War (1837-40), the Mexican War (1848), and the Santee Sioux Uprising (1857-58). During the summer of 1862, three high ranking Confederates were briefly held at the fort, General William G. Harding, General Washington Barrows, and Judge Joseph C. Guild. They left in September, and the fort was abandoned during the rest of the Civil War. They did not return until August 1867. The lone exception was Ordnance Sergeant William Marshall, who stayed to maintain the arms, ammunition, cannon, and other military hardware and supplies stored there. In fact he spent more years at the fort than any other man, arriving in 1848 and staying until the early 1880s.

In the post 1812 period, the soldiers drilled for two hours a day, six days a week. They had to prepare for inspections of their uniforms and weapons frequently and for the fort about once a year. For a while one of the soldier's highlights was the firing of his musket at a target located behind the fort at the end of his guard duty. A gill of whiskey was awarded to the soldier who made the best shot each day. The men had to engage in various duties to maintain the fort and work for their sustenance. They frequently worked on constructing buildings in the fort. For a long time they traveled to Bois Blonc Island to cut down firewood and haul it back to Mackinac to heat their quarters during the cold season. The amount of work this entailed is illustrated by the winter of 1834-35 in which they cut over six hundred cords of wood. They then transported the wood to the island shore through two feet of snow and over twelve miles of ice to Mackinac Island. Yet for all their hard work, the men ate very well, in fact better than many civilians on the island. This was due to the bountiful gardens, which they maintained to supplement their diet including beans, beets, cabbage, carrots, corn, cucumbers, lettuce, onions, peas, radishes, squash, potatoes, tomatoes, and others. Despite their good food, like all soldiers they were restricted to their post as they had to receive permission to leave the fort.

The soldiers at Mackinac had improved conditions as the nineteenth century progressed. Early in the history of the fort, desertion had always been a problem, and some had even died in the attempt. Efforts were made to improve their recreational facilities. The old wood officer's quarters was converted to a canteen in 1889 with three large rooms. One room contained a bar and a lunch counter, two other rooms had billiard tables, including one fifteen foot table. A board of officers also oversaw the Sutler's operations to ensure that the soldiers could purchase quality goods at fair prices. Some of the men raised families at the fort. They also involved themselves in the village life, attending church, going to dances, and various other activities. Throughout most of the nineteenth century, the island population ranged from five hundred to a thousand people. In 1886 Captain Gooddale commented that the men were "more contented than at any post I have ever seen."

The soldier's routine in 1874 as posted by Captain Charles J. Dickey was as follows:

Reveille	5:00 a.m.
Breakfast call	5:30
Surgeon's call	6:30
Fatigue call	7:00
Guard mounting	
1st call	7:50
2nd call	8:00
Drill call	10:00
Recall from drill	11:00
Recall from fatigue	11:30
Orderly call	11:45
Dinner call	12:00 p.m.
Fatigue call	1:00
Drill call	2:00
Recall from drill	3:00
Recall from fatigue	one hour before sunset
Dress parade	20 minutes before sunset
Tattoo	9:00
Taps	9:30

Sundays

Inspection	
1st call	7:50 a.m.
2nd call	8:00
Guard mounting	immediately after inspection
Church call	10:30

A private had earned $5 a month in 1812. By 1872 he received $13 a month and earned a raise each month if he reenlisted. By contrast a captain earned $40 per month in 1812 and $150 per month by 1882. Officers sometimes held more than one job for which they received additional pay; for example an officer could have the position of both paymaster and quartermaster. The soldiers received their pay once every two months. Many of the soldiers who served at Mackinac were immigrants. They usually outnumbered the native born. Depending on the current source of immigrants, they may have been Irish, German, or Scandinavian. In 1850 for example, out of thirty-seven enlisted men at the fort, seventeen were Irish. By the 1860s the Germans were dominant.

It was not until 1880 that native born soldiers equaled the number of foreign born.

In March 1875 the federal government established Mackinac Island as the nation's second national park, three years after Yellowstone. Consequently, in addition to his regular duties, the fort commander now held the job of park superintendent. The soldiers from the fort also spent some time doing work projects to benefit and provide safety for the tourists. For example they built a fence around "Robinson's Folly" to prevent anyone from falling and constructed a twenty foot high observation tower on Fort Holmes Hill. In 1895 the state of Michigan acquired Mackinac Island from the federal government, making it Michigan's first state park. That year the last soldiers departed. For the next sixty years the state leased many of the fort buildings for use as summer cottages in order to raise revenue for the upkeep of the park.

Twentieth Century to Present

A monument to Dr. Beaumont was erected in 1900. In 1915 the first Fort Mackinac museum opened in the old officers' stone quarters. In it both Indian and pioneer artifacts were put on display including axes, arrowheads, guns, snowshoes, kettles, pipes and bear claw necklaces. In 1904 Fort Holmes was rebuilt. It burned in 1933, but an authentic reproduction was built in 1936. The Civilian Conservation Corps (CCC) also did much work in restoring and reconstructing other buildings in the 1930s. The fort buildings were converted to a historical museum after a revenue bond program was started in 1958.

The north blockhouse is devoted to the British attack and occupation of the fort during the War of 1812. The other buildings contain various other paintings, dioramas, and products depicting people, events, and life at the fort. A professional museum staff was hired in 1958, and the historical objects that had been collected over the years were catalogued. By 1972 restoration work had been done on the barracks, post headquarters, quartermaster's storehouse, schoolhouse, three blockhouses, old hospital, and commissary, and most were opened to visitors. The officer's stone quarters is the oldest building in the state of Michigan, built by the soldiers originally in 1780 when they moved from Fort Michilimackinac to Mackinac Island.

Today there are nearly twenty thousand objects including artwork, decorative objects, furnishings, tools, equipment, personal items, archival material, and photographs. Many of these items are on display. Currently, a visitor can see and experience the fort in much the same way as the soldiers did before they departed in 1895.

The Fort and Museum are open seven days a week in the season from May through October. The hours are as follows:

May 6 – June 6	9:00 a.m. to 4:30 p.m.
June 7 – August 23	9:30 a.m. to 7:00 p.m.
August 24 – October 12	9:30 a.m. to 4:30 p.m.

There is a Tea Room Restaurant in the fort with lunch, desserts and beverages. In addition there are many shops in the village below the fort. Some of the daily events held at the fort are rifle firing, cannon firing, soldier life tour, military music, court-martial re-enactment, and children's program.

Image credit: Mackinac State Historic Parks Collection

Note on Mackinaw coat

After the British vacated Fort Mackinac in 1796, they moved to St. Joseph Island and built a fort. There the Mackinaw coat originated in 1811. After the last supply ship of the season failed to reach the fort—leaving the garrison without overcoats for the winter—Captain Charles Roberts approached the Indian storekeeper, John Askin, and acquired his stock of Hudson Bay blankets. Every woman of the island, white and Indian alike, lent her skills in transforming these blankets into the now famous coats. Short, bright, and warm, the coats arrived just in time for Christmas. The Mackinaw coat proved to be practical for outdoorsman and has remained popular ever since.

Fort Massac

The earliest legends pertaining to the vicinity of the site of Fort Massac say that in 1542 the Spanish explorer Hernando De Soto passed through the area while wandering throughout the southeastern United States. This legend seems to be quite a stretch as no one has ever verified any factual evidence to support it.

The first real documentary evidence on the occupation of the site concerns Sieur Charles Juchereau St. Denys, a French entrepreneur. Having obtained a grant of land from the King of France at the mouth of the Ohio River, he arrived at the peninsula between the Ohio and Mississippi River with about twenty-five men late in 1702. The De Gannes memo places the location of the fort about two leagues (approximately six miles) up the Ohio from the mouth in the vicinity of what is now Mound City, Illinois. It has been estimated that the fort was located not too far south of the old Halliday House Hotel site. Though there are no remains of the fort, the men evidently were very productive in that location. They accumulated thousands of skins and buffalo hides. It has been stated that 30 Frenchmen killed about 13,000 buffalo in the vicinity during a three year period. Juchereau also had a tannery here to ship buffalo hides to European markets. Missionary Father Mermet, a member of the original party, reported Juchereau's death in the fall of 1703. In 1705, Indians attacked the settlement and the fort, killed most of the French, and carried off what wealth had been accumulated—buffalo hides, furs, and other provisions. Thus they ended the history of the first fort in the area.

Fort Construction under the French

Years later the French again realized the strategic value of a fort located in the vicinity, and in 1745, Bernard de Verges, assistant engineer for the Colony of Louisiana, recommended that a masonry fort be built on a bluff overlooking the Ohio. He argued that a fort there would inhibit Indians and their European allies from accessing the Mississippi. Not until the French and Indian War, when Governor of Louisiana Louis de Kerlerec sought authority to build a fort near the mouth of the Ohio, was any action taken to thwart a possible British attack or contain potential Cherokee or Chickasaw invasions down the Tennessee River.

In 1757, the Illinois commandant Macarty-Mactigue, stationed at Fort de Chartres, ordered Captain Charles Philippe Aubry to travel up the Ohio River to the mouth of the Tennessee River. With his force of 110 Frenchmen, 100 Indians and 3 artillery pieces, he was to reconnoiter the Tennessee in search of a rumored Anglo-Indian attack and to establish a retrenchment to hold 50 men. Aubry decided to build on the site de Verges had recommended. By June 20, 1757, his men under the direction of French engineer De la Gautraye built a fort on the north bank of the Ohio River, northwest of the mouth of the Tennessee River, and cleared a four hundred yard wide space surrounding it. The fort was called "Fort de L'Ascension" because they began to place the first piles on the holy day in the Roman Catholic calendar. De Verges wrote that it was built

> in the form of a square flanked by four bastions of twenty six toises, one pied, six puces [approximately 168 feet] on each front, from the flanked angle of one bastion to the flanked angle of the other, with the wall made of two rows of stockaded tree trunks, joined together; those of the outer row being thirteen feet in length and eleven to twelve inches in diameter, and those of the inner row, placed against the joints of the former, being nine feet in length and six to seven inches in diameter, the whole planted in earth to a depth of three feet, with a banquette along the interior two feet height, for firing through the loopholes which have been cut at a height of six feet in the outer wall; and with platforms raised at the flanked angles of the bastions for placing the guerittes, and some cannon en barbette, with two buildings of pied en terre, covered with clapboards for lodging the garrison.

Archaeologists later found remains outlining two buildings of the original fort that were approximately twenty-five by sixty feet in area.

After he left most of the Frenchmen and an unknown number of Indians to garrison the fort, Aubry reconnoitered up the Tennessee River. Finding no enemy other than an English colonist, he returned to the fort. Subsequently, in the autumn a large party of Cherokee attacked the fort. Aubry's men repulsed the attack and put them "totally in flight". This was the only known attack to be made against the fort. Though the defeat of the Cherokee removed the immediate danger, the Indians constantly threatened the soldiers when they ventured outside the fort. By December

1758, fifteen of the garrison, plus an officer and a sergeant, were missing. Cherokees or Chickasaws probably killed most of them.

The original construction used inferior local wood, probably willow or cottonwood, which deteriorated so fast that Macarty had to repair and rebuild the fort only two year later in 1759. This time he built two parallel walls separated by several feet and filled the space between with earth and stone. Macarty also added a ditch with sharpened pickets jutting outward. In addition, he may have built a battery close to the river—an idea originally proposed by de Verges—to control the river traffic with the eight artillery pieces that he now possessed. Afterwards he named the fort Massiac in honor of the French Minister of the Marine, the Marquis de Massiac.

The French utilized Fort Massac, the anglicized name used by the Americans, to maintain communications with and supply all the needs for the forts of the upper Ohio. Additionally, the fort helped feed their Indian allies. One authority estimated that keeping two thousand Indian soldiers in the field actually required feeding six thousand to support all their families. The Illinois grain crop was especially critical to maintaining the garrison at Fort Duquesne: "the support and maintenance of the posts in the Ohio country came to depend almost entirely upon the conveyance of Illinois flour and other provisions up the Ohio River." The French sent the first convoy to Fort Duquesne in 1753, and annually until the fall of the fort in 1758. Convoys of fifteen or more bateau transported flour, biscuit, maize, fats, bacon, tobacco, salt, and lead to the distant fort. A military guard left with the convoys from the Illinois settlements in mid-March and arrived about three weeks later at Fort Duquesne. Though supplies had been sent to Fort Duquesne in 1758, by September only eighteen days worth was left. Late in November the 400-500 French who garrisoned the fort evacuated just prior to the arrival of the 2,500 man British army under General John Forbes.

In the spring of 1760, Neyon deVilliers, now in command in Illinois, sent fifty additional soldiers under Sieur Philippe Francois de Rastel de Rocheblave with supplies to Fort Massac, relieving Sieur Declouet of command. Anticipating the fall of Quebec, one writer suggested that the French surrender, evacuate Canada, and resettle in Louisiana, which included the French settlements in Illinois. Thus Fort Massac would have been an important center of French power. However, due to their severe defeats and weak bargaining position, at the Treaty of Paris the French relinquished all claims to land east of the Mississippi. After the treaty of 1763, the French reduced their garrisons in Illinois. The French crossed the Mississippi with most of their men and artillery leaving only one officer—twenty-one-year-old Francois Saucier (son of engineer of Fort Chartres by the same name)—and fifteen men in Fort Massac. Saucier was authorized to surrender the fort; and in mid-summer of 1764, the French finally evacuated Fort Vincennes and Fort Massac.

The British had planned to garrison the fort with a captain and sixty men in 1764, but were delayed until 1765 due to the hostilities of Pontiac's Rebellion. When Captain Thomas Stirling with the Forty-Second Royal Highland Regiment finally arrived to garrison the fort, all he found was the burned ruins that the Chickasaw Indians had left. Stirling and his men continued on to Fort Chartres to accept its surrender. Thus, the British never occupied Fort Massac for Stirling continued on to Fort Chartres to accept its surrender.

American-built Fort

Though the site remained unoccupied, it still played a role in important events during the following years. An overland route called the Massac Road led from the site to Kaskaskia. In late June 1778, George Rogers Clark stopped at the fort and raised the American flag. Then he marched for one hundred miles northwest on the Massac Road on a campaign to take Kaskaskia for the Americans.

Clark referred to the fort as "Fort Massacre," perhaps in reference to a legend written down by John Todd Burris of Virginia during a visit to the area in 1773. The story goes that many years in the past, Indians dressed in bear skins lured three Frenchmen and four servants from their dug-out fort to the Kentucky side of the river. When the rest of the garrison left their quarters to watch the spectacle from the Illinois side, the Indians ambushed and massacred all the men on both sides of the river.

From 1787 through 1791, the Spanish government attempted to convince General James Wilkinson and others to secede from the eastern states and establish an "Independent Government." They offered to pay $200,000 and supply twenty cannon and munitions. According to the plan, Fort Massac was to be occupied and used as a base for operations against the other western posts. Perhaps due to the example of Benedict Arnold, Wilkinson never followed through, though he continued to entertain various offers from the Spanish and receive money from them. He even schemed with the Spanish after becoming commander in chief of the army after General Anthony Wayne's death in 1796. Many Spanish coins have been found in and around the fort, suggesting that Spanish soldiers may have occupied the fort for a short period after the French evacuation.

In 1790 and 1791, the United States suffered two humiliating defeats at the hands of the Ohio Indians under the leadership of Little Turtle of the Miami and Blue Jacket of the Shawnee. In 1794, as Anthony Wayne was preparing his army for what would culminate in a victorious campaign against the Ohio Indians at the Battle of Fallen Timbers, he received orders to refortify the site of Fort Massac. The Americans believed the site was well situated to defend against Indian attack, to control the trade on the Ohio River, and to guard against any French plans for detaching any of the Illinois territory from the United States in light of the Genet Affair. Edmond Genet had been trying to recruit men to invade Canada, Spanish Florida, and Louisiana in the hope of restoring a French presence in North America. Additionally, President Washington was concerned about threats from the Spanish, who now controlled much of the land west of the Mississippi River.

On Wayne's orders Major Thomas Doyle and Captain Isaac Guion's company of the First Sublegion, plus a detachment of artillery, departed from Cincinnati on May 24, 1794, to build a new fort on the site of Fort Massac. His men began rebuilding the fort in June 1794, and he reported to Wayne that his men had completed the work by October 20, 1794. The best description of the fort comes from Victor Collot, who visited in 1796, and stated that the fort had four blockhouses surrounded by a ditch and was about seventy feet above the river at low water. The structure was believed to be approximately forty-six yards square on each side with palisades of upright logs twenty feet high. In 1796 the fort had eight cannon, all 12-pounders, to bolster its defenses.

Indian trouble threatened the area during this period. In April 1795, Indians thought to be Potawatomi and Kickapoo massacred the party belonging to Colonel Samuel Chow. They killed him, four white men, a white woman and child, and eleven slaves just a few miles north of the fort on the Ohio River. Potawatomi and Kickapoo also attacked a camp of Cherokee and Chickasaw. The danger from Indians in the area eased somewhat when reinforcements under Captain Zebulon Pike arrived and took command of the fort later in the year. He worked to prevent war from breaking out among these tribes and engaged in extensive repairs to the fort. At this time the Chickasaws helped supplement the garrison diet with game. Along with the Choctaw and Cherokee, they traded venison and bear oil for flour.

The Spanish government posed a concern for American authorities in the late 1790s. Spain had tried to limit American territorial acquisition since the Revolutionary War and feared continuing expansion. During this period the Spanish sent a vessel to patrol the Mississippi as far north as the Ohio River. Other Spanish activities and policies threatened the Americans. The Americans heard rumors that the Spanish planned to build a new fort near the mouth of the Ohio and a new sawmill in the area. The Spanish lured Indians and some Americans to their side of the Mississippi to bolster their own strength. Allegations loomed that the Spanish were plotting to take Fort Massac. Thus the Americans were wary of Spanish activities in inciting Indian warfare and curbing American power.

Upriver from Fort Massac in Hardin County, Illinois, thieves, river pirates, murderers, and counterfeiters operated out of Cave-in-Rock. Cave-in-Rock is a cave along the Ohio River about fifty-five feet wide at its base with a semi-elliptical opening that extends back from the opening about 160 feet with an average width of 40 feet. It was a natural hideout for criminals preying on travelers down the Ohio River. In the late 1790s, a counterfeiter by the name of Duff made it his base. Eventually he met his end due to the action taken by the commander at Fort Massac.

According to the most repeated version, six solders apprehended Duff, his slave Pompey, and three members of his gang upriver from Cave-in-Rock. They put them in a boat, and while descending the river on their return to the fort, stopped at Cave-in-Rock to have dinner. One of them stood guard on the boat. Having only four sets of manacles, they left Pompey free, believing he would not care about his master. Instead, Pompey helped free one of the prisoners, and together they overpowered the guard and freed the other two men. They grabbed the guns stacked near the boat, rushed to the cave, and captured their captors. They then secured all the soldiers into the boat and sent it floating down the river.

The soldiers were sighted while passing Fort Massac and were ordered to stop, which of course they could not. The commander discovered what happened when a skiff he had sent to apprehend them returned. Angered by the outcome, he determined to get his revenge by hiring a Canadian and three Indians to kill Duff. He promised them a reward for a successful mission. They found and killed Duff and his slave, while the rest of the gang fled.

After 1799 the U.S. Treasury operated a customs office from the fort. The office required all commercial boats to stop and pay taxes on their cargoes. Also in 1799, the government started preparations for transferring supplies for the one thousand men bound to Fort Massac. Alexander Hamilton, now a major general, wanted General Wilkinson to prepare for an offensive expedition against the French in Louisiana and the Spanish in St. Louis incase war should erupt with either country. Currently the American and French navies were fighting the so called "Quasi War." In 1798 Congress authorized President John Adams to expand the army and to call up state militiamen to active duty. By 1799 the French had seized more than eight hundred American ships. During that year the American Navy had fought back by capturing eighty-four French ships.

Instead of reinforcing Fort Massac, however, Cantonment Wilkinsonville was erected twelve miles downriver from the fort in early 1801. For a short while this post of over 20 log barracks housing a garrison of 800-1,000 men, and numerous other buildings surrounded by a log palisade, was the largest military outpost in the United States. Established on the banks of the Ohio by the Chain of Rocks between Metropolis and Cairo, Cantonment Wilkinsonville contained one third of the United States Army. At the time these two posts were the most important in the west and were together called "The S. W. Post in the N. W. Territory." The threat of war with France faded when President Adams concluded a treaty with the French in the last day of his administration, and the new president, Thomas Jefferson ordered the posts evacuated.

Tensions flared again in 1802 between America and Spain when Spanish authorities put a stop to American trade down the Mississippi by revoking American rights to deposit their cargoes in New Orleans. The trade was the lifeblood of western America. By 1801 three thousand American ships passed through New Orleans each year. Captain Daniel Bissell with the First Infantry Regiment was ordered to reoccupy and rebuild the deteriorated fort in 1802. His men constructed a new stockade, new barracks, three blockhouses, two officers' quarters and a powder magazine. All the blockhouses used ladders from the first floor to the second instead of stairs in case an enemy entered the fort. The defenders could pull up the ladders and shoot from the gun ports as a last line of defense. In 1803 Bissell and other river post commanders were ordered to oppose any unauthorized forces rumored to be gathering for an attack on Louisiana.

Spain was not really in a position to resist an American attack. The French in Louisiana had rebelled against Spanish authority and were restless. The Spanish army was spread out all over South America, and there were simply not enough troops available to protect Louisiana. In an effort to protect her western territories, Spain agreed to return Louisiana to France in exchange for Etruria (now Tuscany and part of Umbria in modern Italy). In the fall of 1800, in a secret treaty with France's foreign minister Talleyrand, Spain ceded Louisiana back to France. As rumors of the transaction reached the United States, Jefferson began to fear French plotting. Since the 1790s when France began to overrun the countries of Europe and threaten invasion of England, it was thought France might also invade America. Unbeknown to Jefferson, Napoleon had such a plan in mind.

Napoleon planned for a mass colonization of Louisiana in order to provide France with foodstuffs, including grain, sugar, cattle, produce, and cotton. He intended to send an army of 20,000 to take possession of the territory, thereby halting any American expansion west of the Mississippi. Unfortunately for Napoleon outside events intervened. He had already sent an army to put down a guerilla war in Santo Domingo by slaves under the former Toussaint L' Overture. After the French had tricked Toussaint into pledging allegiance to them they whisked him off to prison in France. The slaves and the mosquitoes carrying yellow fever decimated the French army, killing 24,000 men by September 1802. Furthermore, in the fall of 1802, an early arctic blast stormed in and froze a fleet in place for the winter just as it had been readying itself to sail from Rotterdam, Holland, with a French army bound for America. The final blow came when the British threatened war if the fleet left port.

Meanwhile, President Jefferson had ordered his secretary of war to make preparations for a military expedition against New Orleans. However, in an attempt to avert war, he sent James Monroe on a voyage to France and Spain for the purpose of purchasing New Orleans for a price of up to 5 million livre ($9,375,000). In the end, war was avoided when Napoleon, frustrated by his recent setbacks, unexpectedly offered to sell the entire Louisiana Territory. After three weeks of negotiations, the Americans paid only $15 million, amounting to pennies an acre, doubling the size of the nation.

In its first steps to cross the continent, the Lewis and Clark expedition stopped at Fort Massac from November 11-13, 1803, where they had been authorized to recruit from the garrison. They were disappointed in the quality of the men there and only recruited George Drouillard, John Newman, and possibly Joseph Whitehouse for their Corps of Discovery. Drouillard played a key role on the expedition as an interpreter and a hunter. The fort commander, Captain Bissell did not want to let him go because he was so valuable as a hunter, messenger and interpreter. Drouillard may have been who Major Doyle referred to as the "George" who spoke seven Indian languages. Fort Massac also played a role in the exploration expedition of Zebulon Pike (whom Pike's Peak is named after). Zebulon, as an ensign, served under his father of the same name, who commanded the fort from 1795-1797. He later recruited some members of his expedition from Fort Massac.

Early in 1805 St. Louis became the new military headquarters for western troops and Bissell's company was transferred there. Nathan Heald of later Fort Dearborn fame took command there with another company. Later that year Bissell returned to resume command of the fort. In November 26, 1806, President Jefferson ordered post commanders along the Ohio River to arrest former vice-president Aaron Burr's expedition, which had begun its descent of the Ohio in the autumn of 1806. Aaron Burr and General James Wilkinson met at Fort Massac in 1805, but little is known about their meeting. It has been surmised that Burr planned to invade Mexico, divide the nation, or set up a colony on the Washita River. Though Wilkinson's role is unclear, it is known that Spanish agent Tom Powers had given him $9,000 and that Spain wanted to detach the western states from the country. At some point Wilkinson decided to withdraw from the plot, reported it to President Jefferson, and aided in the arrests of the conspirators that followed. Later, Henry Clay defended Burr, who was acquitted. Wilkinson was also tried for treason and acquitted. Wilkinson became known as "the general who never won a battle and never lost a court-martial." Bissell allowed Burr's expedition of sixty to one hundred men in ten boats to pass by on December 29. His reasons for allowing Burr to pass must have satisfied his superiors as he was promoted from the rank of captain to lieutenant colonel in 1808.

In the years prior to the War of 1812, the threat of an Indian war increased. The great warrior and Shawnee statesman Tecumseh and his brother Tenskawatawa, the Prophet, strived to unite the Eastern tribes to resist further white acquisition of Indian lands. First Lieutenant Samuel Price, who had taken over command of Fort Massac in 1809, proceeded to make the fort ready for war. In preparing for war, the fort was used for assembling western recruits.

In the War of 1812, the government utilized Fort Massac as a training center for western recruits, who were sent east to fight the British. The fort had received some damage from the December 1811 through February 1812 New Madrid earthquakes; the extent of the damage is unknown. However, Lieutenant E.A. Allen, the post commander, did make at least two requests for funds to repair the fort. After William Henry Harrison's victory over Tecumseh and the British at the Battle of the Thames in September 1813, the center of the war effort moved further north. The fort was no longer necessary for support of the troops in the field and was evacuated in 1814. By 1817 the fort had been dismantled by local inhabitants, who had used the wood for their own buildings and as fuel for steamboats on the Ohio River. Only stones remained where the fort once stood.

After the War of 1812

In 1838, Fort Massac received consideration from a commission of army officers appointed by the secretary of war to select a location for a western armory. Surgeon General Lawson headed the commission that visited Nashville, St. Louis, Cincinnati, Louisville, Rock Island, and many other places. While at the Fort Massac site, they took surveys of the surrounding area. On their return to Washington, they recommended Fort Massac as the most favorable site for a national armory. However, the Western Armory was later built at Rock Island, Illinois. The final use of the Massac site by the military took place early in the Civil War. Camp Massac was established to thwart any Confederate forces that may use the Ohio River, but it was soon abandoned after a measles outbreak killed a substantial number of troops in 1861-1862.

Through the efforts of the Daughters of the American Revolution, the state of Illinois purchased twenty-four acres surrounding the Fort Massac site in 1903. Finally, on November 5, 1908, official's dedicated the Fort Massac site as Illinois' first state park. In 1939 a team of archeologists directed by Paul Maynard began excavations at Fort Massac. These continued through 1942 and further work was done again in 1966, 1970, and 2000. A replica of the 1794 American fort was reconstructed in the early 1970s near Metropolis, Illinois, about a mile west of the original site. It was dismantled in the fall of 2002. The state of Illinois built a historically accurate replica of the 1802 American fort in 2003, which stands to the east of the original French forts and the American forts built over them. Only the earth works of archaeological excavations remain of the original forts. The current fort consists of a stockade wall, three blockhouses, and a picketed dry moat with an officer's quarters and two barracks. The officer's quarters is a sixteen by twenty-two foot two-story building built on a stone foundation, constructed of white oak timber, with a brick fireplace on each floor. There are two barracks for soldiers, the east one is eighteen by seventy-five feet with a porch, and the west one is twenty-two by seventy-five feet. Both consist of two stories with four rooms each with fireplaces inside. A sixteen by sixteen foot two-story blockhouse is on the northwest corner. A twenty by twenty by twenty-four foot two-story blockhouse is on the southwest corner and is the same as the 1794 style. The southeast blockhouse is sixteen by sixteen feet and has three floors. The third floor is a lookout tower over the Ohio River.

An onsite museum open daily from 10:30 a.m. until 5 p.m. displays the fort's history. A statue of George Rogers Clark also stands on the grounds. For two days each October the Fort Massac Encampment is held. This event, which recreates the lifestyles and atmosphere of the late 1700s, attracts as many as 130,000 people. The fort is part of a 1,450-acre park that has facilities and opportunities for picnicking, camping, hiking, boating, and hunting. Call 618-524-4712 for more information.

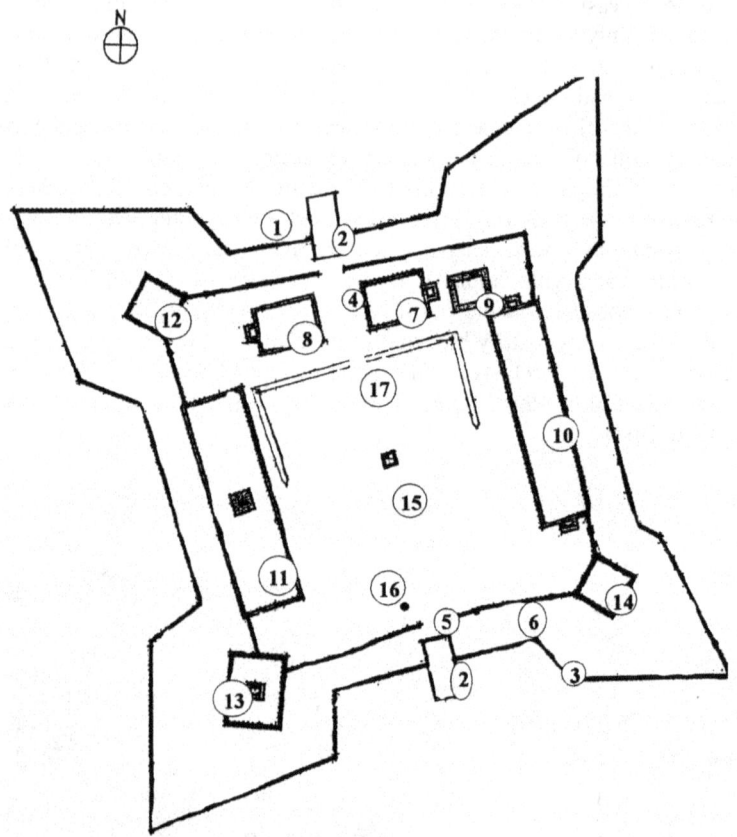

Image credit: Illinois Department of Natural Resources

1. Dry Moat with Pickets
2. Wooden Bridge over a Dry Moat
3. Pickets or Fraising
4. North Gate – back door of the fort
5. South Gate – Ohio Riverside, front of the fort
6. Stockade Walls
7. Officers' Quarters
8. Foundation of Officer's Quarter
9. Foundation of Powder Magazine
10. East Soldiers Barrack, with a porch
11. West Soldiers Barrack
12. Northwest Blockhouse
13. Southwest Blockhouse with Fire Places
14. Southeast Blockhouse with Viewing Tower
15. Well
16. Flag Pole
17. Drainage Ditch

Fort de Chartres

In roughly a forty year period three forts named de Chartres were built in the same vicinity approximately four miles west of what is now Prairie du Rocher in Randolph County. In 1718, the site was selected by a Lieutenant Pierre Duque de Boisbriant to be the center of the French administration in the Illinois country after its jurisdiction was transferred from Canada to Louisiana. King Louis XV had granted the Company of the Indies a charter to run the government and appoint necessary officials. This grant included jurisdiction over forts, posts, and garrisons. In order to establish a civil government in the Illinois country, the Company sent Boisbriant (a cousin of Le Moyne de Bienville, governor of Louisiana), several other officials, Captain Pierre d' Artaguiette, four lieutenants, about seventy soldiers of marine infantry, several new settlers, and workmen in October 1718. Boisbriant first established himself at Kaskaskia and lodged with a part of his force there for three years while the fort was being built. Boisbriant also sent out exploring parties to locate mines, hoping to find riches in the form of silver. However, they were unsuccessful.

Over the next eighteen months, his men constructed the first Fort de Chartres, named presumably after the Duc de Chartres, the king's son. They completed the fort in the spring of 1720 at a location about eighteen miles north of Kaskaskia and about three-quarters of a mile from the Mississippi River. The French built palisades of squared logs with earth in between and bastions built diagonally from opposite corners. They also constructed several buildings: barracks for the soldiers, powder magazines, a store house and the commander's home. They surrounded their works with a dry moat. However, the fort deteriorated rapidly due to frequent flooding from the river. In 1723 the fort and its surroundings were described by Diron d' Artaguette (Louisiana's intendant) as follows: "Fort de Chartres, is a fort of piles the size of one's leg, square in shape, having two bastions, which command all the curtains....There is a church outside the fort and some dwellings a half league lower down on the same side as well as half a league above as far as a little village of the Illinois where two Jesuit fathers, missionaries, who have a dwelling and a church."

One of the first arrivals was Philippe Francois de Renault, the French director-general of the mining operations for the Company. He brought with him a body of two hundred miners and laborers, and five hundred Santo Domingo Negroes, thereby introducing African slavery into the Illinois country. Though in search of precious metals, all he found was lead. A large quantity was discovered about an hour south of the future site of St. Louis along the Merameg, a small stream which entered the Mississippi River, an area known today as "Old Mines." The mines produced a ton and a half of lead a day by 1725. Eventually the French found lead in other locations including near present day Galena, Illinois.

Due to the frequent flooding, the French decided to move inland from the Mississippi and started building a new fort in 1725. The Mississippi must have moved closer to the fort. In October 1721, Father Xavier de Charlevoix had described the fort as being only "about a musket shot from the river." Eight soldiers of the garrison contracted to build the new fort. With about 160 feet on each side, the new fort consisted of four buildings on the inside: the residence for the commandant and storekeeper, another house, barracks, and a guard house. Other structures were also built in each corner bastion, including a powder magazine, a stable, a prison, and chicken house. The fort was reported to be in good condition still in 1732, but by the late 1730s had fallen into severe disrepair, however the garrison repaired and maintained it until 1747.

The village that grew beside the fort was called La Nouvelle Chartres. Not only was it the center for administration of the Illinois colony, but it was an important center for trade and agriculture. It served as a depot for goods shipped from New Orleans bound for Vincennes, Peoria, and Cahokia. Since the land was so rich, corn, wheat, and rye were produced in far greater abundance than required by the inhabitants. The colony served as a granary for New Orleans, shipping thousands of pounds of flour with as much as 50,000 to 100,000 pounds in a single convoy. Trips from Illinois took two to three weeks to reach New Orleans and three to four months to return. Travel on the river proved dangerous and many made their wills before risking a journey filled with the hazards of currents, snags, and Indians.

The inhabitants of the village built homes of upright posts with a mix of clay and straw filled in between, on lots 192 feet square. The homes averaged sixteen by twenty-five feet with two doors and windows, divided into two main rooms. They had roofs covered with thatch or wood shingles and a fireplace or two made of stone for heat. A porch and a small cellar completed the home, which would have a life span of about twenty years. The inside walls were whitewashed, while some had paneling or plaster for a finish. Many dwellings included billiard rooms for the very popular game that was different than that played today. An archaeological dig at Kaskaskia turned up an ivory ball used in the game. Each French village had its own church. St. Ange at Chartres was thirty by fifty feet with walls eleven feet high. There the Jesuits had a flourishing mission which served the nearby principal village of the Kaskaskia Indians. Also during the first few years of the Illinois colony, the still existing village of Prairie du Rocher was established.

The French needed protection from at least some Indians who were hostile and had killed Frenchmen, especially the Fox tribe (also known as the Outagami or Mesquakie) with whom the French had been at war since 1712 and fought against until the 1730s. One primary source of the conflict was the Fox determination to be the middle men in the trade between the French and the Sioux. They killed Frenchmen who attempted to pass through their territory (Wisconsin and Illinois) to trade directly with the Sioux. The Fox and the Sioux had threatened the settlement at Cahokia in the spring of 1723 and killed two Canadian hunters near the walls of Fort de Chartres. In the summer of 1730, Robert Croston de St. Ange, then the commander at the fort, brought ninety Frenchmen and three hundred Illinois warriors with him to join a French and Indian force that surrounded and almost completely wiped out a large portion of the Fox tribe (about one thousand members) on the Illinois prairie as they tried to journey to New York to join the Iroquois. Most of the remaining free Fox were so decimated that they joined with the Sauk tribe with whom they remained bound in their subsequent history.

Over the years of French occupation, various other expeditions also had marched out to defend France's North American empire. Men from the garrison and the local militia went on expeditions against the Natchez in 1729 and against the Chickasaw in 1736 and 1739. All able bodied habitants joined in the local militia. They and the garrison suffered severely in the 1736 expedition. Under orders from Governor Le Moyne de Bienville, Major Pierre d' Artaguette with thirty soldiers, one hundred volunteers, and two hundred Indians marched out to join him in a military expedition against the hostile Chickasaws. He met Chevalier Vincennes, from the fort of the same name with reinforcements of 20 men and another 106 Indians. Together, without waiting for Bienville they ventured an attack against the Chickasaws stronghold. The Chickasaws ambushed and defeated the French and captured D'Artaguette, Vincennes, many other officers, and about sixteen soldiers. Scores of soldiers were killed in the battle. Failing to receive a ransom for them, the Chickasaws then proceeded to roast them at the stake, taking an entire day to complete the process. In 1739, the next commander at Fort de Chartres, Alphonse de la Buissoniere led another more successful expedition against the Chickasaws.

Generally there was one company of government soldiers of about fifty men and four officers known as *Compagnies franches* stationed at Fort de Chartres after 1732. The officers consisted of one captain, one lieutenant, one ensign, and one cadet who was training to become an officer. The company also included two sergeants, three corporals and two drummers. The men were equipped with a sword and a flintlock musket with its bayonet, officers carried a spontoon and a sword. The soldiers wore coats that were grey-white with blue cuffs and lining; vests, breeches and stockings were blue. According to the description related by one Swedish visitor in the 1750s, the regular soldiers lived a comfortable life:

> The soldiery enjoy such advantages here as they are not allowed in any part of the world....They get every day a pound and a half of wheat bread....They likewise get plenty of peas, bacon, and salt or dried meat....All the officers kept cows....The soldiers had each a small garden outside the fort, which they were allowed to attend and to plant in its whatever they liked...and planted all kinds of vegetables. In time of peace the soldiers have very little guard duty....Each soldier got a new coat every two years; but annually, a waistcoat, cap, hat, breaches, cravat, tow pair of stockings, two pair of shoes, and as much wood as he had occasion for in the winter.

Failing financially, in January 1731 the Company relinquished Louisiana back to the king. During the period surrounding King George's War (1744-1748), the governor general of Canada Marquis de la Galissoniere expressed his concern that the king should not neglect the Illinois area. He said, "The little colony of Illinois ought not to be left to perish; the king must sacrifice for its support. The principal advantage of the county and its great productiveness and its connection with Canada and Louisiana must be maintained." However by 1747 the fort was in disrepair and the garrison abandoned it and moved to Kaskaskia.

Second French Fort

The French knew that they needed a strong fort to defend their interests in the Illinois region, the breadbasket of Louisiana, with its rich bottom land producing abundant crops and nearby lead deposits on the west bank of the Mississippi. After years of hesitation and argument over the best location (the government had seriously considered Kaskaskia) to build a new stone fort, authorities heeded the local commandant's advice to build near the old location.

Construction began in the years following the installation of a new commander, Richard Macarty, an Irish soldier of fortune and major of engineers, in 1751. The new fort was probably begun in 1753 as a letter dated May 15, 1753, from a Captain Bossu of the French Marines states, "The Sieur Saussier, an engineer, has made a plan for constructing a new fort here according to the intention of the court." Utilizing the plans drawn by engineer Lieutenant Jean Baptiste Saussier the workmen built limestone walls fifteen feet high and over two feet thick with forty-eight loopholes at regular intervals and two port-holes for cannon in the face and two in the flank of each bastion. There was a fifteen foot high arched gateway, with a stone platform above the gate. The fort contained a powder magazine, a storehouse two stories high and thirty feet by ninety feet in size, a prison with four dungeons, barracks and quarters for officers, bake ovens, a chapel and missionary quarters, and two large wells. When completed it ranked as the best fortification the French had built in the Mississippi Valley.

Over four hundred soldiers would be able to live in the fort enclosing over four acres of land and built at a cost of over 5 million *livres,* or about $1 million. The workmen hauled limestone by oxen and floated it on rafts from bluffs more than four miles away. The work proceeded very slowly. Desertions by two stonemasons and a carpenter in 1752 coupled with a lack of competent workers hampered progress. Finally, in June 1760 Louisiana's chief fiscal officer reported that by the end of the year the fort would be completed. At least one historian believes the fort was built partially to enrich corrupt French officials as there was no real need for such a strong fortification, though the fort would have served to protect the French administration in the Illinois country and to protect the road from Cahokia to Kaskaskia. The governor of Louisiana Louis de Kerlerec was later put in prison for having spent too much money. Nevertheless, by the time of its completion, the French would have little use for the fort as Canada fell to the relentless advances and crushing defeats of British armies.

In the early 1750s, the French attempted to shore up there interests in the Ohio valley by building additional forts. One detachment journeyed to the forks of the Ohio (present day Pittsburgh) to construct a fort. There they encountered a British force engaged in the same purpose and drove them away. The British brought word to George Washington, then serving as a colonel in the British Army, while he was building a military road on his way to protect the men at work on the fort. Washington learned of a small French force in the vicinity. He surrounded and attacked the thirty-three man party at Little Meadows, Pennsylvania, killing the commander, Ensign Joseph Coulon de Villiers de Jumonville, in the engagement on May 28. Washington then retreated and began building Fort Necessity at Great Meadow, Pennsylvania. The French in overwhelming force attacked him there. Washington surrendered after losing one third of his men killed and wounded. The French sent him and his men packing back to Virginia, allowing them to keep their arms. After that engagement the British government decided to send reinforcements to the colonies and the French and Indian War began in earnest.

In September 1755, the second in command at Fort de Chartres, Captain Neyon de Villiers, led a convoy of 120 tons of flour and 40 tons of salted pork up the Ohio for the troops at Fort Duquesne. Once there he learned of his brother's death. Desiring vengeance, he received permission from the commander at Fort Duquesne to attack George Croghan's stockade. Instead, with twenty-two men and thirty-three Indians he attacked Fort Granville with its thirty-eight defenders. He obtained the fort's surrender by starting the fort on fire. He then transported the captives all the way back to Fort de Chartres. Once there, he ransomed the captives from his Indian allies and sent them to New Orleans.

Other contingents from Fort de Chartres played important roles during the war. In 1758 Charles Philippe Aubry departed for Fort Duquesne with seventeen bateaux carrying troops and supplies. While there in September he led the Illinois contingent in routing a British force of 840 men under Major James Grant, capturing Grant in the process. This would be the last real French success during the war. It only delayed the larger army under General John Forbes from capturing the fort, which was burned and abandoned in November.

Aubry, who had returned to Illinois after Duquesne was abandoned, journeyed with four hundred men up the Ohio again in 1759. This time he met with disaster after joining a force under Captain de Ligneris in an attempt to relieve the siege of Fort Niagara by Sir William Johnson's army. A British and Iroquois force of 1,200 attacked and routed the French. Aubry was captured. In the defeat the Illinois contingent suffered a loss of six officers, thirty-two soldiers, fifty-four militiamen, and several Illinois warriors.

One who escaped the debacle was Philippe Francois de Rocheblave. By the fall of 1761, Illinois was the only French territory in North America not yet subdued by the British. They thus prepared for a British assault. In May, Neyon de Villiers, now in command of the fort, sent Rocheblave to Fort Massac with fifty soldiers to reinforce the garrison. Sometime in the spring, Sieur de Beaujeu-Villemonde arrived with 132 soldiers from Fort Michilimackinac after learning that New France would soon be surrendered to the British.

British Occupation

While the French waited to learn the details of peace negotiations, Pontiac organized an uprising against the British west of the Alleghenies in the hope that the French would help him resist British control. Though he initially achieved great success against the British, he had been unable to capture the fort at Detroit. In October 1763, Cadet Dequindre from the garrison at Fort de Chartres arrived at Detroit and brought the news that no French armies would be coming to his assistance. Pontiac and other Indians were invited to move across the Mississippi to land still held by the French. Pontiac found it difficult to believe the French would not assist him. Many Frenchmen had married Indian women. They lived their lives among the various tribes as relatives, friends, and advisors. They had enthusiastically encouraged Indian resistance to the British. In April 1764 he came to Fort de Chartres to seek assistance, at the same time seeking allies among the Indians west of Lake Michigan. Rebuffed by Villiers he pleaded, "My father, we pray the king to have pity on us....All thy children, my father, even when beat and conquered by the English love better to die than to fail the French in anything." He again returned in August to seek assistance from the new commander, St. Ange de Bellerive, who also refused him aid. Bellerive was simply holding the fort until he could turn it over to the British.

Several British attempts to reach Fort de Chartres from both the Ohio and Mississippi Rivers were turned back by Indians. It was not until October 1765, more than two years after the French surrender of North America to Britain at the Treaty of Paris, did Captain Thomas Stirling and the Forty-Second Royal Highland Regiment take possession of Fort de Chartres. Eight months later a Major Farmer arrived with the Thirty-Fourth Regiment of Foot. He renamed Fort de Chartres "Fort Cavendish," a name that did not stick. The British had recognized the great strength of Fort de Chartres. (In 1766 Captain Philip Pittman of the Royal engineers had stated, "It is generally allowed that this is the most commodious and best built fort in North America.") However, they had seen little value in maintaining a location no longer considered strategic and which the Mississippi menaced by continually eroding the south side walls. In addition, they needed to keep a closer watch on Kaskaskia, which was the center of the French power in the region. Thus the British only garrisoned the fort until 1772 when Commandant Major Isaac Hamilton transferred his soldiers to Kaskaskia, where they remained until 1776 when they were recalled due to the colonial rebellion that matured into the American Revolution. Before vacating the fort, the British partially destroyed it and made it easier for the Mississippi to complete the work. The very next year, after its abandonment, the Mississippi swallowed up the south wall and its bastions. The fort was never again occupied by soldiers.

Apparently the French did not trust British words assuring them of good treatment. Thomas Gage, commander-in-chief of the British forces in America, had written the following proclamation to them:

That His Majesty grants to the inhabitants of the Illinois the liberty of the Catholic religion, as it has already been granted to His subjects...That His Majesty, moreover, agrees that the French inhabitants, or others who have been subject of the Most Christian King, may retire, in full safety and freedom, whereas they please, even to New Orleans, or any part of Louisiana....That those who choose to retain their lands and become subjects of His Majesty, shall enjoy the same rights and privileges, the same security for their person and effects and liberty of trade, as the old subjects of the King: They are commanded by these presents, to take the oath of fidelity and obedience to His Majesty, in presence of Sieur Sterling, Captain of the Highland Regiment.

Instead of staying to enjoy the privileges granted to them by His Majesty, many of the French opted to leave for either New Orleans or the west bank of the Mississippi, where Pierre Laclede and his fifteen-year-old assistant had begun constructing a trading post in February 1764 that would be the future site of St. Louis. When the British arrived at Fort de Chartres, the forty families that had lived in the adjacent village had all departed. Many also left Prairie du Rocher, Cahokia, and Kaskaskia. The French who remained lived without any civil government, though Captain Stirling had appointed a judge and militia captains. Their relations with the British generally were acrimonious and characterized by mistrust. One British officer, a Lieutenant Fraser, expressed the British opinion that the remaining French were all drunkards and could only be expected to be cruel and dishonest. However, enough French stayed that many of their names such as Bienvenu, Dirousse, Duclos, Roy, Gilbert, Aubuchon, Robert, and Barbeau still exist in Illinois communities today.

American Occupation

During the American Revolution, George Rogers Clark's conquest of Kaskaskia on July 4, 1778, brought the Illinois French under the control of the American government. Clark never proceeded to Fort de Chartres since the British had evacuated the fort years ago. In the years from Clark's conquest until the organization of the Northwest Territory in 1787, the still slow influx of Americans into the French settlements began a power struggle resulting in much conflict between the two peoples. The situation, which resembled anarchy, was made more difficult by the lack of a local civil government with authority derived from a central government. During this time, once again many of the French abandoned their homes in the area. For example, Kaskaskia contained 194 heads of household when George Rogers Clark arrived.

By 1790 only 40 remained. French domination soon ended under an avalanche of American pioneers.

As settlers moved into the area surrounding the abandoned fort, they dismantled it to procure stone for their own uses. In 1812, Governor Ninian Edwards took five cannon from the Fort's ruins and mounted them at Fort Russell. Later visitors to the site described the fort's reversion to nature with large trees growing inside houses and undergrowth and brush connected with the walls and cannon lying around half buried. The Mississippi had also retreated and was described in 1879 as being a mile or more distant from the fort, about the same distance it is in the present day. When the State of Illinois purchased the site in 1913, the powder magazine was the only standing original structure. No part of the fort walls was visible above grade level.

Image credit: Illinois Historic Preservation Agency/Ft. de Chartres State Historic Site

To the Present

Soon the state began rebuilding parts of the fort. First, workers restored the powder magazine about 1917, considered by many to be the oldest building in Illinois. In the 1920s they exposed portions of other buildings and wall foundations. In the 1930s the Works Progress Administration reconstructed the gateway and two stone buildings. Today visitors can see a partially reconstructed north wall with bastions, a gatehouse, musket ports, and embrasures. Other structures include the guards' house and the king's storehouse, which houses the Piethman

Museum containing items discovered in archaeological research of the area. The building also contains a library and office. In 1993, Fort de Chartres once again succumbed to the mighty power of the Mississippi River as water fifteen feet in depth inundated the fort. Volunteers and staff refurbished the site.

Today one can visit the site from 9:00 a.m. – 5:00 p.m. daily. The site is closed Thanksgiving, Christmas, and New Year's Day. The Fort is located four miles west of Prairie du Rocher, Illinois, on state Route 155. Phone 618-284-7230 for additional information.

Apple River Fort

In 1804 the combined Sauk and Fox tribes occupied land in what became western Illinois, eastern Iowa, and southern Wisconsin. Their boundaries were roughly the Wisconsin River on the north, about the middle of present-day Illinois on the east, the Missouri River on the south, and the watershed between the De Moines and Missouri Rivers on the west. That year the chiefs had come to St. Louis to rectify a potentially explosive situation created by a few Sauk braves who had murdered two Americans during the summer. President Jefferson seized the opportunity to gain control over land that the tribes occupied and to reduce the activities of British agents and traders. Secretary of War Henry Dearborn instructed Governor of the Indiana Territory William Henry Harrison to try to gain land cessions from the tribes.

A message written by the United States Indian agent at St. Louis gives no indication to the chiefs that they would be negotiating a treaty. He wrote them as follows:

> My brothers. The great chief of the seventeen great cities of America, having chosen me to maintain peace and union between all the Red skins and the government of the United States, I have in consequence just received the order from the great Chief of our country, who has just arrived from the post of Vincennes, to send for the chiefs of your villages with some important men, and to bring with them those of you who recently killed his children; I enjoin you to come at once, and if some great reasons prevent you from bringing the murderers with you, this is not to prevent you from obeying the orders which I transmit to you. When you carry them out, you will be treated as chiefs and you will go home after having listened to the word of your Father, and then you can make it understood by your elders and your young people so open your ears and come at once. You will be treated as friends and allies of the United States.

Upon their arrival, the delegation of Quashquame, Pashipaho, and three others turned over one of the murderers and then tried to pay Harrison for his release. However, he only agreed to meet their demand after a cession of land. Harrison readily supplied the chiefs with whiskey and succeeded in persuading them to sign away over 15 million acres of land—a portion of what is now Missouri, and all of their land east of the Mississippi in Illinois north of the Illinois River and extending into southern Wisconsin. It has been called one of the cheapest land acquisitions ever made by the United States in the Old Northwest Territory. The terms of the treaty allowed the tribes to remain on the land until the government sold it, yet the Indians would eventually have to move across to the west side of the river. In addition to the more than $2,000 spent on the tribal delegation in St. Louis, the government would pay annuities of $1,000 a year, supply the services of a trader and a blacksmith, and send someone to teach them how to farm.

After the Sauk and Foxes learned that they were to lose their land, about 150 of them traveled to St. Louis in 1805 to complain. The new governor, General James Wilkinson, distributed more gifts and tried to assure them that the United States would not intrude onto their territory. However, they left very embittered and distrustful of the Americans.

Following the War of 1812, the Sauk and Fox, many of whom had fought on the British side, made peace with the United States. Signing treaties in 1816 and 1825, they seemed to accede to the terms of the Treaty of 1804. They never physically resisted its enforcement. However, it is highly doubtful they understood its full implications. They probably believed that they would continue to use the land as they had in the past, though the U.S. claimed political sovereignty. They had experienced something similar with the French and the British where nothing had changed. They definitely would not have knowingly sold their villages and best hunting grounds, and they always insisted that they had not sold any land north of the Rock River in Illinois.

In the years after the war, the Americans built Fort Armstrong near Saukenuk, where conflicts arose as more settlers moved closer. There would soon be a reason for the U.S. government to finally enforce the terms of the Treaty of 1804 and move the Sauks further away.

Drawn by the plentiful amounts of lead, many miners moved into southwestern Wisconsin and the Galena area in northwestern Illinois in the 1820s. Pressure began building to open up the land in northern Illinois for settlement. In 1827 the governor of Illinois Ninian Edwards wrote to the secretary of war demanding that the Indians be removed to the west side of the Mississippi River. The government surveyed the land adjacent to Saukenuk in 1828, and squatters began to move onto the land. Saukenuk had more than one hundred lodges, forty to sixty feet long, and each occupied by several families. At that time the total Sauk and Fox population was around six thousand to seven thousand with about two thirds being Sauk. In May 1828, the Indian agent Thomas Forsyth told the Sauk that they would have to relocate across the Mississippi by the following spring. Later that year the Sauk and Fox left their village of Saukenuk at the mouth of the Rock River—today's Rock Island, Illinois—and moved west of the Mississippi to hunt for the winter. During their absence settlers began to move onto the lands they had occupied. The settlers would soon have to contend with hostile Sauks.

In the spring of 1829, a portion of the Sauk and Fox returned under the leadership of Black Hawk. Black Hawk was one leader who always remained anti-American. He was born in 1767 at Saukenuk, the Sauk village located at the mouth of the Rock River. Though he was not a civil chief, he earned much respect as a great warrior against the Osages, Cherokee, and other enemies. He directed war parties of more then five hundred warriors on long campaigns against far away enemies when he was only in his early thirties. During the War of 1812, he led two hundred Sauk and Fox to fight for the British. He participated in the Battle of the River Raisin and the sieges at Fort Meigs and Fort Stephenson. In July 1813, he also led warriors in attacking reinforcements bound to besiege the British held fort at Prairie du Chien. Then with British assistance he repelled another expedition under Zachary Taylor. He even tried to continue warfare against the Americans for awhile after the British signed the Treaty of Ghent ending the War of 1812.

Black Hawk and his followers now found that settlers occupied many of their lodges. The Sauk and Fox moved into empty lodges and began planting. There was friction between the two peoples that threatened to explode into serious violence. Forsyth again warned the Indians to leave the area. In July the government announced that it would be putting the land around Saukenuk up for public sale. Black Hawk's band finally departed with Black Hawk declaring that he would return the next spring.

In October three thousand acres, mostly in the Indian settlement area, were sold. Black Hawk lived up to his word and once again returned in 1830. A tense situation erupted as clashes between both peoples occurred when each group broke down fences and allowed their animals to wander into each others fields. Again Black Hawk said he would return the next spring. This time the government brought force to bear on the Sauk soon after they reappeared in Illinois. The night before General Edmund Gaines bombarded Saukenuk, Black Hawk's band retreated across the Mississippi. The next day Gaines summoned Black Hawk and his followers and persuaded him to sign "Articles of Agreement and Capitulation," whereby they promised never to return to Saukenuk. In return the settlers were to provide the Indians with corn so that they would not starve.

The settlers did not live up to the agreement, and the Indians grew restless. The Indians resented the government's interference in their affairs, the continual trespassing of whites onto their lands, and the forceful eviction from their homes. For these reasons, some of Black Hawk's band encouraged him to lead them home again. His chief lieutenant, a warrior named Neapope, stated that the British would assist him. Wabokieshiek, the Winnebago, prophet assured him that the Potawatomis, Chippewas, and Ottawas would also come to his aid. So in the end, determined to hold on to his home where he had been born, Black Hawk moved across the Mississippi in early April 1832.

After a warning from the Winnebago prophet that the United States military was moving against him, and an invitation to come to his town to wait for further reinforcements, Black Hawk moved his band of about one thousand women and children and between five hundred to six hundred warriors another forty miles further up the Rock River. From the Prophet's village, the band moved even further up the river to near present-day Rockford, Illinois, to meet with the Potawatomis and the Winnebagos. In the meeting Black Hawk finally realized that neither the British nor other supposedly allied tribes would render him any assistance if it came to fighting. Hence he decided to make peace with the Americans and return to the Iowa side of the Mississippi. Since his people had not committed any hostile actions toward the whites, Black Hawk thought he could negotiate with the Americans.

War Begins

Meanwhile Governor John Reynolds had called out the militia. Around two thousand men responded, including twenty-three-year-old Captain Abraham Lincoln. With about 1,500 of the militia joining his army of 1,000 regulars, General Henry Atkinson had started in pursuit of Black Hawk's band up the Rock River on May 10. Learning that the army was only about twenty-five miles away from Black Hawk's band, Major Isaiah Stillman, in command of 275 militiamen, received permission on May 14 to advance in front of the main army in pursuit of the Indians. When Black Hawk's scouts informed him that Stillman's men were only about eight miles away, he sent three of his braves as ambassadors to try to parley with the Americans. Another five followed after them to watch. The first three entered Stillman's camp in the early evening. When the militia saw the other five observing from a distance, they concluded that an attack was immanent and raced toward the five warriors, shooting two of them. The rest escaped and informed Black Hawk. Meanwhile the militia killed one of the three ambassadors and the other two escaped. (The above and what follows is Black Hawk's version, Stillman's story is quite different).

Black Hawk reacted angrily that his men had been killed under a flag of truce. He only had about forty warriors who were presently with him, but he yelled out to them, "Some of our people have been killed! ....We must revenge their death!" In his autobiography he then described what happened next:

> In a little while we discovered the whole army coming towards us in full gallop! We were confident that our first party had been killed! I immediately place my men in front of some bushes, that we might have the first fire, when they approached close enough. They made a halt some distance from us. I gave another yell, and ordered my brave warriors to charge upon them—expecting that we would all be killed! They did charge! Every man rushed and fired, and the enemy retreated! in the utmost confusion and consternation, before my little, but brave band of warriors!

The rout was on as the little band of Indians chased the whites who were many times their number back to their camp. In the ensuing battle since known as Stillman's Run, Black Hawk lost three men while killing eleven of the whites. The war had now begun. Arrayed against Black Hawk and his band of several hundred warriors were almost 12,000 soldiers, plus militia, in Illinois and surrounding states.

All across northern Illinois and southern Wisconsin settlers fortified their homes, erected blockhouses, gathered together for safety, or fled. For example, in Plainfield, Illinois, approximately sixty miles from Stillman's defeat, residents forted up at the home of Rev. Stephen R. Beggs. They later fled to Chicago after hearing of the Indian Creek Massacre in LaSalle County, where men, women, and children of the Hall, Daviess, and Pennigrew families were murdered. Two of the Hall girls, Rachel and Sylvia, were hauled into captivity and later ransomed.

Apple River Fort

Meanwhile, rumors that Black Hawk and his warriors had begun an Indian uprising spread. Residents of the Apple River Settlement at present day Elizabeth, Illinois—about fifteen miles southeast of Galena (where residents also built a stockade)—gathered together to build a fort around already existing cabins. According to one author, they built the fort in a day. The fort was very small. The residents enclosed a 48' by 68' 6" area (3,300 square feet) with walls 12 feet high around the cabins. The logs used for the stockade have been estimated at approximately 8" to 10" in diameter, in which case about 250 would have been required to construct the walls. The logs were irregular and varied in size. The space in between them allowed the men to fire through them; in addition several sentinel stands were also built along the wall. Two log houses were on the southwest and northeast corners. One was converted into a two-story blockhouse as well. There were probably several crude small shanties or huts within the wall and tents for shelter. In addition there were several buildings in the vicinity of the fort. In preparation for hostilities, the settlers collected foodstuffs into the fort, gathered other necessary supplies, molded extra bullets, and cast a crude cannon made from lead. By May 23 they had finished making preparations for an Indian attack. During the day families went to their own homesteads, at night they returned to the safety of the fort. Twenty-two men, mostly miners, and twenty-three women and children resided at the fort.

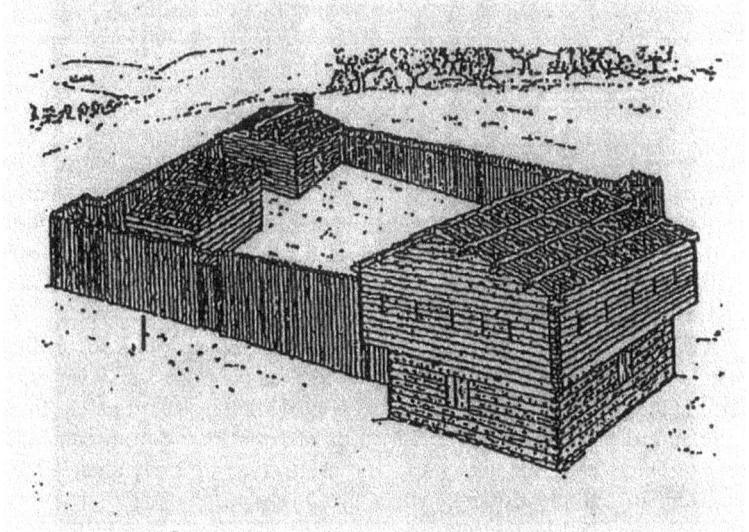

Image credit: Illinois Historic Preservation Agency/Apple River State Historic Site

In the ensuing days Indians stole horses from a corral outside the fort; on June 8 they stole fourteen horses and again on June 17 took off with ten more. The settler's fear of attack would become reality on the evening of June 24, 1832. Unknown to them, Black Hawk and between 150 to 200 warriors arrived in the afternoon. They would soon be making the only attack on a fort led by Black Hawk during the four month war. Deciding first to survey the situation, Black Hawk concealed his warriors in the forest surrounding the fort.

Four men, Frederick Dixon, George W. Herclurode (Also spelled Hercleroad), Edmund Welch, and a young man with the last name of Kirkpatrick, left the fort on their way to General Atkinson's headquarters on the Illinois River. After they had ridden only about three hundred yards from the fort, the braves fired at them from ambush. They wounded Welch in the leg, and he fell off his horse. He fired his gun as they advanced with raised hatchets. At great risk to themselves, the others rode up to Welch, halted the Indians from advancing further by waving their empty guns, helped to lift him up from the ground and onto a horse, and hastily returned to the fort. As the yelling Indians chased them toward the fort, the now alerted settlers also raced to the fort. At the time many of them, including virtually all the women and children, were outside the fort picking gooseberries near the river. The warning averted a massacre as everyone managed to run inside the fort, closing the gate just as the Indians came rushing into view.

As Captain Flack described it to John A. Wakefield, "The Indians pursued these men within firing distance of the fort, all on horseback, they rode up, dismounted and hitched their horses, and I think in about three minutes the fort was surrounded by about 150 Indians, with all the savage ferocity and awful appearance, that those monsters could possibly appear in." They took cover in the houses that were near the fort and began firing.

Many of the men were away from the fort out hunting. To resist the attack, militia captain Clack Stone commanded twenty-two men, mostly miners. According to one of the defenders, Oliver Emmell, "the women and children were panic-stricken, crying and wringing their hands." Elizabeth Armstrong calmed them, saying, "It was worse than folly to give up to fear." She soon rallied the twenty-three women and children to help the men keep up a barrage of fire. The women and girls as young as eight years old molded musket balls, made cartridges, and loaded the guns so the men could maintain a heavier fire than their actual numbers indicated. One participant, Mr. Kirkpatrick, stated that every man, woman, and child actively participated in the defense of the fort during the attack. During the battle the Indians managed to wound one defender in the head, Josiah Nutting, and to kill another, George W. Herclurode— the proud owner of the only percussion cap rifle among the defenders, shot in the neck as he raised his head above the palisade to get a better shot at the Indians. Captain Flack noted that he had seen several warriors carried away during the battle and that blood was found on the ground surrounding the fort.

Later, Black Hawk related in his account of the battle: "One of their braves, who seemed more valiant then the rest, raised his head above the picketing to fire at us, when one of my braves, with a well directed shot, put an end to his bravery." Thinking there were many more defenders than there actually were, Black Hawk broke off the battle, which had begun between four and five o'clock in the afternoon and lasted for about forty-five minutes to an hour of continuous firing by both antagonists. In his autobiography Black Hawk states,

> Finding that these people could not all be killed, without setting fire to their homes and fort, I thought it more prudent to be content with what flour, provisions, cattle and horses we could find, than to set fire to their buildings, as the light would be seen at a distance, and the army might suppose that we were in the neighborhood, and come upon us with a force too strong. Accordingly, we opened a house and filled our bags with flour and provisions—took several horses, and drove off some of their cattle.

Again as Flack relates,

> The Indians got into those houses before spoken of, and knocked out the chinking and kept up their fire until they got discouraged. They then commenced plundering the houses, chopt, split and tore up a quantity of fine furniture. There was scarcely a man or woman that was left with a second suit of clothing. They went into my father's house; there was a large bureau full of fine clothes, they took six fine cloth coats and a number of fine ruffle shirts, with their tomahawk's they split the drawers and took the contents. They ripped open the bedticks, emptied the feathers, took all the bedclothing, and broke all

the delf in the cupboards. Some of the out houses were kept for the purpose of storing away provisions; they got into those houses where a number of flour barrels were stowed away; they would lie down on their faces and roll a barrel after them until they would get into a ravine, where they were out of danger; they then would empty the barrels of flour, after they had destroyed this necessary article, and when they found they could not succeed in taking the fort as they expected, they then commenced the warfare upon the stock; they killed all the cattle that were near the fort and took a number of fine horses to the number of about twenty, which were never got again by the owners.

By one account, during the darkness after the battle, Kirkpatrick snuck out of the fort, evaded the Indians, and rode to Galena to get assistance. In another, Mr. Dixon, one of the couriers in the initial ambush, on the return to the fort had not stopped, but rather had just continued on to Galena. He had feared that the fort could not hold out against the large number of Indians. In any case, the next day a militia company of about one hundred men, commanded by Colonel James Strode with Abraham Lincoln as one of its members, arrived at the fort at about eleven o'clock the next day.

The War Ends

Following the battle Black Hawk's band moved away from the fort the next day to the east where they killed five and wounded three of Major John Dement's militia force at the second Battle of Kellogg's Grove. Black Hawk then moved his people to the Four Lakes region of central Wisconsin. Emboldened by Black Hawk's success against Stillman's force, small parties of Potawatomi, Winnebago, and Kickapoo began attacking isolated white settlers. In one incident, the previously mentioned Indian Creek Massacre, some Potawatomi killed fifteen people. Now that hostilities had begun, Black Hawk also sent out war parties. To protect the women and children, he sent them to a hiding place in the Four Lakes country around present day Madison, Wisconsin. Soon, his people began to grow hungry for lack of food, and Black Hawk, with the knowledge that American forces were pursuing him, decided to follow the Wisconsin River down to the Mississippi and cross back into Iowa where he hoped to find peace and safety.

In the meantime, Colonel Henry Dodge, in command of a force of about 3,500 men, had been pursuing Black Hawk but had lost the trail. Some Winnebagos approached Dodge with the information that they knew where Black Hawk could be found. Taking five hundred men, Dodge caught up to Black Hawk's band as they were crossing the

Wisconsin River. Taking cover Black Hawk and fifty warriors, in what has been called the Battle of Wisconsin Heights, held off the Americans until dark, allowing the Indians to escape. Lacking any means to cross the river, and low on supplies, Dodge broke off pursuit.

Black Hawk's discouraged and starving band, now reduced to about five hundred, finally reached the Mississippi on August 1 just south of the mouth of the Bad Axe River. Unfortunately for them, while they were making canoes and rafts to cross the river, the steamboat *Warrior* appeared. Thinking that the Indians were going to attack, the Americans began firing at point-blank range with a six-pounder for about two hours, killing twenty-three of them. The band now split when Black Hawk and about fifty followers headed further north to seek refuge among the Chippewa, and the rest continued their preparations to cross the river where they were. The arrival of General Atkinson's army of 1,300 on August 3 further compounded the sufferings of the Indians. In the misnamed Battle of Bad Axe, really a massacre, they attacked the Indians, killing every man, woman, and child they could reach. In addition the *Warrior* returned to add its firepower to the overwhelming force that was slaughtering the remainder of the Indians. At the end of eight hours of massacre, the Americans, who had lost thirty-three killed and wounded, held only thirty-nine prisoners, all women and children. Several hundred of the Indians managed to cross the Mississippi River where the waiting Sioux killed most of them. The entire war had lasted just under four months, directly causing the deaths of seventy Americans. However, hundreds more died from a cholera epidemic that had spread across the Atlantic and then to the theater of war by way of the troops shipped from the East coast.

With the war now having essentially ended in total disaster for his band, Black Hawk willingly agreed to surrender at the urging of Winnebagos who had caught up to him near the Wisconsin Dells. He returned to Prairie du Chien. Both Zachary Taylor and Jefferson Davis oversaw his transportation to Jefferson Barracks where he was imprisoned. He was later released and toured eastern cities before returning home where he died in 1836. As a result of the war, the peaceful Sauk and Fox under Keokuk were pressured during treaty negotiations to relinquish all their remaining land—six million acres along the Iowa side of the Mississippi—holding on only to a small reservation.

In a celebration of the victory at Bad Axe and the end of the war, the Apple River settlers suffered one more casualty. When they fired their lead cannon, which they had loaded to the muzzle, it unexpectedly burst and killed a nearby soldier.

Image credit: Illinois Historic Preservation Agency/Apple River State Historic Site

Past to Present

After the war, two squatter families, by the name of Hawk and Davis occupied the fort. The hastily built fort itself lasted until 1847 when George Bainbridge purchased the land from the federal government. He dismantled the fort and used the lumber to construct a barn.

In honor of her heroism, the town of Elizabeth was named for Mrs. Armstrong. The Illinois State historical Society in Jo Davies County erected a replica fort in 1934. In 1995 the Apple River Fort Historic Foundation determined to locate the original fort site. Archaeological excavation of the site recovered numerous artifacts. In 1996, volunteers rebuilt the fort's two cabins, erected a surrounding palisade of fourteen to fifteen foot logs placed in a two to three foot trench, constructed firing stands on two corners accessed by hand-hewn ladders, and added a two-story blockhouse with the upper story projecting two feet over the lower story.

The fort is open today for self-guided tours and hosts special events throughout the year. Among these are Living History Weekends where costumed interpreters portray frontier life during the period. They demonstrate hearth cooking, gardening, lead bullet molding, wood splitting, and more. A two-story Interpretive Center and Museum Shop close to the fort relates the history of the Apple River Fort and the Black Hawk War, and highlights the roles of many of the famous men who participated in the war, including General Winfield Scott and future presidents Abraham Lincoln and Jefferson Davis. Exhibits also display artifacts uncovered at the site, give the archaeological story of how the fort was located, and show photographs of the fort's rebuilding. In addition a fifteen-minute video recounts the story of the Black Hawk War. The National Register of Historic Places lists the Apple River Fort among the significant places in American history.

The fort is open year-round, Wednesday – Sunday, 9:00 a.m. – 4:00 p.m. Call 815-858-2028 to confirm. Today, there is also a historical marker on the north side of US 20 about one half mile east of Elizabeth.

(See Appendix III for a list of settlers at the fort during the battle)

Fort Howard

The first white man to step foot in Wisconsin, Jean Nicolet, entered at Green Bay in the 1630s. He was in search of a people he had heard were without hair or beards. Thinking that he would be meeting Chinese, he wore a Chinese robe when approaching them. In this he was disappointed for they were Winnebago. However, it would be the start of a long and for the most part friendly relationship. In time the Winnebago became firm allies and devoted trading partners with the French.

It was not perhaps until 1684 that French soldiers established themselves at Green Bay near the future site of Fort Howard. They erected a stockade with quarters for soldiers just below the rapids of De Pere, near the St. Francis Xavier mission established by Jesuit Father Claude Allouez in 1671. They named their new construction Fort St. Francis. Hostile Indians burned it down in 1687, and a new Fort St. Francis was built in 1717, but was only garrisoned intermittently. The fort was also named St. Philippe at one time but was most commonly known as Fort La Baye. The mouth of the Fox River emptied into Green Bay (*La Baye Verte*), which was named for the greenish color it exhibited at certain times of the year. It was also called *La Baye de Puants* (Bay of Bad Odors). The name was derived from The Winnebago Indians, called Puants by the French (Ho-Chunk today). Another reason may have been the odor from the large numbers of dead fish that frequently scattered the shores.

The French fought the Fox tribe periodically from early in the 1700s until the late 1730s. The Fox resented French attempts to trade (especially firearms) with their enemies the Sioux to the west of them. In response, they killed Frenchmen attempting to travel the Fox-Wisconsin River route to the Mississippi to trade with the Sioux. In 1727 the new governor-general of Canada, the Marquis de Beauharnois, decided to put an end to Fox interference and aggressiveness, which was hurting French trade and prestige. The Fox had recently murdered eight French soldiers, and Beauharnois had learned that the Fox had declared that they would not allow any French to be among them. Beauharnois sent Constant Marchand deLignery in command of an expedition against them. When Lignery arrived at Green Bay, a Potawatomi chief warned the Fox of French intentions to attack them. Thus warned, the Fox retreated from Lignery's force. Unsuccessful in confronting the Fox, Lignery returned to Fort LaBaye and burned it before he departed for Mackinac.

Later in 1730 the French and their Indian allies severely defeated the Fox on the Illinois Prairie. A large segment (about one thousand) of the Fox had decided to seek safety by emigrating to New York to settle among their friends, the Seneca of the Iroquois Confederacy. On their journey some Cahokia Indians spotted them and sounded the alarm. Soon the French and their allies—Illinois Indians, Mascouten, Potawatomi, Kickapoo, Miami, and others—surrounded the heavily outnumbered Fox, who fortified themselves in a wood grove. After a month of siege, the Fox tried to escape during a storm, but were trailed by 1,200 French and their allies. Only about fifty Fox warriors escaped. After the destruction of the Fox (it was thought that only about 450 remained alive), the governor sent Antoine Coulon de Villiers to rebuild the fort at Green Bay.

The famous Charles de Langlade (Father of Wisconsin) came to Green Bay with his father Sieur Augustin de Langlade in the 1740s. The Langlades settled on the east side of the river near its mouth, becoming the first permanent white settlers in the area. (Some historians do not believe the Langlades settled there permanently until 1765). It is believed that Langlade came in 1746 after the commandant at Fort Mackinac allowed him to purchase a trading license for one thousand Francs.

LaBaye post served as an important center for trade for the French. The garrison was quite isolated. The commandant, who usually served for a three year term, only heard from higher authorities about once a year. Most of the commandants attempted to enrich themselves off the fur trade. Starting in 1742 the French government auctioned off licenses for trading at the western posts. This resulted in higher prices for trade goods, and the Indians became dissatisfied with the French, especially during King George's War (1744-1748) when it was difficult to obtain any goods from the French due to British naval domination on the high seas.

Governor Marquis de la Jonquire arrived in Canada in 1749 and reinstituted the licensing system that had prevailed before 1742. Unfortunately, he awarded the trading licenses to mostly corrupt cronies. Finally, in 1758, the formerly staunch French allies the Menominees rebelled. They killed eleven Frenchmen at LaBaye and plundered the warehouse. They had planned to kill the commandant Hubert Couterot, but he managed to escape. Peace was made the following year. The corrupt system, where the owners of the licenses did not deal fairly with the Indians, continued until the French defeat in 1760.

After the French defeat in Canada, the British replaced the French at Green Bay. They rebuilt the St. Francis fort and renamed it Edward Augustus for the brother of King George III. Lieutenant James Gorrell commanded the garrison of one sergeant, one corporal, and fifteen privates. Gorrell made friends with the Indians by borrowing wampum, beads, and trinkets from the squaws while the warriors were absent, and then giving the items as gifts to the warriors upon their return. He succeeded so well in establishing friendly relations with the local Foxes, Sauks, Menominees, and Winnebagos despite total inexperience in dealing with them, that when Pontiac's war began, his post was the only one in the entire Northwest Territory that was not attacked. After the capture of Mackinac, the fort commander, George Etherington, sent him a letter with orders to bring his garrison to L'Arbre Croche. Gorrell then told the surrounding Indians in a council that he had to abandon the fort and would leave it to them.

The local Indians did not like the French and were not supportive of Pontiac. To assist Gorrell, they sent a delegation with him to negotiate with the enemy Ottawas and Chippewas. At Michilimackinac, Gorrell persuaded the hostile Ottawas to take the remaining Michilmackinac garrison prisoners along with his men to Montreal to receive a large reward rather than keeping them under guard. Once at Montreal the prisoners were released and the Indians received a generous reward from General Thomas Gage. The British returned after Pontiac's War and continued their authority in the Green Bay area until the War of 1812 settled the question of British occupancy on U.S. territory.

As part of the American plan to block British use of the Fox, Wisconsin, and Mississippi rivers after the War of 1812 and to woo the Indian trade away from them, the War Department ordered Colonel John C. Miller with four companies of infantry, two companies of riflemen, and a detachment of artillery to build a fort at Green Bay. The men arrived at Green Bay in August 1816 to an unexpectedly friendly reception since it had been rumored that the inhabitants would resist American occupation. The British and French inhabitants also feared the American arrival because they had served in the British militia and supplied the British with food during the war. Upon his arrival Miller went to visit Tomah, the nearby Menominee chief, and asked for his consent to build a fort. Tomah replied, "My Brother! How can we oppose your locating a council-fire among us? You are too strong for us. Even if we wanted to oppose you, we have scarcely got powder and shot to make the attempt." The strong force of five hundred men under Miller's command plus a few pieces of artillery undoubtedly discouraged any thought of resistance. Miller thanked Tomah and offered some spare provisions to him. The advent of the Americans opened up a new market to the local inhabitants, and the people peacefully accepted their presence.

Miller with Major Charles Gratiot of the engineers began construction of Fort Howard, named for General Benjamin Howard, who had been governor of Missouri Territory. Howard had commanded in the west during the late war and had died in 1814 in St. Louis. Lieutenant Colonel Talbot Chambers assumed command when Miller and Gratiot quickly departed for Mackinac. Chambers and his soldiers built the fort on the site of the old French fort on the west side of the river near the mouth during the fall and winter. Under the guidance of Lewis Morgan, the government-sent superintendent of fortifications, they constructed a timber stockade thirty feet high, later cut in half when the Indian threat subsided, with barracks on three sides and block houses mounted with guns at the angles. Also within the three acre enclosed quadrangle was a parade ground and separate quarters for the commanding officer. They constructed additional houses outside the fort for the surgeon and the quartermaster.

Image credit: Photo donated by Heritage Hill State Historical Park

Zachary Taylor became the second commander of the fort when he arrived with five hundred men of the Fifth United States Infantry in the spring of 1817. Taylor brought his family with him and some fine furniture and china. His quarters became the social center for the community as he hosted balls and theatrical events at the fort during the winter. Taylor also continued work on the fort, plastering the officer's quarters and whitewashing the entire fort. Under Colonel Joseph Lee Smith preparations were made to build a new fort of stone about three miles up the river on the south side on the top of Allouez ridge in 1820. However, at Camp Smith, as the site was known, work did not progress rapidly. A new commander, Colonel Ninian Pinkney, arrived in 1821 and under orders from Washington moved the troops back to Fort Howard in 1822.

Pinkney and his troops came to the fort on *Walk-in-the-Water*, the first steamboat to traverse the upper Great Lakes. This was only one of the many firsts in Wisconsin history to take place at Fort Howard and the surrounding community; others include the first hotel, frame house, school, church (besides the French mission at St. Xavier), and lighthouse on the upper Great Lakes, among others. Several famous men lived at the fort at one time or another, including Winfield Scott, William J. Worth, David Twiggs, and Kirby Smith; also Jefferson Davis visited the fort. Doctor William Beaumont, famous for his medical experiments on Alexis St. Martin, was stationed at the fort from 1826-1828.

Sometimes the commanders of Fort Howard were brought into court by civilians for enforcing the laws, particularly when they tried to enforce the Indian intercourse acts, or tried to close down the many grog shops in the vicinity of the fort. They were also guilty of excessive interference in civilian affairs. In the 1820s one commanding officer tried to control the operation of a ferry run by John B. Arndt, arresting him when he did not salute the fort. The United States court fined those who had arrested him. All of the commanders had difficulty controlling the whiskey trade which greatly affected their garrison. One traveler to the fort remarked of the men "that I have seen more cases of drunkenness than ever I saw among any troops in the world." The whiskey greatly affected the men's health in the form of liver disease, dropsy, consumption, apoplexy, palsy, and other ailments. In 1825 the surgeon general reported that of the 116 deaths in the army that year, 40 could be traced to the effects of alcohol. The army tried to solve the problem by ending the daily liquor ration in 1830 and paying an allowance instead. Two years later the army substituted coffee and sugar for the liquor ration, but nothing was totally effective. The wives of soldiers even sometimes smuggled two-quart canteens of whiskey into the fort in large kettles filled with sugar.

Observers of the army have noted that many of the soldiers came from the bottom of society. One Frenchman observed that "The recruits are generally men, who, as laborers and mechanics, receive much higher compensation than in the military service. They must, therefore, be infected with some moral infirmity, which renders them unfit for a useful and laborious life." Many soldiers were foreigners, for example, from 1821-1823 fully one quarter of all enlistees were foreign born. It did not help that enlisted men could not advance to the rank of an officer as all of the officers entered from West Point. As a result many soldiers deserted. The number of desertions in 1823 equaled nearly one-fourth of the enlistments for the year. In 1825 it was worse yet, with desertions rising to almost one-half of the number of new enlistments. To put this in perspective, an estimated 1,450 men deserted in 1831, when the total strength of the army was less than 6,000 men. The army did take steps to improve the situation in 1833. The term of enlistment was cut from five to three years with a two month bounty offered for reenlistment. The pay was increased from $5 to $6 a month and whipping was restored as punishment for desertion. These measures did help.

As previously mentioned, the men spent a great deal of time working on projects that would not be considered a part of soldiering in order to obtain food, fuel, and to maintain shelter. This was no different at Fort Howard, where in 1826 permission was sought to hire an extra clerk to assist in directing the work of the many men involved in non-military activities. In 1828, under Major David Twiggs, troops from the fort assisted in the erection of Fort Winnebago. Also in 1828, the Fifth Infantry moved from the Jefferson Barracks near St. Louis to Fort Howard, garrisoning the fort for the remainder of its useful life. Brevetted Major Nathan Clark commanded at the fort during the Black Hawk War. An inspection report of the fort in 1830 revealed that the decayed condition of the buildings would prohibit continued occupation without extensive repairs. Yet the fort would remain in use until 1841. For awhile it was feared that Black Hawk and his band might attempt to pass through Green Bay while escaping to Canada. As a safety precaution during the war, the women and children from Fort Winnebago came to live at Fort Howard. From 1835 through 1837, three companies of men from Fort Howard worked on constructing the road to Fort Winnebago, which continued on to Fort Crawford. This was during the command of General George Brooke who served longer than any other commander at Fort Howard, from 1833 through 1838. He also oversaw extensive repairs to the fort during his tenure.

After the Black Hawk War, the government removed the Winnebago Indians from the Fox River Valley, and in 1836 the Menominee Indians ceded land to the north and east of the Fox River. The land office at Green Bay had also begun selling tracts of land in southern Wisconsin to settlers in 1834. Thus with the threat of Indian hostilities reduced and greater settlement, the need for Fort Howard declined. After 1838 only one company, under Captain Moses Merrill, garrisoned the fort, and this garrison finally vacated the fort in 1841 to participate in the Seminole War. Major Ephraim Shayler remained to care for the fort. Eventually, settlers took over Fort Howard, occupying and dismantling its buildings when it was completely abandoned in 1845. The fort was garrisoned for a brief period at the close of the Mexican War until May 1852 when the commander, Lt. Colonel Benjamin Bonneville, abandoned the fort for the last time, departing with the garrison for California. After 1866 railroad yards covered most of the fort grounds.

Today one can visit Heritage Hill State Historical Park, a forty acre site where Camp Smith once stood, and see four buildings that partially represent the original Fort Howard. The Fort Howard Hospital is the original building as constructed outside the fort walls in 1834-35. The Company Kitchen/Orderly Room is also original and was built between 1831 and 1835. The Officer's Quarters building is a replica built in 1975. Finally a replica school house built in the same style of architecture represents Fort Howard's first school, built sometime before 1824 for officers' children and those of the area. While at the park one can also see many other historical buildings, including a Fur Trader's cabin and the Roi-Portier-Tank Cottage, the oldest building still standing in Wisconsin, first erected in 1776. Costumed interpreters explain the uses of each building. Special events are also held their, for example the French and Indian War encampment in June each year.

Image credit: Photo donated by Heritage Hill State Historical Park

The Park is open from 10:00 a.m. to 4:30 p.m. from Memorial Day through Labor Day. Call 800-721-5150 for further information.

Fort Crawford

For many years on a plain a few miles north of where the Wisconsin River flows into the Mississippi, Indians gathered to trade. When American Jonathan Carver passed through the region of the future site of Prairie du Chien, Wisconsin, in 1766-1768, he noted about three hundred families lived there. He stated, "This is the great mart, where all the adjacent tribes, and even those who inhabit the remote branches of the Mississippi annually assemble about the latter end of May, bringing with them furs to dispose of to the traders." At the gatherings the Indians refrained from violence even against their traditional enemies.

During the American Revolution, the British gathered groups of Indians at Prairie du Chien and sent them to help their armies in the east. In 1776 Colonel Arent Schuyler De Peyster, the commander at Mackinac, ordered Charles Langlade to gather French-Canadian Indians and bring them to help General Carleton, but they arrived too late to do anything. In the spring of 1777 both Langlade and Charles Gautier brought Indians from Prairie du Chien to aid General John Burgoyne. The Indians did not like Burgoyne and departed from his army after only a month. In May 1780, De Peyster at Mackinac used Prairie du Chien as a rendezvous location to mount an expedition against the Spanish and the Americans at St. Louis and Cahokia, Illinois, respectively. Spain had declared war against Great Britain in May 1779, and De Peyster feared Spain might also fight against British forces in the North America, where Spain controlled most of the land west of the Mississippi. Captain Emmanuel Hesse, who owned a trading house at Prairie du Chien, along with the Chippewa chief Machiquawish led a mixed force of 750 (accounts vary from 750 to 1,400), including traders, Chippewa, Foxes, Kickapoo, Menominee, Ottawa, Potawatomi, Sauk, Sioux, and Winnebago. In both places the Spanish and the Americans each received advance warning from the trader Pierre Prevost.

In St. Louis the Spanish commander Governor Don Fernando de Leyba built a stone tower mounted with cannon and constructed about a mile of entrenchments. The Spanish repulsed the British-Indian attack that lasted about two hours. In the attacks the Winnebago lost one chief and three warriors. The St. Louis defenders lost sixty-eight killed while three were killed in defending Cahokia. The so called "Battle of Fort San Carlos" was the only battle of the Revolution fought west of the Mississippi River. The Spanish also received help from some of George Rogers Clark's men. Clark had brought about four hundred men to Cahokia. He later claimed that he saved St. Louis for the Spaniards. Clark's force around Cahokia barely avoided an ambush and repulsed an enemy force of approximately three hundred men. An American force of 350 men, under Colonel John Montgomery pursued the retreating British forces for over 250 miles and defeated the Sauks on the Rock River in Illinois. After this defeat British forces made no more military use of Prairie du Chien during the Revolution.

Three Frenchmen—Pierre Antaya, Augustine Ange, and Basil Giard—were granted the first formal possession of land at Prairie du Chien by British Governor Patrick Sinclair at Mackinac in 1781. Nine square miles of prairie two leagues above the mouth of the Wisconsin River had been obtained from the Foxes for permanent settlement. Since Spain still held the land on the west bank of the Mississippi, they kept a watch on Praire du Chien and other settlements that threatened their territory after the war ended. The Spanish employed a gunboat with a forty man crew on the Mississippi to protect its territory and trade from American and British intruders. In 1797, Don Carlos Howard, in command of the gunboat, planned on enlisting the Fox to assist him in attacking Prairie du Chien. However, Wabasha, a Sioux chief, brought reinforcements to the traders there and Howard cancelled the attack.

In 1805 Lieutenant Zebulon Montgomery Pike became the first American military man to enter Prairie du Chien. General James Wilkinson had ordered him to explore up the Mississippi to locate its source, to select locations for future military posts, to gather information about British traders operating in the area, and to make peace between the Chippewa and the Sioux. Pike stopped at Prairie du Chien both in 1805 and 1806 with about twenty American soldiers. American soldiers would not come again until the War of 1812.

In 1813, General Benjamin Howard, commanding officer of the Western Department of the United States Army, and Governor Ninian Edwards of Illinois Territory had sought permission from Secretary of War John Armstrong to establish a fort at British-held Prairie du Chien. Finally, in May of 1814 Governor William Clark of the Missouri Territory (and of Lewis and Clark fame) launched an expedition against Prairie du Chien. After a month ascending the Mississippi, on June 2,

1813, Clark and Lieutenant Joseph Perkins arrived there with 61 regulars of the Seventh infantry and 125 volunteers serving for a term of sixty days. The pro-British inhabitants fled with the arrival of the Americans, who occupied the town without firing a shot. The Americans soon commenced building a fort, which they named Shelby in honor of Isaac Shelby, the first governor of Kentucky. While still working on the fort, a force of British and Indians arrived and demanded their surrender. The official report by Perkins regarding this endeavor is in part as follows:

> On the 5th the Govr. fixed on a place for the Fort which was a small mound back of the Village and one of the most commanding spots about the place. On the 6th I commenced building the Fort under the order and directions of the Govr. who left us for St. Louis on the 7th. On the 19th I had the Fort so far advanced that I moved into it and mounted a six-pounder in one Block house and a three in the other. I continued working on the Fort until the 17th of July when a large body of British and Indians made their appearance in the Prairie (about three miles distant from us) about twelve o'clock a flag arrived at the fort and demanded a surrender of it to his Majesty's forces unconditionally, which demand I refused, at ten minutes past one a fire commenced from the enemy's Gun (a Brass four) on the Gun Boat, which had been left by Govr. Clarke to aide and assist in the defence of the Post, would it be attacked, which was immediately answered from the fort and Gun Boat, about two hours after the action commenced the Govr. Clarke turned down stream and we in short time lost sight of her, but I had no idea that she had gone off and left us. The British, Indians and citizens kept up a constant fire on the fort until the evening of the 19th, finding the boat did not return and we had expended the most of the fixed ammunition for the six and three pounder, the water in the well had so far exhausted that we could scarcely get any to drink, and in attempting to sink, it caved in so that I had to give it over those circumstances together with the enemy's approaching us by undermining, I thought it best to capitulate on the best terms I could, and after consulting G. J. Kennerly the former aid to the Govr. And the latter Lieut. Of Militia, doing duty under me, the conclusion was to send out a flag which was borne by Mr. George Kennerly, and the following capitulations was entered into first the lives of the officers and soldiers to be protected from the Indian our private property respected, and to send us home as prisoners of War not to take up Arms against Great Britain or their Dependencies until regularly exchanged, during the three days and two nights engagement, I had five men wounded and no hospital stores, medicine, nor physician to give them relief; we surrendered at 8 oclock in the morning of the 20th though was permitted to stay in

the Fort for our safety as the Puants [Winnebagos] had devised many plans to murder us; the Commanding officer finding them so much disposed to mischief was induced to place a strong guard of the Sioux and Cippaways around the fort to keep them off, we were kept in the situation for two or three days when they were sent off, after which time we could walk out without any kind of danger, On the 30th were all paroled except four men, two deserters from the British and two Canadians, who was claimed as their subjects, the Commanding officer furnished me with a Boat and Provisions for the Trip; I embarked my men at two oclock and set out for St. Louis accompanied by two British officers, a strong guard and a piece of artillery, who accompanied us as far as the mouth of the Rock river, where we landed on August 2nd. The comdr. Of the Gun Boat went to the Village and after councilling with the Indians who were stated to be four or five hundred in number they agreed to let us pass, we set out about dark with one of the officers an interpreter and six soldiers who accompanied us as far as the lower Rapids where they left us and returned, we pushed on night and day and landed at this place on the morning of the 6th all is good health except the wounded who are like to recover...The force against us I think was about 1200 in all.

In reality, Major William McKay, the British officer in charge of the expedition that captured the fort, led a force of about 120 Michigan Fencibles, 2 companies of voyageurs, Canadian volunteers, and 530 Indians—mainly Sioux, Winnebago, Fox, Sauk, and Kickapoo. He also brought along one three-pounder for artillery, at the insistence of the Indians, under the direction of Sergeant Keating of the Royal artillery. On the seventeenth McKay sent a message demanding Perkins to surrender immediately or to defend himself "to the last man." When Perkins refused McKay began the battle by concentrating the three-pounder on the American gun boat *Governor Clark,* firing eighty-six rounds at it in three hours and finally forcing it to withdraw downriver after a number of hits. Having expended all but six rounds of shot, McKay spent the next day casting new cannon balls out of lead and constructing breastworks 450 yards from the fort. Just when McKay had readied red hot shot to fire into the fort, on the evening of the nineteenth Perkins sent out a flag and requested terms. Though Fort Shelby mounted six cannon, they had been unable to disable the British gun. For McKay the most difficult part of the entire operation was the task of controlling his Indian allies, who pillaged the village and surrounding area.

General Howard knew that Prairie du Chien was isolated and surrounded by thousands of pro-British Indians and that the British would undoubtedly attempt to recapture the fort. Thus in early July he sent Major John Campbell with about one hundred men to reinforce

Prairie du Chien, even before he knew that the fort had fallen to the British. Upon reaching the Rock River, Campbell held a council with the Sauk, who promised to fight for the Americans it they received aid. However, right after the council, they learned that the American garrison at Fort Shelby had surrendered to the British. They quickly reversed their loyalty and the next day about four hundred to five hundred warriors attacked Campbell after he had been forced to land on the Illinois side of the river. In two hours of battle Campbell's boat was set on fire and he was forced to retreat downriver with the loss of sixteen killed and twenty wounded. On his retreat from Prairie du Chien Captain Yeizer arrived on the scene during the fighting, he then assisted in salvaging supplies.

Campbell's men and those of the gunboat *Governor Clark* reached St. Louis, still unaware of Fort Shelby's surrender. Upon their arrival, General Howard immediately dispatched Major Zachary Taylor and 350 men with orders to relieve and evacuate the fort. Meanwhile the British prepared to meet another American advance. Captain Thomas Anderson, whom McKay had left in command of the newly renamed Fort McKay, sent thirty men with a three-pounder and two swivel guns to the Rock River. There in conjunction with 1,200 Indians they waited for Taylor's force. On September 5 the Indians fired on the Americans. As Taylor maneuvered to land and assault the Indians, the British opened up with their hidden artillery on Taylor's boats. In the face of artillery, Taylor knew he could not advance and abandoned the effort with the loss of eleven wounded and several killed. Upon reaching the mouth of the Des Moines River, he began the construction of Fort Johnson. The Americans never threatened Fort McKay again.

With the signing of the Treaty of Ghent in December 1814, Fort McKay was to be handed back to the Americans. When General Thomas A. Smith arrived on June 20, 1816, with six companies of a rifle regiment, he found that the British had burned the fort when they evacuated. A new fort was begun on July 3 under the direction of Colonel William Sutherland Hamilton. The new log fort was to be named for William H. Crawford, the current secretary of war. Hamilton left Captain Willoughby Morgan in command when he left in July, and it was Morgan who mostly planned and built the fort, which was completed in October. Morgan would command the fort periodically until he died there in 1832. In fact he commanded at the fort five separate times, in 1816 as a captain, 1818 as major, 1822 and 1826 as a lieutenant- colonel, and 1830-32 as a colonel.

In 1817 Major Stephen H. Long described Fort Crawford as follows:

The work is a square of 340 feet on each side and is constructed entirely of wood as are all its buildings except the magazine which is of stone. The enclosure is faced principally by the quarters and other buildings of the garrison so that the amount of all the palisade work does not exceed over 350 feet in extent. The faces of the work are flanked by two block houses, one of which is situated in the south east and the other in the northwest corner of the fort. The block houses are two stories high with cupolas or turrets upon their tops. The quarters, storehouses, and so forth are ranged along the sides of the garrison, their rear walls constituting the faces of the work. The buildings are constructed with shed roofs, sloping inwards so that their outward walls are raised 20 feet from the ground. The buildings are all rough shingled, except the block houses which are covered with smooth shingles. The magazine is 24 x 12 feet in the clear, the walls four feet thick, and the arch above supported by strong flooring of strong timbers.

In order to halt British trading with the Indians after the War of 1812, the government prohibited foreign merchants from engaging in the fur trade on its territory. It also gave Indian Agents sole authority to issue licenses to traders, whom army commanders assumed the responsibility of regulating. To further control the trade for the greater benefit of the Indians and to bind them to the United States, the government had established a factory system at different posts. In 1816 the government established a factory at Fort Crawford to regulate trade. However, the government factors were not allowed to extend credit; they were not allowed to sell whiskey; and the goods they sold were inferior to those offered by private traders. John W. Johnson, who had been the factor at Fort Madison, ran the government factory at Fort Crawford. Realizing it could not compete with private traders and John Astor's American Fur Company, the government abolished the factory system in 1822.

Periodically in the years after the War of 1812, there were minor troubles with Indians as white settlement increased. Indian threats multiplied as Americans expanded their mining activity around Galena, and several whites were killed. Ever since a Miami chief had informed Nicolas Perrot to the presence of lead, men had worked the mines in the region about sixty miles south of Prairie du Chien. The Indians placed a high value on the mines. They exchanged lead for manufactured goods. In 1810 alone they removed 400,000 pounds of lead from the mines. Old Indian men and the squaws did most of the hard labor. When white men began to intrude, conflict erupted sometimes resulting in loss of life.

The attitude of the Indians became more recalcitrant with their refusal to hand over those accused of murder to white jurisdiction. In the spring of 1827, the half-breed wife of sub-Indian agent John Marsh informed him that the Winnebago planned to kill the Americans living in Prairie du Chien. This news came less than a year after Colonel Josiah Snelling had ordered the garrison to abandon Fort Crawford and reinforce his men at

Fort Snelling. With the military presence lessened and with rumors that some Winnebago prisoners at Fort Snelling were to be turned over to the Sioux to be killed, the Winnebago decided to strike.

Winnebago Chief Red Bird and several accomplices attacked the Gagnier family, killing Registre Gagnier, a baby, and an old discharged soldier, Solomon Lipcap, who lived with them. Another party of Winnebago attacked two keelboats, *Oliver Perry* and the *Gen. Ashley*, in late June, losing ten to twelve killed, while killing two and wounding four of the boat crews. Thereafter Prairie du Chien residents formed a militia and sent for help. General Henry Atkinson arrived with troops from Jefferson Barracks in late July. In early September he and General Henry Dodge met with the Winnebago and made an agreement. The Winnebago turned over Chief Red Bird and his accomplices who attacked the family, as well as turning over two other leaders who had participated in the attack on the boats. The Indians were imprisoned at Fort Crawford. Chief Red Bird died while imprisoned; his accomplices were sentenced to be hanged but were pardoned by President John Quincy Adams, and the others were released. Meanwhile the Winnebagos agreed not to interfere with the mines at Galena and Wisconsin. General Atkinson issued a peace proclamation on September 22 thus officially ending the so called Winnebago War. Fort Crawford, which had been occupied after hostilities started, was ordered to be re-garrisoned in September.

The New Fort Crawford

After the fort was reoccupied that September, Major General Edmund Gaines, commander of the Western Department of the Army, inspected the fort. He reported that the fort had suffered extensive decay and could be made habitable only through extensive repairs. Much of the damage had been caused by flooding. In 1822 and 1826 the garrison had to vacate the fort because of flooding and did so again in 1828. Gaines considered the site unhealthy and recommended that a new fort should be erected on the Iowa side of the river. However, the War Department did not implement Gaines' recommendations.

Major Stephen Watts Kearny took over command in 1828 and in 1829 received orders to select a location for new barracks. Kearny selected and began preliminary work on a two hundred acre site on an old Indian Mound south of the old fort with access to the Mississippi. Lieutenant Colonel Zachary Taylor assumed command in July 1829. Taylor, who was on furlough for two years (1830-1832), and Willoughby Morgan, who commanded during his absence, both supervised the majority of the construction of the fort, which was not completed until late 1834 or 1835. The fort buildings for the most part were built of rock obtained within a mile of the fort. During this period the garrison spent so much time working on the fort as laborers that they had little time for being soldiers. To assist in building the fort, skilled civilians were even hired, including a master carpenter, a master mason, and a master millwright.

Author Bruce Mahan has described the fort as follows:

> The new Fort Crawford was an imposing work. It consisted of an enclosure, rectangular in shape, the north and south sides of which consisted of a stockade of pine logs each one foot square and sixteen feet high. The east and west walls of the fort were each formed by two barracks thirty-five feet wide and one hundred and seventy-five feet long, separated by a sally-port twenty-six feet wide. These barracks were constructed of stone and consisted of an elevated basement and one story. Inside the stockade and forming the north and south limits of the enclosed parade ground stood the buildings used for officers' quarters and store-rooms, each thirty-five feet wide and two hundred and forty-two feet long. These likewise were constructed of stone and consisted of an elevated basement and one story. A shingled gable roof covered each of these buildings, and these roofs projecting inside the fort formed the roof of a paved porch ten feet wide facing the parade ground.

In addition, the southeast corner of the fort contained the stone powder magazine, nearby a tall flag staff stood in the parade ground. Inside the west barracks at the south end was a room designed as a theatre. The garrison water needs were met by a sixty foot deep well six feet in diameter in the north east corner. The commandant's framed house was outside the fort to the north and the large hospital constructed from stone was south of the fort walls. The west wall of the fort was situated on a ridge about fifty feet above the river and a few hundred feet away.

The soldiers of the fort did most of the work. One famous resident who had contributed to the work for the New Fort Crawford was Lieutenant Jefferson Davis, who supervised a sawmill operation.

In the years prior to the Black Hawk War, Fort Crawford had been the site of three major Indian treaties. Five thousand Indians from almost a dozen tribes gathered there in 1825 for one of the largest Indian Councils ever held in United States history. At this time the U.S. government tried to end clashes between tribes of the Upper Mississippi region by establishing boundaries between them, especially between the allied Fox-Sauk tribe and the Sioux, and between the Chippewa and the Sioux. Governor Cass, of Michigan Territory, proclaimed to the assembled Indians, "We tell you again your Great Father does not want your land. He wants to establish boundaries and peace among you." In

1829, treaties with the Chippewa, Ottawa, and Potawatomi resulted in the purchase of an additional eight million acres for the United States. In 1830 the U.S. government again attempted to force peace between the allied Sauk-Fox tribe and the Sioux, this time by separating them. The U.S. commissioners established a forty mile wide neutral zone from land ceded by both tribes. Other tribes also ceded land along the west side of the Mississippi to be used for reservations for eastern tribes.

In 1832, detachments from Fort Crawford participated in the Black Hawk War. After Black Hawk and his band crossed the Mississippi River into Illinois, General Henry Atkinson threatened to pursue and chase them back to Iowa. Colonel Taylor led two companies of the First Infantry from Fort Crawford down to Fort Armstrong to join Atkinson. They then served under General Atkinson in pursuing Black Hawk's band. Taylor and his men of Companies A, B, and G of the First Infantry and some companies of the Fifth and Sixth Infantry also took part in the slaughter of Black Hawk's band at the Battle of Bad Axe. General Winfield Scott arrived at Fort Crawford on August 7 a few days after the final battle of the war had taken place. Though he had arrived too late to direct the war as ordered by President Andrew Jackson, he did negotiate a treaty with the Winnebago by which they gave up all of their land east of the Mississippi and agreed to settle in the Neutral Ground in Iowa, where they would receive their annuities. The Sauk and Fox also ceded a fifty mile wide section of land on the west side of the Mississippi.

After Black Hawk surrendered, he was brought to Fort Crawford as a prisoner under Taylor's care until he was moved to Jefferson Barracks in St. Louis by a detachment under Jefferson Davis. Davis had not participated in the Black Hawk War as he had been on leave of absence from March 26, 1832, until August 18. Interestingly Davis courted Taylor's daughter Sarah while at the fort. He married her in Kentucky in 1835 without Taylor's approval. Taylor had opposed her marriage to a soldier because of his opinion of the low caliber of the men under his command.

In the period following the Black Hawk War members of the garrison were kept busy evicting squatters from the Dubuque mines to keep peace with the Fox Indians. Three Companies from the fort also helped build a road between Fort Crawford and Fort Winnebago at Portage, Wisconsin. In 1840 General George Brooke led a detachment from Fort Crawford in assisting General Atkinson in removing the Winnebago from Wisconsin. They moved them to a place on the Turkey River in present day Winneshiek County, Iowa. There they helped to construct quarters for a new fort soon to be named Atkinson, which was completed in 1842. For a few months starting in September 1845, Fort Crawford stood empty after its garrison had been ordered to Texas for a build up of regular troops. However, in December troops reoccupied the fort to remove Winnebago who had returned to Wisconsin and were causing trouble to settlers. Troops were again withdrawn from the fort in the summer of 1846 to fight in the War with Mexico. Territorial volunteers then moved into the fort. After the government forced the removal of the Winnebago from the Neutral Ground in Iowa to a new location in Minnesota, it was thought that Fort Crawford was no longer needed. The garrison evacuated the fort in April 1849 and departed for Fort Snelling, leaving a single caretaker in charge of the fort.

When the regulars departed from Fort Crawford in 1849, local editors suggested that the property could be used for a railroad depot or for a college. Before anything was done, troops reoccupied the fort in 1855. Brevet Lieutenant Colonel E. R. S. Canby led 11 officers and 247 men of the Tenth Infantry from Fort Snelling in October. They had come because of reports that Winnebago Chiefs Dandy and Little Hill had left their dwellings in Minnesota to return to Wisconsin. Reports also circulated that the Indians were stealing animals and committing other depredations on settlers. Soldiers were needed at Fort Crawford to protect the settlers and to force the Indians to return to their residences in Minnesota. After the reports proved false, the soldiers remained at the fort until June 1856 when they returned to Fort Snelling.

Just prior to and after the 1855-56 reoccupation, several civilians attempted to gain possession of the fort. B. W. Brisbois and Ira B. Bunson rented out buildings and even allowed several workshops to operate in the barracks. Their attempts to purchase the fort eventually failed. Soldiers enlisting the Thirty-First Wisconsin Infantry used the fort as an assembly point during the Civil War. The fort was also used as a hospital for a time in 1864-1865. The government finally put the fort up for sale at a public auction in 1868. John Lawler purchased the property and established himself in the commandant's former home. He thought it best to use the property for a school, and in 1872 construction began on the first building for Saint Mary's Academy. This girl's school later evolved to became St. Mary's College and Academy, and eventually only St. Mary's College.

Life at the Fort

It has already been mentioned how much manual labor the soldiers engaged in to meet the requirements of maintaining a fort instead of attending to what would be considered formal soldier duties. In fact when Inspector General George Croghan visited Fort Crawford in 1831, he could not complete a regular inspection because four-fifths of the garrison was engaged in various work projects. One soldier (not necessarily from Fort Crawford) expressed his complaint in 1838:

> I am deceived; I enlisted for a soldier; I enlisted because I preferred military duty to hard work; I never was given to understand that the implements of agriculture and the mechanic's tools were to be placed in my hands before I had received a musket or drawn a uniform coat. I never was told that I would be called on to make roads, build bridges, quarry stone, burn brick and lime, carry the hod, cut wood, hew timber, construct it into rafts and float it to the garrisons, make shingles, saw plank, build mills, maul rails, drive teams, make hay, herd cattle, build stables, construct barracks, hospitals, etc. etc. etc.; which makes more time for their completion than the period of my enlistment. I never was given to understand that such duties were customary in the army, much less that I would be called on to perform them, or I never would have enlisted. I enlisted to avoid work, and here I am, compelled to perform three or four times the amount of labor I did before my enlistment.

Sometimes the troops even apprehended civilian criminals and brought them to the Fort Crawford guardhouse, which served as a county jail. The official county jail had proved unreliable in keeping prisoners from escaping. (Other forts, notably Snelling and Ripley in Minnesota, were utilized as county jails).

For relief many of the soldiers turned to whiskey. There were many traders around the fort to supply the desire. The abundance of whiskey maddened various commanders as it affected soldier's performance. General Hugh Brady inspected the fort in 1830 and concluded that the enforcement of discipline and subordination was more difficult there than at any other post. In 1836 Colonel Taylor reported that the post was "completely surrounded with whiskey establishments occupied by individuals of the most dissolute habits and character, whose object and business is to debauch the Soldiers, and in which in great measure may be attributed the desertions which annually discharged on Surgeon's certificate of disability." The men devised ingenious schemes for smuggling the whiskey into the fort. In one trick, men working at the washhouse by the river would soak a blanket with whisky and carry it into the fort with their wet clothes; once inside the fort they would squeeze it out. Another stratagem attempted, probably unique to the fort, failed at least once when two officers intercepted what looked like an approaching cat. The Major stooped down to pick it up and discovered that it was only skin wrapped around a bladder full of whiskey. At one time "The Fort Crawford Temperance Society" was begun to stem the flow of liquor, but the problem was never really solved.

Commanders utilized various punishments to keep the troops in line. When soldiers disobeyed orders or broke regulations the commanders confined them to the guardhouse, ordered them to serve extra police duty, or withheld privileges. However, Colonel Taylor devised the most unique punishment called "Wooling," whereby he would take hold of both ears of a guilty man and then shake him severely. One time it backfired on Taylor. When a big German recruit with poor understanding of English failed to obey his commands, Taylor went up to him and began "Wooling" him. In a moment, the resentful man knocked Taylor down with a strong blow. Other soldiers rushed to Taylor's rescue with the intent to kill the German. Taylor quickly ordered them away saying the man would make a good soldier. He later proved Taylor's assessment by performing well throughout the Black Hawk War.

Besides performing daily drills, inspections, and fatigue duty, the soldiers had leisure time for other pursuits like their colleagues on other posts. They worked in the garden, went hunting and fishing, played games, read a book from the library, and went to dances. The soldiers of the fort even performed in amateur theatricals to which the public was invited.

Present

During the 1930s under the Work's Progress Administration, Fort Crawford was reconstructed. Until 1995 the State Medical Society of Wisconsin owned and operated the fort hospital as the Museum of

Medical Progress. Presently the fort is known as The Prairie du Chien Museum at Fort Crawford and features extensive exhibits on the history of medical progress in Wisconsin.

The Museum is open Wednesday through Sunday, May through October, 10:00 a.m. to 5:00 p.m.

(See Appendix III for a list of men surrendered at Fort Shelby)

Fort Madison

Though Fort Madison stood for only five years (1808-1813) before Indians burned it down during the War of 1812, it is noteworthy for being the first post that the U.S. military established on the upper Mississippi River. The United States did not realize a reason to build a fort in the area until Indiana Territory Governor William Henry Harrison signed a treaty with five Sauk and Fox chiefs in November 1804. The chiefs had come to St. Louis to rectify a potential crisis created by a few Sauk braves who had murdered two Americans during the summer. President Jefferson seized the opportunity to gain control over land that the tribes occupied in northern Illinois and southern Wisconsin and to reduce the activities of British agents and traders. Secretary of War Henry Dearborn instructed Harrison to seek land cessions from the tribes.

Upon their arrival, the delegation turned over one of the murderers and then asked Harrison to set him free. However, he only agreed to meet their demand after a cession of land. Having supplied the chiefs with whiskey, Harrison succeeded in persuading them to sign away over 15 million acres of land in a portion of what is now Missouri, Illinois, and Wisconsin. The terms of the treaty allowed the tribes to remain on the land until the government sold it, yet the Indians would eventually have to move across to the west side of the river. In addition to the more than $2,000 spent on the tribal delegation in St. Louis, the government would pay annuities of $1,000 a year, supply the services of a trader and a blacksmith, and send someone to teach them how to farm—all in all, a bargain for the United States. After the Sauk and Foxes learned that they were to lose their land, about 150 of them traveled to St. Louis in 1805 to complain. The new governor, General James Wilkinson, distributed more gifts and tried to assure them that the United States would not intrude onto their territory. However, they left very embittered and distrustful of the Americans.

A Fort Is Built

The government's first effort to carry out one of its treaty obligations was the building of a factory (trading house) to supply the Indians with manufactured goods they desired. The factory was built at Fort Belle Fontaine a few miles above the mouth of the Missouri River, but the location proved to be too remote for practical trade with the Indians. In 1808 the government decided to build a trading house further north at the confluence of the Des Moines and the Mississippi. Colonel Thomas Hunt, who was to lead the expedition to build the trading house and a new fort, died six days before the expedition's scheduled departure from Fort Belle Fontaine—leaving the job to First Lieutenant Alpha Kingsley, who had never previously commanded a post or built a fort.

Image credit: Ted Kolbet

Instead of locating the new fort at the mouth of the Des Moines, where the government had purchased a three square mile tract of land and where Burlington, Iowa, now stands, Kingsley moved upstream to what is now the modern town of Fort Madison, Iowa, before settling on a location. To persuade the Fox, Sauk, Ioway, and Sioux to part with the site, he paid them $300 worth of merchandise. He had judged the designated location at the Des Moines as prone to flooding. Unfortunately, his inexperience led him to choose a location that, while situated on an elevation safe from flooding with an excellent spring of water, was subject to attack by any enemy that occupied the dominating ridge behind the fort. This would prove fatal when the Indians later besieged the fort. Nevertheless, in a letter to the secretary of war, Kingsley touted the excellent choice that he had made: "This situation is high - Commands an extensive view of the river and the adjacent country, also an excellent spring of water, and I believe there is no place on the river which will prove more healthy, and none more advantageous to the Indian trade." In the winter of 1808-1809, Kingsley began to build a fort only twenty five feet from the Mississippi. It was slightly different than the standard 120 square foot palisade and contained two-story blockhouses on each corner. The main gate faced the river from the center of a 110 foot parallel stockade wall. From the blockhouses on each corner of this wall, stockade walls went back at right angles about 125 feet before angling inward to intersect at a rear blockhouse.

Indian Threat

Though the Sauk and Fox had desired a trading house to exchange their furs and lead mined along the Mississippi for the white man's manufactured goods, they perceived the fort to be a threatening military force directed at them. In the spring of 1809, as the Sauk and the Fox migrated north from their winter homes along the Wyaconda River to their summer homes near the mouth of the Rock River in Illinois, they planned to attack the garrison. By one account, in April the tribes appeared on the bank across the river from the fort. Several men warned Kingsley that the Indians planned mischief, and a young Ioway brave, who the fort sutler had befriended at Detroit, warned that an attack would soon be made. Forewarned, Kingsley avoided a treacherous attack when he refused Black Hawk and Chief Pashepaho's request to enter the fort and do a dance for the soldiers. The chiefs had complained that the ground outside the fort was too rough and bumpy for such a dance.

According to Black Hawk's autobiography, no premeditated attack had been planned on the fort. Instead, he claimed that a group of men (including himself) went to the fort to see what the soldiers were doing. After awhile, some of the young braves followed an armed work party from the fort. Once they set down their guns and went to work with axes, some of the Indians sneaked up and stole the guns. Then they gave a yell. The soldiers threw down their axes and ran for their guns. At this point the young braves surrounded them, then laughed at the soldiers and returned the guns. On account of this incident the fort commander called for a council with the Indians. All the Indians gathered around the fort, which had low walls at the time. At the head of dancing braves, Black Hawk approached the fort and requested entrance to perform a dance for the soldiers. Kingsley, already on the alert for trouble, had his soldiers ready with their arms, one standing by the previously loaded cannon with a match ready to fire. Speaking through an interpreter, Kingsley said,

"Tell Chief Pashepaho that the first man who steps over the gate sill will be fired upon. That is my answer to his request." Subsequently the braves turned away, raised the war clubs they had concealed under their blankets, yelled out war cries in frustration and quickly left. One witness noted that "in twenty minutes not an Indian was to be seen on the north side of the river." Black Hawk later admitted that if they had entered the fort they probably would have killed the entire garrison.

After the Indians departed, Kinglsey's men worked hard to complete the stockade's fourteen-foot high pickets, which they did on April 14. Kingsley initially named the fort Bellevue due to its scenic location; but in a letter written to Washington soon after the fort's completion, Kingsley renamed his new post Fort Madison in honor of the recently elected president James Madison. It was not the first fort named after the president, but the third one—following one on the Arkansas River and one in Annapolis harbor. The fort would continue to change in the five years of its existence. Kingsley added a fourth blockhouse on the ridge to the rear of the fort with a covered path connecting it to the fort in the summer. Though the sizes of these blockhouses are not known, the standard set by the secretary of war was twenty feet square, two stories high, with loopholes in each story, and portholes on the second story for small cannon. In addition there were officer's quarters and barracks, a magazine, some outlying buildings for traders and hired men, and a factory. The fort had two gates, one in the rear towards the forest and one in the front facing the river. In 1809 the new commander of the fort Captain Horatio Stark, who had replaced Kingsley in August, wrote that fort was the best constructed of any he had ever seen. Under Stark, the trading post or factory building—a twenty by fifty-two foot, two-story, log structure—was constructed outside and to the west of the fort. In late 1812 or early 1813, another blockhouse was built near the river and connected to the fort by an underground passage. During this period the garrison numbered forty to fifty men as evidenced by the forty five new jackets delivered to the fort in 1811.

Life at the Fort

The men who served a Fort Madison were recruited mostly in East Coast cities. Primarily, they were men who had a difficult time making it in the world and were considered "the dregs of American society." At a time when the average wage was forty cents a day, a private received $7 a month (later reduced to $5 in 1812 due to lack of funds). This compared to a captain's pay of $40 per month and a lieutenant's pay of $30 per month. The men were paid every two months in the warm seasons. They were not paid in winter, but received pay for six to eight months in the spring. Half of their pay could be charged at the Sutler's store where it cost $4.50 for a blanket or 6 ½ cents for four ounces of whiskey. A recruit did receive an enlistment bounty of $12, of which he received half after signing up and the remainder after completing two months of basic training. He had to sign up for a minimum of five years and had to be between the ages of eighteen and thirty-five. Before 1820 blacks or mulattos could enlist, but were afterwards forbidden to prevent runaway slaves from joining. Twenty percent of the army was foreign born.

The men at Fort Madison lived in two-story barracks, where separate twenty by twenty foot rooms held twelve men each. The rooms contained three two-tiered bunks, each three to four feet wide and six foot in length, with solid planks underneath. The bunks were sometimes called "cribs" because of their raised sideboards. Each bunk was shared by two men, and hence the term "bunky" was applied to those who shared a bunk. The bed sack was made of cotton or linen and filled with thirty-six pounds of straw. The men refreshed the sack with eight pounds of straw every sixteen days and replaced all the straw every thirty-two days. The soldiers possessed only rudimentary furnishings, consisting of benches, mess table, dishes, perhaps a clock, lamp, or candlesticks, and a few safety and health items such as a fire barrel, water bucket, police tub (urine bucket), and wood spit box. They cleaned daily and more thoroughly on Saturdays; however, they still dealt with a persistent bed bug problem. Infractions, such as urinating on a wall or spitting were punished by spending time in the guardhouse. Usually garrisons employed women to do laundry, but there is little mention of any women at Fort Madison. Officers could bring their families, but could only house them in a twenty by twenty foot room. For example Captain Stark brought his wife to the fort. Shortly after her arrival in September, history was made when she gave birth to a baby daughter named Rozanna, who is believed to be the first white child born in what is now the State of Iowa. Though the record is not clear as to where the baby was born, it was probably at the fort. Besides officers, sometimes a few senior enlisted men were allowed to bring their families to live at a fort

The men worked up a hearty appetite, their daily ration generally consisted of "One pound and one quarter of beef, or three quarters of a pound of salted pork, eighteen ounces of bread or flour, one gill of rum, whiskey or brandy, and at the rate of two quarts of salt, four quarts of vinegar, four pounds of soap, and one pound and a half of candles, to every hundred rations." This was predominantly the standard ration for soldiers with minor variations for the entire period from 1798 to 1812. They also received a one-pound loaf of bread each day from the post bakery. In addition, the garrison had a garden and could supplement their diet by hunting deer, rabbit, wild turkey, and other game; by fishing; or by purchasing other foods from the Sutler. They received their liquor ration (whiskey, brandy or rum) in formation at breakfast and lunch. However, the army stopped serving a liquor ration in 1830 because "the habitual use of ardent spirits by the troops has a pernicious effect upon the health, morals and discipline."

If a soldier at Fort Madison was wounded, felt sick, had a fever, or was weak, he reported to Dr. Simpson, the fort physician. In line with the primitive medical opinion of the day, the doctor would more than likely tell you that your body's nerve stimulation was out of balance. Either a patient suffered from excessive stimulation or insufficient stimulation. Excessive stimulation raised the body temperature and increased the pulse due to the spasms of the blood vessels and muscles caused by nerve irritation. The increased pressure had to be reduced by bloodletting. The physician slit a patient's wrist vein above the palm then placed the wrist into hot water to let the blood flow freely. This procedure often weakened the patients further. Unfortunately, the medical profession believed that the human body contained twelve quarts of blood rather than six, which is the actual average. In the case of George Washington, when he fell ill of an infected throat, his physicians drained nine pints of his blood within twenty four hours. If the doctor thought a soldier suffered from too little stimulation, he might proscribe a nerve stimulant such as leaves of foxglove. Even today no synthetic drug has duplicated the effect of the glycosides in foxglove, which is used as a cardiac stimulant for heart patients.

Garrison life followed a disciplined set routine as can be seen from the following typical schedule:

6:00 a.m.	*Reveille.*
6:10 a.m.	The men fall out for the first roll call, then take care of personal hygiene, then clean the barracks.
6:40 a.m.	Soldiers who are sick report to the dispensary at this time.
6:50 a.m.	*Whiskey Drum.* The men receive their first half of their liquor ration for the day.
7:00 a.m.	*Call to Breakfast.*
7:30 a.m.	*Fatigue Drum.* The garrison does general clean up, chopping and hauling of wood, etc.
8:00 a.m.	*First Call.* This second roll call marks the beginning of the work day and men march off to their assigned duties in the garden, kitchen or elsewhere. Fatigue would include any carpentry, masonry, or painting necessary to maintain or repair the buildings, for example, making shingles for the roofs, lime for mortar, or other building work. For special construction projects authorized by the quarter-master general that last more than ten days, the men earn fifteen cents a day extra pay.
9:00 a.m.	The guard changes at the guard house. The new guard leads the prisoners to work and the old guard puts on work uniforms.
12:30 p.m.	*Recall.* The men return to the barracks to clean up for their mid-day dinner. They also can buy items from the sutler's store, which is open for an hour.
12:50 p.m.	*Whiskey Drum.* Yet another roll call muster where the men receive the second half of their liquor ration.
1:00 p.m.	*Dinner Call.*
1:30 p.m.	*Fatigue Drum.* The men attend to their assigned work for the afternoon.
5:00 p.m.	*Recall.* The men clean and store tools and other equipment at the end of the work day.
5:10 p.m.	The sutler's store reopens for the soldiers to buy food or liquor.
6:00 p.m.	*Supper Call.* Upon completion of their meal any man not on guard or special duty has free time until evening parade.
7:30 p.m.	*Drummer Call* for the evening parade.

7:40 p.m.	The men muster on the parade ground.
7:50 p.m.	Roll call and orders for the next day are read.
8:00 p.m.	The men assemble once again for parade and the firing of the evening gun and lowering of the flag. Afterwards they are dismissed for free time prior to tattoo. Those who desire to can take a bath in the wooden tubs in the barrack's kitchen at this time.
8:55 p.m.	The men are in their barracks for the Drummers Call for the final company roll call of the day.
9:00 p.m.	*Tattoo.* Lights are extinguished and all men are supposed to be in their assigned barracks room.
10:30 p.m.	Those given an evening pass to fish in the Mississippi River return to their barracks.

Weekends were somewhat more relaxed. The workday ended at 12:30 p.m. on Saturday, though the men had to spend the afternoon preparing for the Sunday inspection of their barracks and equipment. Following the 10:00 a.m. Sunday inspection, the men drilled until noon. The rest of the day, all soldiers except those on guard duty enjoyed free time to do as they pleased. During their leisure time, most of them hunted, fished, gambled, played indoor table games, outdoor sports, or drank whiskey. They were allowed up to twelve ounces of whiskey a day, including the four ounce ration they received. The hard work, low pay, and strict discipline of army life gave reason for some to desert. The desertion rate at this time averaged between 10 to 33 percent annually. However the rate at Fort Madison was lower, since two hundred miles of wilderness separated Fort Madison from St. Louis, the nearest civilized haven.

Relationship with the Indians

In addition to the garrison, three civilians served at the fort. Nicholas Boilvin served as the Indian agent, Alexander Willard worked as the blacksmith, and John Johnson represented the government as the fort's factor. Johnson, who supervised trading under the Office of Indian Trade, had been instructed as follows: "The principal object of the Government in these establishments being to secure the Friendship of the Indians in our country in a way the most beneficial to them and the most effectual & economical to the United States, you will avail yourself of every proper means & opportunity of impressing these people favourably toward the Government. ...."

In this Johnson must have succeeded on the whole. When war came most of the Sauks, Foxes, and Ioways stayed neutral. The tribes had come to appreciate the goods they acquired through trade. They traded for muskets, traps, fabric, fishhooks, butcher knives, axes, hoes cooking pots, scissors, beads and many other items. The tribes brought in many furs to trade for the goods they no longer desired to live without. An example of the goods the Indians traded to the fort is found in this list of items that Johnson sent to St. Louis in 1809:

> 274 packs deerskins – 38,131 pounds
> 7 packs beaver furs – 100 pounds
> 17 packs bearskins – 347 skins
> 30 packs raccoon – 3,610 skins
> 2 packs muskrat – 1,330 skins
> 2 packs otter – 176 skins
> 60 deerskins covering raccoon packs
> 44 bearskins covering various packs
> 9 kegs tallow
> 1 keg beeswax
> 43 dressed deerskins
> 3 bags feathers

The Indians also mined lead along the Mississippi. In the part of the year after he arrived at the fort in 1809, Johnson collected 48,000 pounds of lead. In 1810 he collected 80,000 pounds. Lead had become such an important item for trade that the Sauks and Foxes had to a great extent abandoned hunting for mining. Johnson traded fairly with the Indians. He charged 120 percent of cost and extended credit to the Indians. He did not always receive full payment. One private trader mentioned that he always charged the Ioways more since they usually only paid back about half of what they owed. The Ioway's agent Nicolas Boilvin also reported on how the Indians complained that the American's traded shoddy goods. For example they said, "The traps were good for nothing; the blankets were small and thin, weighing but half the weight of an English trader's blanket, and the calico would not from age hold together, it would seem that all the old goods of our cities were bought up as good enough for the Indian."

Altogether, Indians killed at least eight men during the fort's short occupation. Prior to the War of 1812, the first killed was a man by the name of James Leonard, whom the Indians killed only a half mile from the fort. After killing him they cut off his head and arms and removed his heart. Winnebagos probably committed the act, as Black Hawk reports in his biography that some went to Fort Madison and returned with several scalps.

Though the War of 1812 began with official declaration on June 12, the fort's new commander Lieutenant Thomas Hamilton did not know of any specific threat in July. John Johnson, the fort's factor, used one trusted Sauk to spy for the Americans. Mellesello reported that there had been a nine-nation council of Winnebagos, Sauks, Kickapoos, Potawatomis, Shawnees, Miamis, Menominees, Sioux, Ioways, Otoes, and Foxes at the Sauk village on the Rock River, where a Kickapoo chief had presented a wampum belt as the Shawnee Prophet's representative. Real news of war arrived on August 24 when an Indian brought news of the fall of Fort Dearborn. Two days later a party of Sauks and Foxes warned Hamilton that he would be attacked within ten days to two weeks. He quickly requested reinforcements from Colonel Daniel Bissell of the Second Infantry Regiment at Fort Belle Fontaine. Bissell immediately ordered Captain Stark back to his old command at Fort Madison with nineteen men. Bissell also picked up eighteen members of a company of Rifle Rangers, raised by Daniel Boone's son Nathan, at Fort Mason. The name Rifle Rangers stemmed from the "rifled barrels" they were issued, the first of any U.S. Army unit to receive rifled long arms.

Fighting did not begin around the fort until September 5. As Black Hawk related, he joined a Winnebago war party that had decided to go against the fort. They sent spies out and observed that only about fifty men occupied the fort. They concealed themselves near the fort at night and planned to rush in when the gate was opened and a signal given. They had previously observed the entire garrison frequently drilling outside the fort, and they hoped to surprise them. After daybreak one young man walked out of the fort to the river and returned, but Black Hawk did not rush the gate because he feared his party was not ready. A short time later, four men left the fort and walked down to the river to gather wood. While they were gone, Private John Cox then came out, and when he was only twenty-five feet outside the fort walls, a Winnebago fired on him, killed him, and scalped him. The other men heard the firing and ran toward the fort; two of them did not make it back. Black Hawk's warriors then kept shooting at the fort all day. Later Black Hawk proudly recounted an event on the second day when he shot the flag cord in two, preventing the soldiers from raising it. He left out the fact that it took a reported four hundred shots to finally bring the flag down. On the same day the Indians also killed all of the cattle, hogs, and chickens that the garrison kept outside the stockade. The next day they impaled Private Cox's head and heart on stakes buried in the mud near the river.

During the siege the Indians tried unsuccessfully to set the fort on fire but were thwarted by the soldiers who kept the shingles too wet to ignite and kept putting out other fires by utilizing old muskets as "squirts." Fearful that the Indians may be able to burn the fort by starting the trading house on fire when the wind was blowing toward the fort, Lieutenant Hamilton sent a soldier to start it on fire during a lull in the fighting. Slipping through the garden when the wind was calm, the soldier succeeded in his mission, and the house burned down without harming the fort. Factory losses were a different matter. Johnson listed his losses at $5,500 including 120 bear skins worth $10 each.

Though the Indians controlled a ridge that overlooked Fort Madison from which they could rain down musket balls or arrows at anyone who moved from blockhouse to blockhouse, they succeeded in only wounding one of the garrison in all of their shooting before they broke off the siege on September 9 when they ran out of ammunition. They did burn all the buildings outside the fort, and Black Hawk's attack succeeded to the extent that he had ended the reason for the fort's existence by destroying the factory. Stark, who had regained his command, sought permission from his superiors to abandon the fort. Bissell even wrote in February 1813 that the fort would be evacuated in the spring. However, the secretary of war wrote to William Clark stating that the fort should remain. In March, Bissell sent fifteen men from the company of Rifle Rangers to Fort Madison. Also in March, he again sent Stark back to the fort (he had left the previous November) with forty men. However, Captain Stark departed from the fort in May, after receiving a promotion to be a major in the Sixth Infantry Regiment.

The strength of the garrison was now brought up to one hundred men. They did not have to wait long for the Indians to attack again. Almost a year after their first attack on the fort, on July 8 Sauk and Winnebago warriors fired on a fatigue detail that was cutting logs for the new blockhouse being constructed by the ravine. The attack killed two and wounded three. A week later Indians attacked four men guarding the now nearly complete blockhouse, killed all of them, and continued firing from the bluff behind the fort. Knowing that the Indians could surprise him at any time, and fearing continued harassment, Hamilton again sought permission to abandon the fort. He wrote Colonel Bissell, "If I do not hear from you by the 20th August and the Indians continue to harass me in the manner they appear determined to do, I do not know but that I will take the responsibility on myself, that is if they will still permit me to go away. It is impossible for us to do the duty long in this manner that I have adopted." He finally ordered the abandonment of the fort on the night of September 3. The men crawled to the river through an escape trench and onto two keel boats. Hamilton sent a few soldiers on a mission to burn down the fort, and then they departed. The fort was never rebuilt.

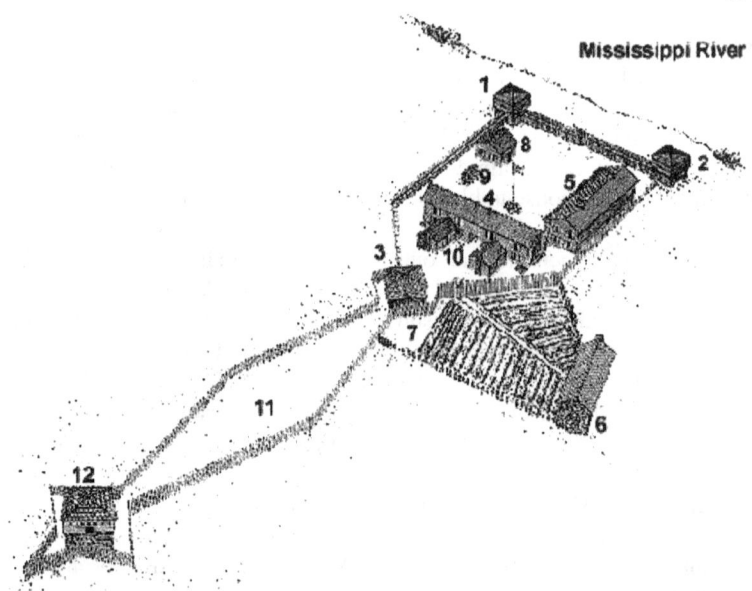

Image credit: The City of Fort Madison

1. and 2. The corner blockhouses, which had shooting platforms on both floors with "loop holes" on the first floor for the soldiers to fire through and openings for cannon and small arms on the second floor.
3. The central blockhouse was the main fort blockhouse and troops manned it continuously. It contained a cellar underneath where trade goods were stored for the fort "factory" or store.
4. Up to four officers and some of their families lived in these two buildings which also contained the hospital room.
5. The two enlisted men's barracks were furnished with double bunk beds to accommodate up to seventy men.
6. The fort factory, or trading post, held all the goods for exchanging with the Indians.
7. The fort garden.
8. The fort guardhouse.
9. Stone powder magazine.
10. Kitchens.
11. The "tail" was a log picket passage that connected the outlying blockhouse to the fort.
12. The tail blockhouse was located on a ridge behind the fort to provide protection from Indians who would have been able to fire into the fort from that elevated location.

Rediscovery to Reconstruction

One traveler noted in 1821 that seven stone chimneys still stood on the site where Fort Madison had once stood. Only one chimney remained when the first settlers arrived to begin a town on the site in 1833. One early settler, General John Knapp, included the chimney into the Madison House—Fort Madison's first hotel. A new owner demolished the hotel in 1856 and with it the last standing remnant of the old fort. It was not until 1935 that one citizen, John Cruikshank, proposed a full-sized reconstruction of Fort Madison. The project never received any further promotion until the local Jaycees took up the cause in 1962. While excavating the Sheaffer Pen Company parking lot to place a new underground water tank, workers unearthed the remains of a fort blockhouse foundation. Additional excavations undertaken by the state uncovered the remains of other buildings, along with many artifacts, fragments of utensils, nails, and beads.

The celebration of Fort Madison's sesquicentennial in 1988 provided the final impetus for the fort reconstruction. John Hansman, one of the archaeologists who had examined the excavations of the fort and chairman of the Sesquicentennial Committee formed in 1983, proposed a reconstruction of the fort. With assistance from the state and the approval of a hotel-motel tax by local voters for the project, construction began in 1985 with the help of inmates from Iowa State Penitentiary, which is located in Fort Madison. The fort opened up to the public in 1988 just a few blocks from the original site. In 1989 the pickets were completed to enclose the fort buildings, and a replica of the trading post was completed outside the fort walls.

Image credit: Ted Kolbet

Today the Parks and Recreation Department of the city of Fort Madison administers the fort. It is open weekends only in May and September, 9:30 a.m. – 5 p.m. and every day except Monday and Tuesday, June 1 through August 31. There are also special events with guest speakers at various times. Authentically dressed historic interpreters perform various duties around the fort including drilling and firing muskets and cannon. Also featured in the fort buildings are artifacts, pictures, much written information, and a short film on the history of the fort. For further information, phone 319-372-770.

Appendix I

Glossary

Bastion. The projecting part of a fortification embedded in a wall or at a corner, arranged so defenders could fire at assailants along the wall. Bastions could also be used for artillery platforms.

Battery. An emplacement of a group of cannon used for combined action.

Blockhouse. A defensive structure constructed of heavy timbers, frequently with a projecting upper story with loopholes in the sides for firing out. Blockhouses could be at corners, along walls, or as stand alone structures.

Curtain. The part of a stockade wall connecting two neighboring bastions.

Embrasure. A small opening in a wall flaring outward to allow for the firing of weapons.

Fort. A fortified place occupied only by troops and surrounded by defensive works as a ditch, rampart, and parapet (Webster's Dictionary).

Militia. An organized force of able bodied citizens enrolled for military service in time of emergency.

Regulars. Professional soldiers of a permanent standing army.

Palisade. A wall of sharpened logs set upright firmly in the earth and close together to form a defensive barrier. Stockade.

Powder Magazine. A building used to store a fort's gunpowder and ammunition.

Sally Port. A passage or gate in a fort that troops used to make a sortie.

Stockade. A wall of sharpened logs set upright firmly in the earth and close together to form a defensive barrier. Palisade.

Appendix II

Additional Fort Sites

Fort Stephenson

Two months after his first invasion of the Ohio country and repulse at Fort Meigs, British General Henry Proctor determined to make another attempt to capture the fort. A ruse planned by Tecumseh failed to draw out the garrison. The combined force of seven hundred British and two thousand Indians pretended to attack a relief column approaching from Fort Stephenson, but the commanding general, Green Clay, did not take the bait despite the urging of his subordinates. Thus, Proctor, with about 385 regulars and an unknown number of Indians, decided to move against Fort Stephenson. He perceived that the fort was weak, and that if he did not make an attack at the urging of his Indian allies, they would leave his army.

Fort Stephenson was located at Lower Sandusky (modern Fremont, Ohio). Colonel Mills Stephenson and Ohio militiamen originally built a fort there in June of 1812. After the fall of Detroit, the Americans abandoned it, and the British and Indians burned it. In early 1813, General Harrison sent Captain Eleazer D. Wood, a West Point graduate and an engineer, to rebuild the fort. Wood supervised the construction of a stockade 100 x 150 feet, with twelve foot high pickets on rising ground. Bayonets were driven horizontally through the top of each picket. The fort contained two blockhouses, bastion, and buildings inside. The fort was surrounded by a ditch eight feet deep and eight to twelve feet wide. The Sandusky River guarded the east side, while woods lined the west side. To the north and to the south of the fort were plains. The fort guarded the approach that the British would have to take to Fort Seneca, about ten miles further down the Sandusky River, Harrison's headquarters and supply depot.

In July 1813, George Croghan brought two companies of the Seventeenth U.S. Infantry, about 160 men, to garrison Fort Stephenson.

Croghan, only twenty-one years old, had been recently promoted from captain to major through the recommendation of General William Henry Harrison due to his courageous sortie against a British battery in the battle around Fort Meigs in early May. Croghan had some reservation as to the defensive strength of the fort. Previously he had requested that General Harrison allow him to shift the fort's location to the higher ground across the east side of the Sandusky River. Harrison refused the request, citing the imminent expectation of British forces entering the vicinity.

As British forces neared the fort on July 29, Harrison wrote a letter to Croghan commanding him to abandon the fort. He sent the message with John Conner at 10 p.m. Conner lost his way in the dark and did not enter the fort until noon the next day. He handed the letter to Croghan. It stated, "Immediately on receiving this letter, you will abandon Fort Stephenson, set it on fire, and repair with your command this night to Headquarters." Croghan then sent Moses Wright through a hail of bullets, his horse mortally wounded, back towards Harrison. In his reply he states, "I have just received yours of yesterday, 10 p.m. ordering me to destroy this place and make good my retreat, which was received too late to be carried into execution. We have determined to maintain this place, and by heavens we can." Incensed at Croghan's apparent insubordination, swearing that he aught to be shot immediately, Harrison sent Colonel Sam Wells with an escort of dragoons to relieve him of his command at once. Wells had to fight his way through an Indian ambush to deliver the letter. Harrison stated in writing, "An officer who presumes to aver that he has made his resolution, and that he will act in direct opposition to the orders of his General, can no longer be entrusted with a separate command. Colonel Wells is sent to relieve you. You will deliver the command to him and repair with Colonel Ball's squadron to this place."

The shuttle back and forth continued. After Croghan was escorted back to Harrison, he explained that he had expected the letter would fall into enemy hands and that it would then be too late to carry out the orders since many Indians already occupied the surrounding woods. Furthermore, he stated that his officers had agreed with him. Harrison allowed Croghan to retain his command. Croghan also wrote the following to a friend prior to the battle: "The enemy is not far distant. I expect an attack. I will defend this post till the last extremity. I have just sent away the women the children and the sick of garrison, that I may be able to act without encumbrance. Be satisfied. I shall, I hope do my duty. The example set me by my Revolutionary kindred is before me. Let me die rather than prove unworthy of their name." (Croghan's father, an Irish immigrant, fought in the Revolutionary War as a major. His mother was a sister of George Rogers Clark.)

The scene was set for an unequal battle. General Proctor sent old Matthew Elliott and Major Peter Chambers under a flag of truce with a message demanding an immediate surrender to prevent the massacre that would inevitably occur with the storming of the fort. Subaltern Edmund Shipp, who had been sent outside the fort to parley, replied as ordered by Croghan: "My commandant and the garrison are determined to defend the post to the last extremity, and bury themselves in its ruins rather than surrender it to any force whatever." Elliott again remonstrates that only surrender will prevent a massacre. To which Shipp replied, "When this fort is taken there will be none to massacre."

The British began firing on the fort on August 1 from gunboats and howitzers on shore, hurling over five hundred cannonballs at the fort. On August 2 Proctor moved three 6-pounders to within 250 yards of the fort and opened up fire, primarily on the northwest angle of the fort. The fire from the bombardment did little or no damage to the fort. Croghan had been shifting around the one artillery piece he had, an eighteenth-century French 6-pound naval cannon known as "Old Betsy" to create the impression that he had more artillery. He stopped firing it in the afternoon because he was getting low on powder. However, he guessed that Proctor would attack the northwest angle and moved "Old Betsy" into position, hidden from the British to rake the north wall. Not seeing anymore return artillery fire, Proctor thought that Croghans' artillery had been disabled. Thinking that the fort was manned by only fifty to sixty men, and with the approach of a thunderstorm, he ordered an assault in the late afternoon.

Proctor sent over three hundred men of the Forty-First Regiment, many of them Wellington veterans, to attack the fort. Under Lieutenant Colonel Augustus Warburton, 160 men moved toward the south side for a feint attack. Leading the assault of 180 men of the Forty-First Regiment on the north side, Lieutenant Colonel William Short and Lieutenant J.G. Gordon made the main attack at about 4 p.m. Their approach could not be seen as dense smoke completely enveloped the force until the men were only twenty feet from the pickets. Musket fire briefly halted the advance, and then Short, who had leaped over the outer works into the ditch, shouted the command, "Give the d—d Yankees no quarter." However, it was the British who needed quarter. Croghan had withheld his men's fire until the British entered the ditch. Scarcely had Short finished uttering his command when the first deadly volley combined with the double-load of grapeshot from "Old Betsy" devastated the British ranks, including Short. Gordon reformed the ranks and was met by another round of murderous fire from "Old Betsy." Though some made it to the wall, they had no ladders and their axes were dull, making it difficult to try to open up a breech in the wall. The deadly American fire quickly filled the ditch with dead and dying bodies.

Appendix II

Within a half hour the British were in full retreat to the surrounding woods, a close ravine also provided many of the troops with some shelter. Firing would continue for another couple of hours, but the battle was already essentially over. The attack on the north wall sputtered out before the south attack, which only resulted in light fire. Left behind were about one hundred dead, wounded, and captured, including Short and several of his lieutenants. The three hundred to four hundred Indians present at the scene for the most part did not partake in the assault. Croghan suffered only one man dead and seven wounded.

The British would never again take the offensive in the Erie region during the remainder of the war. It was the last western battle of the war fought on American soil. Oliver Hazard Perry's victory in September took place on Lake Erie and Harrison's victory at the Battle of the Thames was fought in October near London, Ontario. In addition to decreased morale resulting from the soldier's loss of respect for their commander, the British would also lose disappointed Indian allies who deserted what they perceived to be a losing cause. Finally, General Sir George Prevost wrote Proctor, reprimanding him: "I cannot refrain from expressing my regret at your having allowed the clamour of the Indian warriors to induce you to commit a part of your valuable force in an unequal and hopeless conflict."

His heroic defense catapulted Croghan to the status of a national hero. The president of the United States brevetted him a lieutenant colonel, making him the youngest officer of that grade in the army. Congress later awarded him a gold medal, and the ladies of Chillicothe, then Ohio's state capitol, presented to him a beautiful sword. In addition, the reputation of West Point engineers received a boost as none of the fortifications designed by their graduates were captured by the enemy during the war.

Today, the Birchard Public Library occupies the site where Fort Stephenson once stood. Inside the library, the Fort Stephenson Museum on 423 Croghan Street contains artifacts from the battle in five display cases. The grounds also contain the fort's original armament, "Old Betsy," and the remains of its defender, George Croghan.

Call 419-334-7101 for more information.

Fort St. Joseph

Robert de La Salle first built Fort St. Joseph in modern day Niles, Michigan, near the mouth of the St. Joseph River in 1679. It was situated at the juncture of the Old Sauk Trail, a major east-west Indian trail. In addition, it was only a five mile portage from the St. Joseph River to the Kankakee River, and hence Montreal was connected to the Mississippi River. Thus it was a perfect location for a trading center. In the ensuing years a vigorous trade passed between the French and the Indians here.

In 1693, Sieur de Courmanche was sent to command a small garrison at the fort. A band of Iroquois attacked the fort the next year. Initially they thrust their guns through the palisades, firing at the soldiers. The soldiers fired a volley which forced the Iroquois to abandon their attack. In 1696 Courmanche evacuated the fort under orders of the king. Sometime before 1720 the fort was re-garrisoned and remained so until the French surrender of Canada. During this period the fort remained a great trading center, second only to Fort Michilimackinac. With the French surrender in Canada in 1760, the British gained possession of the fort.

Young Ensign Francis Schlosser, called "the boy" by both soldiers and traders, now commanded a garrison of fourteen men at St. Joseph. On the morning of May 25, 1763, Schlosser learned that a party of nearly one hundred Potawatomis had just arrived from Detroit on a visit to their relatives at the large Potawatomi town across the river and that the visitors also wished to greet him. Schlosser foolishly had shrugged off a warning the night before from a French trader who had lived there for thirty years. Three or four Potawatomis under Chief Washee came to Schlosser's quarters. A Canadian entered behind them and let Schlosser know that Indians exhibiting hostile intentions surrounded the fort.

Schlosser then ran to his barracks to gather his men under arms and proceeded to the grounds to organize the Canadians. Very soon an Indian from among those already in the barracks cried out and Indians rushed to open the gates and allow their co-conspirators to enter. Within minutes the Indians quickly killed eleven of Schlosser's men and captured the remaining three plus Schlosser. Fortunately for Schlosser and his surviving men, they were taken to Detroit and exchanged for Potawatomi prisoners held by the fort commander, Henry Gladwin. Fort St. Joseph was never re-garrisoned.

During the American Revolution, British traders used the fort to conduct their business. Twice expeditions successfully attacked the fort. In late 1780 a small force recruited at Cahokia commanded by Jean Baptiste Hamelin captured the traders and their goods. As Hamelin's force retreated back toward Chicago, they were overtaken by Dagneau De Quindre, also a French officer, but serving with the British. He had been appointed a representative for the English among the Potawatomi Indians. His party of Indians routed Hamelin's, killing most of them and retrieving the goods. In the winter of 1781, the Spanish governor of St. Louis, Francisco Cruzat, sent out a Spanish force under Captain Eugene Poure to forestall an attack from the British in the spring. He successfully surprised and captured the fort in February with his force of 140 Spanish soldiers and Indians. He claimed the region for Spain, and decamped the next day. Spain tried unsuccessfully to use Poure's claim to negotiate for the territory east of the Mississippi River during peace negotiations ending the Revolutionary War. Following the war, the British used the fort as a trading center until they abandoned it under Jay's Treaty in 1795. The fort was probably used through the 1810s by traders, as it was shown on maps of the period.

Presently the fort location is buried under landfill and water from the Niles dam. A museum in Niles houses artifacts from the fort including musket parts, knife blades, trade silver, and other items. The museum on 508 E. Main Street is open Wednesdays through Saturdays, 10:00 a.m. – 4:00 p.m. throughout the year. The Michigan Archaeological Society is attempting to raise money to reconstruct the fort. Call 616-683-4702, ext. 236 for further information.

Fort St. Louis

In 1677 Robert de La Salle had obtained a patent from Louis the XIV, the king of France, granting him the authority to explore and possess the country west of the Great Lakes. Traveling with twenty-nine men and a Mohegan named LeLoup, La Salle reached an Indian village located on the west bank of Peoria Lake on January 3, 1680. After camping a few days in the village, La Salle suspected the Indians of planning treachery. He then selected a site on a low hill on the east side of the Illinois River about two and a half to three miles below the outlet of the lake. There he built Fort Creveceour (which means "broken heart"), containing the first buildings meant for permanent occupancy constructed by Europeans in what would become the state of Illinois. This fort contained a small patch of ground consisting of a few log cabins with officers' quarters, barracks for the men in two angles, a cabin for the priests, and a blacksmith's forge—all surrounded by a stockade. Soon after its construction, LaSalle departed for Canada to obtain additional supplies and men. Henri de Tonti stayed in command of the fort, but soon abandoned it after all but three soldiers deserted. The fort never again experienced European occupation.

According to tradition and the description given by Hennepin, the location of the fort was at a place now called Wesley City in Tazewell County. The Peoria Chapter of the Daughters of the American Revolution established a monument on the perceived fort's location.

In the fall of 1682, La Salle returned to the Illinois River with about forty soldiers under his command. After seeing the devastation wrought by the Iroquois on the Illinois village La Vantum in 1680, La Salle chose to build a fort on what would later become known as Starved Rock, a rocky fortress like hill rising about 130 feet above the south side of the Illinois River, and about a mile north of the Illinois village of LaVantum (on the north side of the river near the town of Utica, Illinois). The French labored hard, removing rock and cutting steps for a pathway to the summit. They also cleared trees from the top to make room for the fort and heaped earthworks around two thirds of the rock's circumference. They then built a blockhouse, a storehouse, and several dwellings out of timbers dragged up the steep slope. To obtain water, they placed a windlass on a platform to lift buckets of water from the river far below. Additionally, on a rampart they mounted a small canon that they had brought with them.

La Salle came to trade, and trade he did. For the meat the Indians provided and for the furs they brought, the French traded blankets, guns, and, steel tomahawks and knives. Additional Frenchmen migrated from Canada and settled nearby to participate in the lucrative trade. Fortunes could be made when a blanket that sold for $3.00 in Quebec could be exchanged for $100 worth of furs. The surrounding Indians flocked to the area until six thousand had settled within a mile along the river. At times there were twenty thousand Indians camping in the vicinity of what had become the first permanent white settlement in the Mississippi Valley. Two years after building the fort, La Salle left Tonti in command and returned to Canada and then sailed to France. He never entered the fort again. His own men killed him in Texas while on an expedition to locate the mouth of the Mississippi. Tonti then conducted the trade at Fort St. Louis for the next eighteen years with La Frost based in Canada.

A large war party of Iroquois raided into Illinois again in the spring of 1684. After robbing a party of fourteen traders and trappers on the Kankakee River, they learned that La Salle had left only a weak force at Fort St. Louis. The Iroquois then headed toward the fort, prompting the Illinois to flee La Vantum when they learned that their dreaded enemies were only about thirty miles distant. About two hundred Iroquois then entered a deserted town. Undeterred, they soon began a six day siege by firing on the fort from a neighboring cliff with little or no effect due to the distance. Tonti, under the overall command of Chevalier de Baugis, defended with fifty French soldiers and about one hundred Indian allies. The Iroquois drew closer and closer finally approaching at close range. The defenders inflicted heavy casualties, firing both muskets and cannons to drive away the Iroquois, who never again raided into Illinois. After waiting in the fort for a few days until they were sure the Iroquois were gone, the defenders once again ventured outside. Gathering together allies they pursued the Iroquois, engaged them to their advantage and returned with many scalps. They would again achieve a vengeful stroke against the Iroquois in 1687 when Tonti along with fifty French and two hundred Illinois warriors joined Canada's Governor Marquis de Denonville in an expedition against the Iroquois.

In 1690-91 Count Ponchertrain, French minister of the colonies, ordered the disbanding of the garrison, leaving the fort only as a fur trading post. In 1699 the French closed their Western forts with their fur trading operations, but kept Fort St. Louis operating. However, the French relationship with the Illinois soon degenerated. In 1702 the governor of Canada took the fort away from Tonti and appointed unscrupulous agents who cheated the Indians by selling inferior goods. The French also abused Indian women through frequent marriages. They would abandon one wife for another young attractive one by offering just trinkets. The men resented the women who only wanted to marry a Frenchman. Having endured enough abuse, the Illinois head chief Jere finally plotted to rid his people of the French. In late summer of 1718, about three hundred warriors entered the fort after the French had spent a night of revelry and debauchery. Upon wakening Captain La Mott, they sent him and his men packing while they burned down the fort, which had stood guard over the Illinois River for thirty-six years. The French fled the area, with some returning to Canada, some settling at Cahokia, and others at the seven-year-old colony by Peoria Lake.

In the 1770s, Ottawa, Pottawatomi, Kickapoo, Winnebago, Miami, and other tribes decided to exterminate the Illinois Indians in retaliation for the death of Pontiac (a Peoria Indian had murdered him in 1769). Retreating in the face of attacks on many of their villages, all the remaining Illinois Indians (about 10,000) consolidated and gathered at their principal village of La Vantum, built fortifications, and waited for their allied enemies. After an initial all day battle in which both sides suffered heavy losses, the remaining 1,200 Illinois retreated to Starved Rock. The allies tried to assault the Rock the following day, but were repelled with heavy losses. Changing to a strategy of attrition, they began a siege, only firing on the Illinois from a safe distance. South of the Rock is another cliff known as Devil's Nose. From here they built breastworks and fired on the Illinois. Though the Illinois had some provisions, they lacked water. They attempted to lower vessels attached to cords to the river below, but Indians at the base of the cliff cut them. After twelve days of starvation, many died, and the air reeked from putrefied bodies; some of the still living had resorted to cannibalism. The allies made a final assault and killed the remaining survivors. One Illinois warrior escaped down a chord and into the river a few days before the siege ended. He was later christened under the name of La Bell and his descendents are now living near Prairie du Rocher, Illinois.

Starved Rock State Park is open daily year round. Call 815-667-4726 for information.

Image credit: Susanna Steilen

Appendix III

Personnel Lists

The Battle of Tippecanoe

The following is a list of casualties of the battle:
    Officers: Colonel Abraham Owen, Aide de Camp, Major Joseph H. Daviess, Captains William C. Baen, Spier Spencer, and Jacob Warrick, Lieutenants, Thomas Berry and Richard McMahan, Sergeants James Martin and Adam Mills, Corporals Stephen Mars and James Mitchell, Thomas Randolph (an enlisted man, but personal aide to General Harrison.

    Privates killed in action on November 7:

James Asberry	John Hutcherson	John Ousley
Springer Augustus	Henry Jones	Kader Powell
Francis Bonah	David Kearns	Samuel Sand
Joseph Burditt	William Kelley	Joseph Smith
Israel Butler	Abraham Kelley	James Summerville
Levi Cary	William H. King	Joseph Tibbetts
Thomas Clendennan	John Maxwell	William Tissler
William Davis	Josh Maxwell	Ira T. Trowbridge
Marshall Dunken	William Mehan	Joseph Warnick
Dexter Earll	John McCoy	Isaac White
Peter Hanks	Daniel McMickle	Abraham Wood
Henry Hickey	Jack Obah	John Yoemans

    Privates who died from wounds following the battle from November 8 until after the return to Vincennes:

George Bently	Dennison Crumby	John Sandborn
John Black	Daniel Fisher	Nathan Snow
Senro Bologna	Daniel Gilman	James Stevenson
William Brigham	James Haskell	Lewis Taylor
Edward Butner	Daniel Lee	Richard Ward
Charles Coger	Isaac M. Nute	Leman E. Welch

Jonathan Crewell   Amos Royce

The complete roll of the Army commanded by Harrison can be found in *Battle of Tippecanoe* by Captain Alfred Pirtle.

Fort Harrison

J.T. Scovell in *Fort Harrison on the Banks of the Wabash 1812-1912* gives the following list of the known persons at the fort during the siege:

Captain Zachary Taylor, commandant, Dr. William A. Clark, army surgeon, Drummer Davis, a deserter from the English army, William Bandy, a Virginian, William Cowen, killed in the fight, Josey Cowen, died from disease, Jonathan Graham and wife, Isaac Lambert and wife, Julia Lafferty Lambert, Mrs. Briggs and her daughter, Mary, Mrs. Isaac Anderson and her daughter, Matilda, Mary Dickson and Joseph Dickson and their young children, Peter Mallory, wife and children, and John Clinton Bradford, a baby about a year old.

Apple River Fort

The settlers known to have been within the fort at the time of the battle were as follows: Captain Clack Stone, John Flack, James Flack, Milton Flack, Washington Flack, James Curtly, Thadeus Hitt, Rebecca Hitt, Hebrew Morris, Nathaniel Morris, Betsy Morris, Jefferson Murdock, John Murdock, Hezekiah Milligan, Granville Mathews, Jesse Lee, Samuel Jamieson, David Armstrong, John Armstrong, Elizabeth Armstrong, Dan Wooten, James Wooten, Elizabeth Winter, Jesse Van Voltenberg, Thomas Killien, Mrs. James Craig, Jessee Van Buskirk, Thomas Van Buskirk, Ishan Hardin, Niman Hardin, William Lawhorn, Mrs. William Lawhorn, Obadiah Rittenhouse, a Mr. Lowry, Samuel Hughlett, Hoseph Vean, Benjamin Tart, Josiah Nutting, Charles Tracey, Ambrose White, Judge Fowler, Jefferson Clark, Peter Howard, Charles Bauers, William Johnson, George Herclurode, Erwin Welch, and a Mr. Kirkpatrick.

Fort Shelby/Crawford

The following is a list of those who were surrendered to the British at Fort Shelby:

The officers: Joseph Perkins, Lt. 24 US Infantry; George Kennerly, Capt. Militia; James Kennerly, Lt. Militia; John McKenzie, Serg. 7th Infantry; Robert Morrison, Serg. 24th Infantry; James Kearns, Serg. 7th Infantry; Henry Hopkins, Corp., 7th Infantry; Easton Nance, Corp., 7th Infantry; Edmund Hollanno, Corp., 7th Infantry; Lot Porter Fifer. Privates; 7th Infantry: John Bryarly; John Bee; David Bigger; Anthony

W. Byard; Edward Brunner; David Brown; Henry Brumer; William Bennet; Peter Benman; Henry Barnhart; Benj. Corp; Booker Davis; James Doherty; James Davourez; John Iford; James Johnson; Thomas M. Jefferson; Daniel Fink; Saml. McBrided; James BcBride; James Murphy; Lewis McCarys; John Martin; Thos. McClaine; Thomas Marshall; William Marsh; John Page; Pleasant Philips; Henry Reese; Epram Richardson; John Runnalds; James Robertson; Harmon Seers; Gustavus Smith; Elisha Trader; Hugh Tranner; Elijah Tuel; Thurston Vaughn; James Kennedy; Samuel Gray; John Gamblin; William Howell; William Heres; Henry Hall; John Hall Thomas Moore; Ely Anderson; Greenberry Baker; Ezekiel Gibs. Total—50 privates, 7th Infantry.

Bibliography

Alvord, Clarence Walworth. *The Illinois Country 1673-1818*. 1920. Urbana and Chicago: University of Illinois Press, 1987.

Andrews, Roger. *Old Fort Mackinac on the Hill of History*. Menominee, WI: Herlad-Leander Press, 1938.

Ankenbruck, John. *Five Forts*. Fort Wayne: Lion's Head Publishing Co., 1972.

Anson, Bert. *The Miami Indians*. Norman, OK: University of Oklahoma Press, 1970.

Antal, Sandy. *A Wampum Denied: Procter's War of 1812*. Ottawa: Carleton University Press, 1997.

Armour, David A., ed. *Attack At Michilimackinac 1763: Alexander Henry's Travels and Adventures in Canada and the Indian Territories between the years 1760 and 1764*. Mackinac Island, MI: Mackinac Island State Park Commission, 1978.

Armour, David A., and Keith R. Widder. *At the Crossroads: Michilimackinac During the American Revolution*. Mackinac Island, MI: Mackinac Island State Park Commission, 1986.

Bakeless, John. *Background to Glory*. Philadelphia: J. B. Lippincott Company, 1957.

Balesi, Charles John. *The Time of the French in the Heart of North America 1673-1818*. Chicago: Alliance Francaise, 1992.

Ballard, Ralph. *Old Fort Saint Joseph*. Berrien Springs, MI: Hardscrabble Books, 1973.

Barry, James P. *Old Forts of the Great Lakes: Sentinels in the Wilderness.* Lansing, MI: Thunder Bay Press, 1994.

Beard, Reed. *The Battle of Tippecanoe.* Chicago: Donohue & Henneberry, 1889.

Beckwith, H.W., ed. "Aubrey Manuscript." *Illinois Historical Collections* n.s. 1 (1903) 165-170.

Berton, Pierre. *Flames Across the Border: The Canadian-American Tragedy, 1813-1814.* Boston: Little, Brown and Company, 1981.

---. *The Invasion of Canada 1812-1813.* Boston: Little, Brown and Company, 1980.

Bird, Harrison. *War for the West 1790-1813.* New York: Oxford University Press, 1969.

Bowen, Angela. *The Battle of Tippecanoe.* Lafayette, IN: Tippecanoe County Historical Association, 2004.

Brice, Wallace A. *History of Fort Wayne.* Fort Wayne: D.W. Jones, 1868.

Brown, Margaret K., and Dean C. Lawrie, *The French Colony in the Mid-Mississippi Valley.* Carbondale, IL: American Kestrel Books, 1995.

Butterfield, Consul W. *History of the Girtys.* Cincinnati: Robert Clarke & Co, 1890.

Caldwell, Norman F. "Fort Massac: The American Frontier Post 1778-1805." *Journal of the Illinois State Historical Society* n.s. 43 (summer 1950): 265-281.

---. "Fort Massac: The Frontier Post, 1778-1805." *Journal of the Illinois State Historical Society* n.s. 43 (winter 1950): 265-81.

---. "Fort Massac: Since 1805." *Journal of the Illinois State Historical Society* n.s. 44 (spring 1951): 47-60.

Carter, Harvey Lewis. *The Life and Times of Little Turtle: First Sagamore of the Wabash.* Urbana and Chicago: University of Illinois Press, 1987.

Chartrand, Rene. *The French Soldier in Colonial America.* Ottawa: Runge Press Ltd., 1984.

Coffman, Edward M. *The Old Army.* New York: Oxford University Press, 1988.

Davis, James E. *Frontier Illinois.* Bloomington, IN: Indiana University Press, 1998.

Davis, Susan Burdick. *Old Forts and Real Folks*. Madison: Zoe Bayliss and Susan Davis, 1939.

De Regnaucourt, Tony. *The Archaeology of Fort Recovery, Ohio*. Arcanum, OH: Upper Miami Valley Archaeological Research Museum, 1996.

Dowd, Gregory Evans. *A Spirited Resistance: The North American Indian Struggle for Unity, 1745-1815*. Baltimore: Johns Hopkins University Press, 1992.

Downes, Randolph C. *Council Fires on the Upper Ohio*. Pittsburgh: University of Pittsburgh Press, 1940.

Edmunds, David R. *The Potawatomis*. Norman, OK: University of Oklahoma Press, 1978.

---. *Tecumseh and the Quest for Indian Leadersip*. Boston: Little, Brown, 1984.

Edmunds David R. and Peyser, Joseph L. *The Fox Wars: The Mesquakie Challenge to New France*. Norman, OK: University of Oklahoma Press, 1993.

Evers, C.W., *History of Fort Meigs—Monument Dedication*. Bowling Green, Ohio: Democratic Print, 1908.

Fortier, John B. "New Light on Fort Massac" in *Frenchmen and French Ways in the Mississippi Valley*. Champaign, IL: University of Illinois Press, 1969.

Gaff, Alan D. *Bayonets in the Wilderness: Anthony Wayne's legion in the Old Northwest*. Norman, OK: University of Oklahoma Press, 2004.

Gilman, Julia. *William Wells and Maconaquah: White Rose of the Miamis*. Cincinnati: Jewel Publishing, 1985.

Gilpin, Alec R. *The War of 1812 in the Old Northwest*. East Lansing, OH: Michigan State University Press, 1958.

Grant, Bruce. *American Forts*. New Your: E. P. Dutton, 1965.

Guthman, William H. *March to Massacre: A History of the First Seven Years of the United States Army*. New York: McGraw Hill, 1975.

Hagan, William T. *The Sac and Fox Indians*. Norman, OK: University of Oklahoma Press, 1958.

Hansman, John. *Every Day Life at Old Fort Madison*. Privately printed, 1990.

---. *Black Hawk at Old Fort Madison and Indians in Prehistoric Lee County*. Privately printed, 1996.

---. *Old Fort Madison on the Mississippi 1808-1813*. Privately printed, 1990.

---. *Physicians, Medicine and Surgery at Old Fort Madison*. Privately printed, 1999.

Havinghurst, Walter. *Three Flags at the Straits: The Forts of Mackinac*. Englewood Cliffs, NJ: Prentice-Hall, 1966.

Heidler, David S. and Heidler Jeanne T. eds. *Encyclopedia of the War of 1812*. Santa Barbara, CA: ABC-CLIO, Inc. 1997.

Hickey, Donald R. *The War of 1812: A Forgotten Conflict*. Urbana, IL: University of Illinois Press, 1989.

Hitsman, Mackay J. *The Incredible War of 1812: A Military History*. Toronto: University of Toronto Press, 1965.

Holmes, John R. *The Story of Fort Steuben*. Steubenville, OH: Fort Steuben Press, 2000.

Hurt, Douglas R. *The Ohio Frontier: Crucible of the Old Northwest, 1720-1830*. Bloomington, IN: Indiana University Press, 1996.

Jackson, Donald. "Old Fort Madison – 1808-1813." *The Palimpsest* (January 1966): 1-62.

---. ed., *Ma-ka-Tai-Me-She-Kia-Kiak, Black Hawk: An Autobiography*. 1955. Urbana: University of Illinois Press, 1990.

Jacobs, James R. *The Beginning of the United States Army 1783-1812*. Princeton: Princeton University Press, 1947.

Kellogg, Louis P., ed. *Frontier Advance on the Upper Ohio, 1778-1779*. Madison: 1917.

Kohn, Richard H. *Eagle and Sword: The Federalists and the Creation of the Military Establishment in America, 1783-1802*. New York: Free Press, 1975.

Krauskopf, Francis, ed. *Ouiatanon Documents*. Indianapolis: Indiana Hist. Socl, 1955.

Lindley, Harlow, ed. *Fort Meigs and the War of 1812, Orderly Book of Cushings's Company, 2nd U.S. Artillery April, 1813-February, 1814, and Personal Diary of Captain Daniel Cushing October, 1812-July, 1813*. Columbus: Ohio Historical Society, 1975.

---., Norris F. Schneider and Milo M. Quaife, *History of the Ordinance of 1787 and the Old Northwest Territory*. Marietta, OH: Northwest Territory Celebration Commission, 1937.

Lossing Benson. *The Pictorial Fieldbook of the War of 1812*. 1868. Somersworth: New Hampshire Publishing Company, 1796.

Mahan, Bruce E. *Old Crawford And The Frontier*. Iowa City, IA: State Historical Society of Iowa, 1926.

---. "Old Fort Crawford." *The Palimpsest* (October 1961): 449-512.

Mahon, John K. *The War of 1812*. Gainesville: University Presses of Florida, 1972.

Matson, Matson. *French and Indians of Illinois River*. 1874. Carbondale and Edwardsville, IL: Southern Illinois University Press, 2001.

McAfee, Robert B. *Siege and Relief of Fort Wayne in the War of 1812*. Fort Wayne: The Public Library of Fort Wayne and Allen County, 1958.

McCoy, Raymond. *The Massacre Of Old Fort Mackinac*. Bay City, MI: Raymond McCoy, 1956.

McCollough, Almeda, ed. *The Battle of Tippecanoe*. Lafayette, IN: Tippecanoe County Historical Association, 1973.

Olmstead, Earl P. *David Zeisberger: A Life among the Indians*. Kent, OH: The Kent State University Press, 1997.

Osman, Eaton G. *Starved Rock: A Chapter of Colonial History*. Chicago: A. Flanagan Company, 1911.

Nelson, Larry L. *Men of Patriotism, Courage, and Enterprise: Fort Meigs in the War of 1812*. Bowie, MD: Heritage Books, 1985.

Palmer, Dave R. *1794 America, Its Army, and the Birth of the Nation*. Novato, CA: Presidio Press, 1994.

Parkman, Francis. *The Conspiracy of Pontiac and the Indian War After the Conquest of Canada*. Boston: Little, Brown, and Company, 1902.

Peckham, Howard H. *Pontiac and the Indian Uprising*. Princeton: Princeton University Press, 1947.

Pieper, Thomas I. and James B. Gidney. *Fort Larens 1778-1779-The Revolutionary War in Ohio*. Kent: Kent State University Press, 1976.

Pirtle, Alfred. *The Battle of Tippecanoe*. Louisville: John P. Morton Co., 1900.

Poinsatte, Charles. *Outpost in the Wilderness: Fort Wayne, 1706-1828*. Fort Wayne: Allen County Historical Society, 1976.

Prucha, Francis Paul, ed. *Broad Ax & Bayonet: The Role of The United State Army In The Development of the Northwest 1815*-1860. 1953. University of Nebraska Press, Lincoln, 1995.

Prucha, Francis Paul. *The Sword of the Republic: The United States Army on the Frontier 1783-1846*. 1969. University of Nebraska Press, 1986.

Quaife, Milo M. *Chicago and the Old Northwest 1673-1835*. 1913. University of Chicago Press, Urbana, 2001.

Rohr, Martha E. *Historical sketch of Fort Recovery*. Portland, IN: The Fort Recovery Historical Society, 1991.

Scamyhorn, Richard and John Steinle. *Stockades in the Wilderness: The Frontier Defenses and settlements of Southwestern Ohio 1788-95*. Dayton: Landfall Press, 1986.

Scanlan, Peter L., ed. *Prairie du Chien: French, British, American*. 1937. Prairie du Chien, WI: The Prairie du Chien Historical Society, Inc., 1998.

Simmons, David A. *The Forts of Anthony Wayne*. Fort Wayne: Historical Fort Wayne, Inc., 1977.

Sugden, John. *Tecumseh: A Life*. New York: Henry Holt and Company, 1997.

Sutton, Robert P., ed. *The Prairie Stat: A Documentary History of Illinois Colonial Years to 1860*. Grand Rapids, MI: William B. Eerdmans Publishing Company, 1976.

Sword, Wiley. *President Washington's Indian War: The Struggle for the Old Northwest 1790-1795*. Norman, OK: University of Oklahoma Press, 1985.

Tanner, Helen Hornbeck. *Atlas of Great Lakes Indian History*. Norman, OK: University of Oklahoma Press, 1987.

Temple, Wayne C. *Indian Villages of the Illinois Country*. Springfield, IL: Illinois State Museum Scientific Papers 2 (2), 1966.

Thornbrough, Gayle. *Outpost on the Wabash, 1787-179*. Indianapolis: Indiana Historical Society, 1957.

Van Every, Dale. *Ark of Empire, the American Frontier, 1784-1803*. New York: Morrow, 1963.

Wallace, Anthony F. C. *Prelude to Disaster*. Springfield, IL: Illinois State Historical Library, 1970.

Widder, Keith R. *Revelille Till Taps: Soldier Life At Fort Mackinac 1780-1895*. Mackinac Island, MI: Mackinac Island State Park Commission, 1972.

Widder, Keith R., and David Armour. *At the Crossroads: Michilimackinac During the American Revolution*. Mackinac Island, MI: Mackinac Island State Park Commission, 1978.

Williams, Gary S. *The Forts of Ohio: A Guide To Military Stockades*. Caldwell, OH: Buckeye Book Press, 2003.

Winger, Otho. *The Potawatomi Indians*. Elgin, IL: The Elgin Press, 1939.

Woehrmann, Paul. *At the Headwaters of the Maumee: A History of the Forts at Fort Wayne*. Indianapolis: Indiana Historical Society, 1971.

Young, Calvin M. *Little Turtle The Great Chief of the Miami Indian Nation*. 1917. Mt. Vernon, IN: Windmill Publications, Inc., 1995.

Index

Adams
    John, 71, 121
    John Quincy, 165
Allouez, Father Claude, 151
Amherst, Jeffrey, 51, 58
Amherstburg, 35
Anderson, Thomas, 163
Ange, Augustine, 160
Armstrong
    David, 200
    Elizabeth, 146, 149, 200
    John, 15–17, 160, 200
Arndt, John B., 155
Arnold
    Benedict, 119
Artaguette
    Diron d', 127
    Pierre d', 130
Articles of Confederation, 21
Asberry, James, 199
Assiniboine, Indian tribe, 89
Astor, John Jacob, 108, 164
Atkinson, Henry, 142, 144, 148, 165, 167–68
Aubry, Charles Philippe, 116, 132, 133
Auglaize River, 31, 35, 45
Augustus
    Edward, 153
    Springer, 199
Bad Axe, battle of, 148, 167
Bainbridge, George, 149
Balfour, Henry, 90
Balme, August de la, 58–59
Barrows, Washington, 110
Bartholomew, Joseph, 74, 82
Bartlett, Joseph, 55
Battle of Tippecanoe, 63, 71, 82–84, 199–200
Battleground, Indiana, 76
Bauers, Charles, 200
Beatty, Ekuries, 18–20
Beaujeu, Louis Lienard de, 90
Beggs, Stephen R., 143
Bellerive, St. Ange de, 133
Bentely, George, 199
Bienville, Le Moyne de, 127, 130
Bigger, James, 76

Bird, Henry, 7, 9
Bissell
    Daniel, 122–23, 182–83
    Russell, 17
Black Hawk War, xii–xiii, 149, 150, 156, 166–68, 170
Black Hawk, Chief, 141–48, 156, 167–68, 175–76, 181–83
Blackfish, Chief, 9
Blainville, Pierre-Joseph Celoron de, 89
Blue Jacket, Indian, 31, 59, 119
Blue Licks, battle of, 1, 97
Boilvin, Nicholas, 180–81
Boisbriant, Pierre, 127
Bologna, Senro, 199
Bonah, Francis, 199
Bondie, Antoine, 64
Boone, Daniel, 1, 97, 182
Bouquet, Henry, 3, 52–53
Bourne, Alexander, 39
Bowman, John, 9
Boyd, John P., 73–74, 79
Braddock, Edward, 57, 90
Bradstreet, John, 53
Brady, Samuel, 3
Brandywine, battle of, 25
Brigham, William, 77, 199
Brisbois, B. W., 168
Brock, Isaac, 104
Brodhead, Daniel, 3, 9
Brooke, George, 156, 168
Brown
    Jacob, 44
    William, 77
Buckongehelas, Indian, 31, 59
Buissoniere, Alphonse de la, 130
Bullock, Richard, 41, 106
Bunker Hill, battle of, 26
Bunson, Ira B., 168
Burbeck, Henry, 25–26, 60, 103
Burditt, Joseph, 199
Burnett's Creek, 76
Burr, Aaron, 74, 123
Burris, John Todd, 118
Bushy Run, battle of, 52
Buskirk
    Jessee Van, 200

Thomas Van, 200
Butler
   Anthony, 108
   Israel, 199
   John, 2
   Richard, 14
Cadillac, Antoine de la Mothe, 87
Cahokia, 97, 129, 132, 135, 152, 159–60, 194, 196
Campbell
   John, 3, 162–63
   Richard, 9
   William, 32
Canby, E. R. S., 168
Captain Johnny, Indian, 16, 31
Carleton, Guy, 28, 96, 159
Carver, Jonathan, 159
Cary, Levi, 199
Cass, Lewis, 166
Charlevoix, Xavier de, 128
Chartres, Duc de, 127
Cherokee, Indian tribe, 74, 116–120, 141
Chickasaw, Indian tribe, 28–30, 49, 50, 89, 116–20, 130
Chillicothe, Ohio, 9, 193
Chippewa, Indian tribe, 3, 14, 24, 28–29, 42, 61, 89–94, 101, 104, 142, 148, 153, 159–60, 166–67
Choctaw, Indian tribe, 28, 29, 30, 74, 120
Chow, Samuel, 119
Cicott, Zachariah, 75
Cincinnati, Ohio, 23, 37, 67, 119, 124
Clark
   George Rogers, 6–9, 14, 53, 97, 118, 125, 135, 160, 190
   Jefferson, 200
   John, 6
   Marston, 76
   Nathan, 156
   William, 60, 160–61, 183
   William A., 84, 200
Clay
   Green, 38, 41–44, 189
   Henry, 123
Clendennan, Thomas, 199
Coger, Charles, 199
Collot, Victor, 119
Congress, 1–2, 4, 13–15, 20–21, 23, 25, 96, 104, 108, 121, 193
Conner, John, 190
Craig, Mrs. James, 200
Cree, Indian tribe, 89
Crewell, Jonathan, 200
Croghan, George, xiv, 47, 51, 53, 106–8, 132, 169, 189, 190–93
Crumby, Dennison, 199
Cruzat, Francisco, 194
Cuppy, John, 5
Curtis, Daniel, 66–67
Curtly, James, 200
Cushing, Daniel, 37–38, 44–46
Daviess, Joseph Hamilton, 74–78, 82, 199
Davis
   Booker, 201
   Drummer, 200
   Jefferson, xii, 148–49, 155, 166, 168
   William, 199
De Peyster, Arent Schuyler, 96–97, 159
De Soto, Hernando, 115
Dearborn, Henry, 139, 173
Delaware, Indian tribe, 1–9, 13, 23–25, 28, 31, 58–59, 61, 63, 71–72, 81, 96, 105
Dement, John, 147
Denonville, Marquis de, 196
Des Moines River, 163
Detroit, Michigan, 1–2, 4, 8, 35, 38, 42, 50–53, 57–58, 62–63, 65, 67, 73, 81, 87, 92, 95, 97, 101, 103, 105–6, 108, 133, 175, 189, 193–94
Dexter, Earll, 199
Digny, Louis, 5
Dixon
   Frederick, 144
   Jeremiah, 14
Dodge, Henry, 147–48, 165
Dold, Samuel, 26
Dousman
   John, 104
   Michael, 104
Doyle, Thomas, 119, 123

Index

Draper, Lyman, 5
Drouillard, George, 123
Dubois, Touissant, 75, 82
Dubuisson, Charles Renaud, 49, 57
Dudley, William, 41–43
Dunken, Marshall, 199
Edwards, Ninian, 136, 140, 160
Elizabeth, Illinois, 143, 149–50
Elliott
    John, 18
    Matthew, 191
Emmell, Oliver, 145
Etherington, George, 92, 94, 153
Eustis, William, 67, 73
Fallen Timbers, battle of, xii, 31, 74, 119
Finney, Walter, 21
Fisher, Daniel, 199
Flack
    Captain, 145–46
    James, 200
    John, 200
    Milton, 200
    Washington, 200
Forbes, John, 118, 132
Ford, Mahlon, 17
Fort
    Crawford, xii–xiii, 109, 156–71, 200
    de Chartres, xi, xiii, 52–53, 116, 127–37
    de L'Ascension, 116
    Dearborn, 63, 66–68, 123, 182
    Deposit, 24
    Duquesne, 117–18, 132–33
    Finney, 16, 21
    George, 106, 108
    Granville, 132
    Greeneville, 25, 26, 31, 61
    Hamilton, 24
    Harrison, 75, 82–83, 85, 200
    Holmes, 108, 112
    Howard, 151–57
    Laurens, xii–xiii, 1–14
    Le Boeuf, 52
    Mackinac, xii, 63, 101, 103–4, 107–8, 110, 112–13, 152
    Madison, xii–xiii, 164, 173–85
    Malden, 35–6, 38, 43
    Marietta, 16
    Mason, 182
    Massac, xi, 115–25, 133
    McIntosh, 3–8, 13, 16
    McKay, 163
    Meigs, xii–xiv, 35–47, 81, 141, 189–90
    Miamis, xii, 28, 31–32, 38, 42, 44, 57
    Michilimackinac, xi, 87–98, 133, 193
    Necessity, 132
    Niagara, 2, 51, 103, 109, 133
    Oswego, 103
    Ouiatenon, xi, xiii, 49–55
    Pitt, 1–3, 8–9, 14–15, 20
    Presqu' ile, 52
    Recovery, xii, 23–32, 59
    Russell, 136
    Sackville, 53, 97
    Shelby, 162–63, 171, 200
    Snelling, 165, 168–69
    St. Joseph, xiv, 193–94
    St. Louis, xiv, 194–96
    Stanwix, 13
    Stephenson, xiv, 37, 45, 47, 107, 141, 189–93
    Steuben, xii, 13, 17–22, 54
    Venango, 52
    Washington, 23, 24, 25, 74
    Wayne, xii, 23, 35, 57, 60–73
    William Henry, 90
Fort Wayne, Treaty of, 63, 71, 73
Fowler, Judge, 200
Fox, Indian tribe, 50, 73, 88–89, 129, 139, 140–41, 148, 151–53, 159–62, 166–68, 173–75, 180–82
Gage, Thomas, 95, 134, 153
Gaines, Edmund, 141, 165
Galena, Illinois, 128, 140, 143, 147, 164–65
Galissoniere
    Marquis de la, 131
Gautier
    Charles, 159
Geiger, Captain, 77
Genet, Edmond, 119
Ghent, Treaty of, 108, 141, 163

Giard, Basil, 160
Gibson
   Alexander, 26–27, 29, 30, 31
   John, 4, 6–8
Gilman, Daniel, 199
Girty, Simon, 6–7
Gladwin, Henry, 50–51, 58, 194
Gordon, J. G., 191
Grant, James, 132
Gratiot, Charles, 36, 154
Greaton, Richard, 26
Green Bay, 52, 88, 90, 109, 15–53, 156
Greenville, Treaty of, 10, 32, 61
Guild, Joseph C., 110
Guion, Isaac, 119
Haldimand, Frederick, 97–98, 101, 103
Half King, Chief, 7
Hall
   John, 201
   Rachel, 143
   Sylvia, 143
Hamelin, Jean Baptiste, 194
Hamilton
   Alexander, 121
   Henry, 1, 6, 7, 53
   Isaac, 134
   Thomas, 181–83
   William Sutherland, 163
Hamtramck, John, 16–17, 20–22, 24, 32, 60–61
Hanks
   Peter, 199
   Porter H., 104, 105
Hardin, 200
Harding, William G., 110
Harmar, Josiah, 15–16, 20–25, 29, 59
Harrison, William Henry, xii, 35–47, 63–67, 71–85, 106, 124, 139–40, 173, 189–92, 199–200
Haskell, James, 199
Heckewelder, John, 1, 4, 6
Henry, Alexander, 90–94
Herclurode (or Hercleroad), George, 144, 146, 200
Hesse, Emmanuel, 159
Hickey, Henry, 199
Hitt
   Rebecca, 200
   Thadeus, 200
Holmes
   Andrew Hunter, 107
   Robert, 58
Hopkins
   Henry, 200
   Samuel, 82
Hoseph, Vean, 200
Howard
   Benjamin, 154, 160, 162–63
   Don Carlos, 160
   Peter, 200
   William, 94
Hughlett, Samuel, 200
Hull, William, 63, 81, 105
Hunt, Thomas, 61, 68, 174
Hutcherson, John, 199
Hutchins, Thomas, 14, 16
Illinois, Indian tribe, 152, 196
Indians. *See* individual tribes
Indian Creek Massacre, 143, 147
Iroquois, Indian tribe, 2, 9, 13, 81, 129, 133, 152, 193, 195–96
Jamieson, 200
Jay's Treaty, 103, 194
Jefferson Barracks, 148, 156, 165, 168
Jefferson, Thomas, 13, 122–23, 139
Jenkins, Edward, 50–52
Johnson
   James, 201
   John, 180–83
   John W., 164
   Richard M., 67
   Sir William, 51, 94–95, 133
   William, 95, 200
Johnston
   John, 62
   Stephen, 64
Jones, Henry, 199
Kaskaskia, Illinois, 53, 97, 118, 127, 129, 131–32, 134, 135
Kaskaskia, Indian tribe, 61, 129
Kearns
   David, 199
   James, 200
Kearny, Stephen Watts, 165

Kekionga, Miami village, xii, 23–24, 53–54, 57–59
Kelley
  Abraham, 199
  William, 199
Kellogg's Grove, battle of, 147
Kennerly
  George J., 161, 200
  James, 200
Keokuk, Chief, 148
Kerlerec, Louis de, 116, 132
Kersey, William, 17
Kickapoo, Indian tribe, 24, 50–54, 61, 74, 77, 82–83, 119, 147, 152, 159, 162, 182, 196
Killbuck, Chief, 8
Killien, Thomas, 200
King George III, 153
King George's War, 50, 57, 89, 131, 152
King Louis XV, 127
King, William H., 199
Kingsley, Alpha, 174–76
Kirkpatrick, Mr., 144–47, 200
Knox, Henry, 15, 24–25, 54, 59
Kumskaukau, Indian, 82
La Salle, Robert de, xiv, 57, 193–96
La Vantum, Indian village, 195, 196
Laclede, Pierre, 135
Lambert
  Isaac, 200
  Julia, 84, 200
Land Ordinance of 1785, 14
Langlade
  Augustin de, 152
  Charles, 89, 90–93, 96, 152, 159,
Laurens, Henry, 1, 4
Lawhorn
  Mrs. William, 200
  William, 200
Lee
  Arthur, 14
  Daniel, 199
  Jesse, 200
Leftwich, Joel, 36–37

Legion of the United States, 25, 28, 29–32
Lernoult, R. B,, 6
Leslie, William, 90–92
Ligneris, Constant de Marchand, 133
Lincoln, Abraham, 142, 147, 149
Little Miami River, 9
Little Turtle, Chief, 23–25, 27, 30–31, 53, 59, 68, 74, 119
Logan, Chief, 4
Logan, John, 64, 67
Long, Stephen H., 163
Louvigny, Louis de la Porte, 88
Lowry, Mr., 200
Lundy's Lane, battle of, 44
Luse, Francis, 17
Macarty, Richard, 116–17, 131
Mackinaw City, Michigan, 88, 98, 99
Madison, James, 71, 176
Marquette, Father Jacques, 87
Mars, Stephen, 77, 199
Marsh, John, 164
Marshall
  Thomas, 201
  William, 110
Martin, 20
  Absalom, 14
  James, 199
  John, 201
Mascouten, Indian tribe, 50–51, 152
Mason, Charles, 14
Mason-Dixon Line, 14
Mathews, Granville, 200
Maumee Rapids, 35–36
Maumee River, 14, 23, 28, 31, 35–38, 41, 57
Maxwell
  John, 199
  Josh, 199
Maynard, Paul, 124
McCoy, John, 199
McCrae, Jane, 97
McCune, Joseph, 44
McCurdy, William, 17
McDouall, Robert, 106–8
McIntosh, Lachlan, 1–9

McKay, William, 106, 162–63
McKee, Alexander, 9, 54
McMickle, Daniel, 199
Mehan, William, 199
Meigs, Return Jonathan, 36
Menominee, Indian tribe, 96, 104, 107, 153, 156, 159
Mesquakie. *See* Fox
Metea, Chief, 64
Metropolis, Illinois, 121, 124
Miami Confederacy, xii, 53, 55
Miami River, 21
Miami, Indian tribe, xii, 23–31, 35, 49–63, 71, 74, 83, 89, 119, 152, 164, 196
Militia, 2–8, 24, 32, 36–45, 54, 55, 60, 74, 76, 82, 85, 90, 106, 130, 135, 142–47, 153, 165
Miller
  Christopher, 28
  George, xiii
  James, 75
  John, 82
  John C., 42, 153, 154
Milligan, Hezekiah, 200
Mills
  Adam, 199
  John, 17, 19
Minavavana, Chief, 90, 92
Mingo, Indian tribe, 6, 7, 9
Mississippi River, xi–xii, 13, 50, 52, 57, 95, 105–6, 115–53, 159, 160, 165–67, 173–75, 180–81, 193–95
Mompesson, John, 97
Montgomery
  John, 160
  Richard, 96
Montreal, Canada, 50, 57, 92, 94–96, 108, 153, 193
Moore
  Hugh, 67
  Thomas, 201
Morgan
  Daniel, 2
  George, 4
  Lewis, 154
  Willoughby, 108, 163, 165
Morris
  Betsy, 200
  Hebrew, 200
  Nathaniel, 200
Morrison
  Robert, 200
Mosby, John T., 37
Muir, Adam, 35, 63
Murdock
  Jefferson, 200
  John, 200
Muskingum River, 3, 6, 16, 23
Napoleon, 122–23
Natchez, Indian tribe, 130
Naylor, Isaac, 75, 77, 80
Neapope, Indian, 142
New Orleans, Louisiana, 52, 122–23, 129, 132, 135
Newburgh Petition, 13
Nicolas, Chief, 57
Niles, Michigan, xiv, 90, 97, 193, 194
Northwest Territory, xi, xii, xiii, 21–24, 53, 58, 67, 71, 135, 140, 153
Norton, John, Indian, 42
Nute, Isaac M., 199
Nutting, Josiah, 146, 200
Obah, Jack, 199
Ohio Company, 21, 23
Ohio River, 6, 13–16, 21, 54, 105, 115–25
Ohio State Archaeological and Historical Society, 32
Ojibwa. *See* Chippewa
Old Britain, Chief, 89
Oliver
  Peter, 64
  William, 38, 41, 64–66
Ordinance of 1787, 21, 23
Osage, Indian tribe, 141
Ostrander, Phillip, 66–67
Ottawa, Indian tribe, 3, 35, 94, 142, 153
Ousley, John, 199
Outagami. *See* Fox
Owen, Abraham, 77, 82, 199
Paris, Treaty of, xi, 13, 103, 118, 133
Parks, James, 3

Pashipaho, Chief, 140
Peoria, Illinois, 35, 129
Perkins, Joseph, 161
Perrot, Nicolas, 164
Perry, Oliver Hazard, 106, 192
Peters, William, 17, 78
Pettit, John, 83
Pickawillany, Ohio, 89
Pickering, Timothy, 13
Pike, Zebulon, 120, 123, 160
Piqua, Ohio, 63–64, 67
Pittman, Philip, 134
Plainfield, Illinois, 143
Pomoacan, Chief, 7
Pontiac, Chief, 51–53, 58, 76, 94, 133, 153, 196
Pontiac's Rebellion, 3, 50, 52, 58, 92, 94, 118, 153
Poure, Eugene, 194
Powell, Kader, 199
Powers, Tom, 123
Prairie du Chien, Wisconsin, 106, 141, 148, 159, 160–65, 171
Prairie du Rocher, Illinois, 127
Prevost
   George, 192
   Pierre, 159
Price, Samuel, 124
Proctor, Henry, 36, 38–39, 41–44, 47, 81, 105–6, 189, 191–92
Prophet, the. *See* Tenskawatawa
Prophetstown, Indian village, 72, 74–75, 80, 81–83
Putnam, Rufus, 14, 23
Quashquame, Chief, 140
Quebec, Canada, 50, 57, 90, 97, 101, 118, 195
Quindre, Dagneau de, 194
Raimond, Charles, 57
Raisin, River, 35–37
Reaume, Simon, 50
Red Bird, Chief, 165
Renault, Philippe Francois de, 128
Reynolds, John, 142
Rhea, James, 61–67
Rittenhouse, Obadiah, 200
River Raisin, battle of the, 41, 141
Roberts
   Benjamin, 95
   Charles, 104–6, 113
Robertson
   Daniel, 102
   James, 201
Rocheblave, Philippe Francois de, 118, 133
Rock Island, Illinois, 124, 141
Rock River, 140–42, 160, 163, 175, 182
Rogers, Robert, 90, 94–95
Ross, David, 3
Roundhead, Chief, 38
Royce, Amos, 200
Russell, William, 1, 85
Sand, Samuel, 199
Sandborn, John, 199
Sandusky River, 2, 6–9, 44, 189, 190
Sargeant, Winthrop, 14
Sauk, Indian tribe, 73, 92, 130, 139, 140–41, 148, 153, 159–63, 166–67, 173–75, 180–83, 193
Saukenuk, Indian village, 140–41
Sault Ste. Marie, 90–91
Saussier, Jean Baptiste, 131
Schlosser, Francis, 193–94
Scott
   Charles, 54
   Winfield, 149, 155, 167
Seneca, Indian tribe, 51, 152, 189
Seydam, Cornelius Ryker, 17, 20
Shawnee, Indian tribe, 2–3, 7, 9, 14, 16, 23–25, 28, 30–31, 38, 41, 50, 54, 58–59, 61–67, 71, 77, 81, 83, 96, 119, 124, 182
Shay's Rebellion, 19
Shelby, Isaac, 161
Sherman, Isaac, 14
Shipp, Edmund, 191
Short, William, 191–92
Sinclair
   Arthur, 107
   Patrick, 97–98, 101–2, 160
Smith
   Gustavus, 201
   Joseph, 155, 199
   Kirby, 155
   Thomas, 163
Snelling, Josiah, 78, 164

Snow, Nathan, 199
Spencer, Spier, 74, 76, 78, 80, 82, 199
St. Ange, Robert Croston de, 129
St. Anne Church, 97–98
St. Clair, Arthur, xii, 24–29, 32, 53, 55, 59, 74, 106
St. Denys, Charles Juchereau, 115
St. Joseph Island, 104, 108, 113
St. Joseph River, 23, 57, 193
St. Louis, Missouri, 73, 97, 121, 12–24, 128, 135, 139–40, 154, 156, 159–63, 168, 173, 180–81, 194
St. Mary's River, 23, 57, 68, 104
Stephenson, Mills, 189
Steuben, Baron von, 15, 17, 19, 103
Steubenville, Ohio, 16, 22
Stevenson, James, 199
Stickney, Benjamin, 64–65, 68
Stillman, Isaiah, 142–43, 147
Stirling, Thomas, 118, 133, 135
Stone Eater, Indian, 77
Stone, Clack, 145, 200
Sullivan, John, 9
Summerville, James, 199
Tart, Benjamin, 200
Taylor
    Lewis, 199
    Richard, 6
    Walter, 76
    Zachary, xii, 6, 82–85, 141, 148, 154, 163, 165–70, 200
Tecumseh, Chief, 38, 41–44, 63, 67, 71–76, 80–82, 106, 124, 189
Tenskawatawa, the Prophet, 77, 80, 81, 124, 142, 182
Terre Haute, Indiana, 74, 85
Thames, battle of the, 81, 106, 124, 192
Tibbetts, Joseph, 199
Tipton, John, 78, 82
Tissler, William, 199
Tonti, Henri de, xiv, 195–96
Tracey, Charles, 200
Trowbridge, Ira T., 199
Tupper, Benjamin, 14
Turner, Daniel, 108

Tuscarawas River, 3–4
Tute, James, 94
Vaudreuil, Philippe de Rigaud, 49, 88
Verges, Bernard de, 115–17
Vernon, Frederick, 9
Villemonde, Sieur de Beaujeu, 133
Villiers
    Antoine Coulon de, 88–89, 152
    Joseph Coulon de (Jumonville), 132
    Neyon de, 118, 132–133
Vincennes, Francois-Marie, 49
Vincennes, Indiana, 6–7, 9, 38, 49, 53, 71, 73–74, 80–81, 85, 97, 118, 129–30, 139, 199
Voltenberg, Jesse Van, 200
Wabash River, 24, 27, 32–35, 49, 53–57, 72, 75, 105, 200
Wabasha, Chief, 160
Wakefield, John, 145
Ward, Richard, 199
Warnick, Joseph, 199
Washee, Chief, 193
Washington, George, 1, 3, 9, 23–25, 103, 119, 132, 155, 176, 178
Waubansee, Chief, 75
Wawatam, Chief, 91–94
Weirton, West Virgina, 16
Welch
    Edmund, 144–45
    Erwin, 200
    Leman E., 199
Wells
    Samuel, 76, 79, 190
    William, 27–28, 30, 61, 63
West Point, 14, 26, 36, 156, 189, 193
Wheeling, West Virginia, 21
Whistler, John, 68
White
    Ambrose, 200
    Isaac, 199
White Horse, Chief, 75
White Loon, Indian, 77
Whitehouse, Joseph, 123
Whittlesey, Charles, 10
Wilcox, Philip, 82, 85

Wilkinson, James, 32, 54–55, 61, 119, 121, 123, 140, 160, 173
Willard, Alexander, 180
Winchester, James, 35–36
Winnebago, Indian tribe, 77, 80–83, 104, 142, 147–48, 151, 153, 156, 159–68, 181–83, 196
Winnemac, Chief, 65–66
Winter, Elizabeth, 200
Wisconsin River, 139, 147–48, 151, 159–60
Wood
   Abraham, 199
   Eleazor, 36–37, 39, 44, 189
Wooten
   Dan, 200
   James, 200
Worsley
   Miller, 108
Wyandot, Indian tribe, 3, 7, 9, 13, 24–25, 28, 31, 38, 59, 61, 77, 81
Wyllys, John, 16
Wyoming Valley, 2
Yoemans, John, 199
Zeisberger, David, 1, 4, 6

ABOUT THE AUTHOR

JONATHAN HALL is a graduate of American Military University with a M.A. in Land Warfare. He is also the author of *Revolutionary Quiz & Fact Book* (1999). He researched extensively both primary and secondary sources and visited most of the sites in this book to describe the history of each fort and how they appear today.

www.ingramcontent.com/pod-product-compliance
Lightning Source LLC
Chambersburg PA
CBHW071228170426
43191CB00032B/1130